Contents

3 Editorial:
A New Journal and A New Centre for Gospels Research

5 *Frank J. Moloney*
An ending and a new beginning: A study of Mark 11:1-25

18 *Darrell L. Bock*
A Note on The Gospels' Jesus Tradition, Memory, and Issues Raised by Bart Ehrman

23 *Peter G. Bolt*
Preparing Israel for the Arrival of the Son of Man. Jesus' Kingship Parable (Luke 19:11-28) in its Historical and Literary Context

42 *James R. Harrison*
Jesus and the Grace of the Cross: Luke 23:34a and the Politics of "Forgiveness" in Antiquity

68 *Debra Snoddy*
Interpreting the Holy One of God in John 6:69: A Tradition-critical Analysis

81 *Sehyun Kim*
Thesis Summary: The Kingship of Jesus in the Gospel of John

Book Reviews

88 Bauckham, R. *Jesus and the Eyewitnesses: The Gospels as Eyewitness Testimony* (Grand Rapids, MI: Eerdmans, 2017, 2nd edition). (David Graieg)

91 Green, J.B., J.K. Brown, N. Perrin (eds.), *Dictionary of Jesus and the Gospels: A Compendium to Contemporary Biblical Scholarship* (Downers Grove: IVP Academic, Nottingham: IVP, 2013, 2nd ed.). (Christoph Stenschke)

93 Hays, C.M. *Renouncing Everything: Money and Discipleship in Luke* (New York/Mahwah, NJ: Paulist Press, 2016). (James R. Harrison)

97 Runesson, A. *Divine Wrath and Salvation in Matthew: The Narrative World of the First Gospel.* (Minneapolis: Fortress, 2016). (George Bishai)

99 Spadaro, M. *Reading Matthew as the Climactic Fulfilment of the Hebrew Story* (Eugene, Or.: Wipf & Stock, 2015). (Peter G. Bolt)

101 Cedric E.W. Vine. *The Audience of Matthew: An Appraisal of the Local Audience Thesis.* (LNTS 496; London: Bloomsbury T&T Clark, 2014). (Ben Cooper)

A New Journal and A New Centre for Gospels Research

The *Journal of Gospels and Acts Research* is an activity of the SCD Centre for Gospels Research, newly launched on 28 September 2017.

A self-accrediting Higher Education Provider delivering excellence in theological education within the Australian Higher Education Sector, the Sydney College of Divinity is structured as an ecumenical consortium of theological colleges, together with a centrally delivered Korean program and Graduate Research School, representing a breadth of Christian traditions, including Catholic, Orthodox, Wesleyan, and various Protestant and Evangelical traditions. Located within this unique educational environment, the Centre will draw upon the strengths of its rich cultural and Christian heritage and the due rigour required of contemporary tertiary education for a rapidly changing world.

This Centre aims to promote research into the four Gospels and, due to the connections with Luke, the Book of Acts. With the aim of better understanding these foundational documents of historic Christianity, the Centre will encourage research from a variety of methodological perspectives, such as historical, archaeological, theological, exegetical, literary, sociological, feminist, or text-critical approaches.

Although based within the SCD, membership of the Centre is open to those researching in the Gospels and Acts in the wider community. The Centre seeks to create networks amongst scholars presently working within the field and also to encourage a future generation of Gospels and Acts researchers. To coincide with the launch of the Centre and its journal, the SCD has already announced a monetary prize for an excellent essay on a subject related to the Gospels or Acts submitted by an SCD student, and plans other encouragements in the future for students to undertake research in the field.

The activities of the Centre will include a regular seminar, as well as colloquia, and conferences. To foster and disseminate Gospels research, it will also publish, through the SCD Press, as the first of its kind, this dedicated journal, the *Journal of Gospels and Acts Research*, as well as occasional monographs.

EDITORIAL: A NEW JOURNAL AND A NEW CENTRE FOR GOSPELS RESEARCH

Despite the changes and challenges of the contemporary world, the significance of Jesus Christ has not diminished. With the rise of a noisy radical atheism in the West, along with a secularism that wants to continue to enjoy the fruits of the Christian heritage while deliberately cutting off the roots, and radical religionists wreaking havoc in so many parts of the globe, there has never been a greater need for Christianity to express itself clearly as it continues to take its part in bringing about a better future for all. Meeting this challenge will involve many different tasks, but, given the importance of the Gospels and Acts as foundational documents of the Christian movement, their rigorous, patient, and long-term study must surely be one of these tasks, and the clear communication of that research must be another.

Peter G. Bolt
Executive Editor

An ending and a new beginning
A study of Mark 11:1-25

FRANK J. MOLONEY

I have argued elsewhere that textual indicators highlight turning points in the Markan narrative (1:1-13: Prologue; 1:14-8:30: the Mystery of the Messiah; 8:31-15:39: Messiah: Son of Man and Son of God; 16:1-8: Epilogue).[1] Further literary strategies can be traced across the narrative, and one of them runs from 11:1-13:37 (Temple worship [11:1-25], the institutions of Judaism [11:27-12:44], the end of Jerusalem [13:1-23], and the end of the world [13:24-37]). This study argues that Jesus' entry into Jerusalem, and his actions in the Temple, along with the words and events associated with the fig-tree that frame the episode, are a symbolic ending of Israel's sacred access to God, and its replacement.[2]

The Literary Structure of 11:1-25

Two major events mark Jesus' arrival in Jerusalem: the entrance itself (v. 11) and Jesus' presence in the Temple (vv. 15-19). These events are circumscribed with Jesus' entry and exit from the city. From Bethany and Bethphage, Jesus prepares his entry (vv. 1-2), and after entering the Temple and looking around at everything, he returns to Bethany (v. 11). He sets out from Bethany on the next day (v. 12), and after his presence in the Temple, in the evening withdraws from the city (v. 19). The following day, he journeys back to Jerusalem (v. 20). His final arrival in Jerusalem is noted in

---

[1] See, most recently, F.J. Moloney, *Gospel Interpretation and Christian Life* (Scholars Collection 3; Adelaide: ATF Theology, 2017), 16-20.

[2] See F.J. Moloney, *The Gospel of Mark. A Commentary* (Grand Rapids: Baker Academic, 2012), 215-16. Most commentators see 11:1-13-37 as a literary unity, framed by the references to the Mount of Olives. See, for example, A.Y. Collins, *Mark* (Hermeneia; Minneapolis: Fortress, 2007), 513. The following study depends heavily upon Moloney, *Mark*, 216-28. It serves as a 'companion piece' to the more historical essay, 'Revisiting the Temple: Mark 11:15-17 and 13:2', delivered at the Sydney College of Divinity Seminar on the Jesus of History on 28-29 September, 2017. In contrast to that essay, the sole concern of what follows is *the Markan narrative and theological agenda* across 11:1-25. J. Marcus, *Mark* (AYB 27-27A; 2 vols.; New York/New Haven: Doubleday/Yale University Press, 2000-2009), 2:767-71, accentuates the mounting hostility across 11:1-13:37, calling this section of the Gospel 'the vestibule to the passion narrative'. I suggest that it is formed by a series of dramatic 'endings'. See Moloney, *Mark*, 215-73.

v. 27.³ A number of encounters between Jesus and other characters take place across 11:27-12:44, but Jesus never leaves the Temple. Thus, the movement to and from Jerusalem in 11:1-25 sets up an uneasy relationship. Tension mounts in those first days of Jesus' presence in the city.⁴ Using Jesus' movement to and from Jerusalem in vv. 1-25, the description of the first days can be outlined as two tripartite structures.

> I – In vv. 1-11 Jesus enters Jerusalem, with reference to Bethany in v. 1 and v. 11.
>
>> a) Preparations for the entry of Jesus into Jerusalem (vv. 1-7a)
>>> b) The welcome as Jesus approaches the city (vv. 7b-10)
>> a¹) Jesus enters the city, visits the Temple, and departs (v. 11).

Jesus journeys from Bethany in v. 12, and he exits Jerusalem in v. 19. He is on the move in v. 20, but his return to the city is not mentioned until v. 27.

> II – In vv. 12-25 Jesus is again in Jerusalem, with reference to a journey from Bethany in v. 12, and the same location in vv. 20-25, in sight of the fig-tree.
>
>> a) The cursing of the fig-tree (vv. 12-14)
>>> b) Jesus in the Temple (vv. 15-19)
>> a¹) The withered fig-tree and *a new way to God* (vv. 20-25)

The literary construction of this report of Jesus' first days in Bethany-Jerusalem-Bethany is the result of careful Markan narrative skill.⁵

Jesus' entry into Jerusalem and the Temple (vv. 1-11)

The approach to Jerusalem is mentioned in association with two villages that lie in close proximity to the city, Bethphage and Bethany. Both villages lie on the way from Jericho (see 10:46) to Jerusalem, although one would arrive in Bethany before Bethphage. The geographical location of these villages, both on the slopes of the Mount of Olives, legitimates the position of Jesus and the disciples *pros to oros tōn elaiōn* (v. 1ab).⁶ From that location, already within sight of the city, he

---

3   Most early witnesses across all text types do not have v. 26 ('But if you do not forgive, neither will your Father who is in heaven forgive your trespasses'). It is universally accepted that copyists inserted the passage, in imitation of Matt 6:15. See B.M. Metzger, *A Textual Commentary on the Greek New Testament* (Stuttgart: Deutsche Bibelgesellshaft, 1994 2nd ed.), 93; W.R. Telford, *The Barren Temple and the Withered Tree: A Redaction-critical Analysis of the Cursing of the Fig-Tree Periscope in Mark's Gospel and its Relation to the Cleansing of the Temple Tradition* (JSNTSup 1; Sheffield: JSOT Press, 1980), 50-54.
4   On the Markan nature of these three days and the use of intercalation within them, see Telford, *The Barren Temple*, 42-49; D. Lührmann, *Das Markusevangelium* (HNT 3; Tübingen: Mohr Siebeck, 1987), 185-86. B. van Iersel, *Reading Mark* (W. H. Bisscheroux, trans.; Collegeville, MN: The Liturgical Press, 1988), 144, suggests that the coming and going reflects Jesus' awareness that his life is under threat. Staying in Jerusalem at night, with the gates closed, Jesus would to be trapped in the city (see Acts 9:23-25). For W.H. Kelber, *Mark's Story of Jesus* (Philadelphia: Fortress, 1979), 62 (and elsewhere), Jesus' moving away from the city shows that Jerusalem and its Temple are not 'his place'. He takes up his abode elsewhere, so that he can turn against the Temple.
5   See Marcus, *Mark*, 2:776-777.
6   Those who wish to make every element in this story point to its messianic meaning, look to 2 Kings 15:32; Ezek 11:23; Zech 14:4-5 and Josephus, *J.W.*, 2.261-263; *Ant.* 20.167-172, for indications that in the first century the Messiah was expected to appear on the Mount of Olives. See, for example, E. Lohmeyer, *Das Evangelium des Markus übersetzt und erklärt* (MeyerK; Göttingen: Vandenhoeck & Ruprecht, 1967 17th ed.), 229.

sends two of the disciples into the village 'opposite' (*katenanti*) (vv. 1c-2a). It is not clear which of the two villages (Bethphage or Bethany) is intended.[7] Jesus' words to the disciples set the theme for vv. 2bc-6. This is the only place in the Gospel of Mark where Jesus is credited with foreknowledge. The disciples are instructed, in considerable detail, where they are to go (immediately entering the village), what they will find (a young ass upon which no one has ridden) and what they are to do (untie it and bring it to Jesus).[8] They are to say that the Lord (*ho kyrios*) has need of it. There is no need to read complicated speculations or an exalted Christology into this use of *ho kyrios*.[9] The strangeness of unknown disciples taking possession of a young ass, and their response to queries about their right to do so as fulfillment of the needs of 'the Lord', indicate that they do what they are told.[10] They are obedient to the man they follow, referred to as 'the master', and once this is made clear they are free to act as they were instructed. This oddness adds to the impression that something more than Jesus, the disciples, and taking possession of a young ass is involved in these preparations. They are further instructed by means of a reported encounter that simulates the direct speech of both the protagonist and the disciples, how they are to respond to any objections to their taking the colt (vv. 2bc-3). The description, in the third person, of what then takes place matches exactly what Jesus had said: they find the ass, untie it, and resolve the objections by saying that their Lord had need of it, and they bring the colt to Jesus (vv. 4-7a).

Jesus' foreknowledge, however, is not the point of the story. After early suggestions about Jesus' destiny (see 2:20; 3:6; 6:14-29; 8:11-12), he has now made it clear that he is going to Jerusalem to suffer, die and rise again (see 8:31; 9:31; 10:32-34).[11] The instructions Jesus gives to his disciples, and the exact correspondence between his instructions and what happens, tells the reader that Jesus accepts his final crossing over from the Mount of Olives to the city of Jerusalem where the Son of Man must suffer and rise (see 8:31; 9:31; 10:32-34). But there is more to it. Jesus' awareness of the events that will bring him into the city points beyond Jesus to God. The passion predictions made it clear that Jesus was responding to God's design, and this thought is carried further in the correspondence between Jesus' orders and what, in fact, happens. Jesus' preparations for his entry into Jerusalem are a further step in the unfolding of God's plan.[12]

---

7   On the villages, see J. Gnilka, *Das Evangelium nach Markus* (EKKNT II/1-2; 2 vols.; Zürich/Neukirchen-Vluyn: Benziger Verlag/ Neukirchener Verlag, 1998 5th ed.), 2:115-16; Collins, *Mark*, 516-17. It is possible that from Bethany, the disciples are sent to the next village, Bethphage (see W.L. Lane, *Commentary on the Gospel of Mark* [NICNT; Grand Rapids: Eerdmans, 1974], 395).

8   The noun *pōlos* can refer to the colt or foal of a horse or of an ass. See Marcus, *Mark*, 2:772. The influence of Zech 9:9 on commentators has led to the universal acceptance that it was an ass.

9   It has been suggested that the expression indicates that the real owner (one of the disciples?) of the ass needs it (see V. Taylor, *The Gospel according to St Mark* (London: Macmillan, 1966 2nd ed.), 455; C.E.B. Cranfield, *St Mark*, 350), or that at this stage of the narrative Mark feels that the full christological 'Lord' (reflecting the LXX's use of *kyrios* for the divine name) can be introduced into the narrative (see H. Anderson, *The Gospel of Mark* [NCB; London: Oliphants, 1976], 261). For a summary, see Marcus, *Mark*, 2:772-73.

10 See M.-J. Lagrange, *Evangile selon Saint Marc* (EB; Paris: Gabalda, 1920), 270-71. Lagrange rightly points out that the promise to return the animal suggests that the disciples are speaking in the name of their Master. That promise (v. 3c: *auton apostellei palin*) is rendered variously in the manuscript tradition. For the variants and its inclusion in this form, see Taylor, *St Mark*, 454; Metzger, *Textual Commentary*, 92. Gnilka, *Markus*, 2:113-15 argues that the passage is made up of two traditions, vv. 1-7, associated with the finding of the ass, built on Old Testament motifs (especially Zech 9:9 and Gen 49:10-11), and already confessing Jesus as 'Lord', and vv. 8-11, a messianic entry.

11 As throughout 11:1-25, also here the Markan literary and theological agenda must drive the interpretation. Jesus' presence in Jerusalem has been delayed until now. See above, n. 2.

12 See A.E. Harvey, *Jesus and the Constraints of History* (London: Duckworth, 1982), 122-23. A close parallel to 11:2-7a is found in Jesus' sending two disciples to prepare for the final meal in 14:13-16. Both passages are used by Mark (perhaps based on a single pre-Markan tradition) to show Jesus' unfailing openness to God's design.

In vv. 1-7a Jesus initiates everything that happens. In v. 7b others enter the action.[13] The disciples throw their garments on the colt (v. 7b), and many (*polloi*) spread their garments and branches on the road. 'Those who went before and those who followed' (author's translation) proclaim the one who comes in the name of the Lord, and the coming of the kingdom of David (vv. 9-10). The only action of Jesus in this passage is to sit upon the colt, fulfilling his earlier words of instruction, that the Lord had need of it (see vv. 3, 6). The disciples' preparation of the colt by decorating it with their own garments, the laying of further garments to form a pathway for the man riding the decorated colt, and the spreading of leafy branches, cut from the field, are gestures that welcome Jesus as a powerful figure.[14] They recall earlier solemn entries to take possession of Jerusalem. The recent freeing of Jerusalem by Simon Maccabeus (142 BCE) comes to mind. 'On the twenty-third day of the second month, in the one hundred and seventy-first year, the Jews entered it with praise and palm branches and with harps and cymbals and stringed instruments, and with hymns and songs, because a great enemy had been crushed and removed from Israel' (1 Macc 13:51).[15] Jesus' teaching on the purpose of his journey to Jerusalem (see 8:31; 9:31; 10:32-24) is ignored by both the disciples who decorate the unridden colt of an ass (v. 7b), and those who strew Jesus' path with garments and branches (v. 8).

The acclamation of Jesus in v. 9 makes explicit the failure of both the disciples and the crowds who prepared Jesus' way. Two groups have been involved in the welcome to this point, those who prepared the way of Jesus (v. 8) and the disciples (v. 7b). The former are called 'those who went before' (*hoi proagontes*) and the disciples are given their familiar title, 'those who followed' (*hoi akolouthountes*).[16] Both groups join in the acclamation (*ekrazon*), 'Hosanna! Blessed is he who comes in the name of the Lord! Blessed is the kingdom of our Father David that is coming. Hosanna in the highest' (vv. 9-10). The initial cry of 'Hosanna' has its roots in Psalm 118:25, and is a petition, asking 'Grant salvation'. In its Markan context, however, it is an acclamation.[17] The remainder of v. 11 cites Psalm 118:26a (see LXX Ps 117:26a). Given the context of the preparation of the colt and the strewing of the roadway, the reader suspects that an acclamation welcoming Jesus as the one who comes in the name of the Lord expresses a false messianic expectation. The

---

13   This change in direction in v. 7b militates against Gnilka's reconstruction of two originally independent pre-Markan traditions, vv. 1-7, vv. 8-11. See above, n. 10.

14   The Markan setting for this event is several days before the celebration of the Passover (see 14:1). On the basis of the text, one could argue for five days (11:1, 19, 20 indicate three days, and 14:1 says 'after two days'). This chronology should not be pushed too hard, neither for strict chronology nor symbolism. See the careful remarks of Lane, *Mark*, 390-91. D.E. Nineham, *The Gospel of St. Mark* (PNTC; Harmondsworth: Penguin Books, 1963), 289-90, sees an already established 'Holy Week' behind Mark 11-16. See also Marcus, *Mark*, 2:768-69. E. LaVerdiere, *The Beginning of the Gospel. Introducing the Gospel According to Mark* (2 vols.; Collegeville, MN: Liturgical Press, 1999), 2:140-41, over-reads the three days of 11:1-20 as 'evoking the days of the passion and the resurrection'. The use of the leafy branches in v. 8 and the proclamation of Psalm 118 has led some to suggest that Jesus may have come to Jerusalem for the celebration of Tabernacles or Dedication. The context is clearly Passover. For the discussion, see J. Ernst, *Das Evangelium nach Markus* (RNT; Regensburg: Pustet-Verlag, 1981), 321; Marcus, *Mark*, 2:774.

15   See also Lohmeyer, *Markus*, 230 n. 8; Taylor, *St Mark*, 456; Harvey, *Jesus*, 125-26; Marcus, *Mark*, 779. There is no direct link between Mark 11:7-10 and 1 Macc 13:51. However, the same expectation – the freeing of Israel of a great enemy – is expressed, as throughout the earlier passages on the disciples' misunderstanding of Jesus' mission to Jerusalem (see 8:32-33; 9:32-34; 10:35-37, 41). It is this moment which is celebrated annually in the feast of Dedication (see 1 Macc 13:52).

16   The reference to two groups, the 'many' from v. 8 and the unnamed disciples from v. 7, resumed in 'those who went before and those who followed' (v. 9a) is seldom noticed by the commentators. See, however, Kelber, *Mark's Story*, 57-58. Collins, *Mark*, 519, finds an unconvincing parallel in Josephus' report of the burial of Herod the Great (*J.W.* 1.33.9 §673). The careful distinction made in v. 9a is more than 'a large crowd going in front of him and following behind him' (J. Painter, *Mark's Gospel. Worlds in Conflict* [New Testament Readings; London: Routledge, 1997], 155).

17   See Morna D. Hooker, *The Gospel according to St. Mark* (BNTC; London: A. & C. Black, 1991), 259-60.

suspicion is confirmed by the words of v. 10. The disciples and the crowd develop what is meant by the one who comes in the name of the Lord (v. 9) with a description of their expectation: he is bringing in the restoration of the kingdom of David (v. 10. See Amos 9:11; Isa 9:6-7).[18] Nothing could be further from the truth. Jesus is bringing in the Kingdom of God, and he has made it clear that this Kingdom will be established by means of rejection, death and resurrection in the city of David.[19] His command to bring an ass, rather than a horse (see v. 2), had set the scene for a humble entry, but it has been transformed by the disciples and the many who have their own understanding of who Jesus is, and what he will do in Jerusalem.[20] The hopes of those who welcome him in triumph, as the one who is coming in the name of the Lord to bring in the kingdom of David, have missed the point. The praise to God (see Ps 148:1) which closes the acclamation cannot save it from having articulated a false messianic expectation. It is another failure on the part of the disciples to accept that Jesus has come to Jerusalem as the Son of Man who will suffer, die, and be vindicated in the resurrection (8:31; 9:32; 10:32-34).[21] 'As far as the followers are concerned, Jesus enters Jerusalem in order to establish the Kingdom in power. That is cause for celebration. As far as Jesus is concerned, he enters into suffering and death. He will not be King until he is nailed to the cross'.[22]

For Mark, the acclamation of the messianic Son of David takes place outside Jerusalem.[23] The entry is held back until v. 11, and even here it is only mentioned passingly. The story-teller's main concern is to report Jesus' entry into the Temple. Jesus is the only active figure in v. 11. After the

---

18   See Harvey, *Jesus*, 121.
19   Lührmann, *Markusevangelium*, 189, makes an interesting distinction. He suggests that the acclamation is half right: he is bringing in the Kingdom, but not the Kingdom of David. He correctly comments, 'König Israels' wie "Sohn Davids" gehören nicht zur eigentlichen Christologie des Mk'. See also Ernst, *Markus*, 322. Marcus, *Mark*, 2:779-80, claims that the entry is messianic, and should be understood as such. His *subsequent* actions will show, however, 'how a Messiah is supposed to act'. Similarly, see Collins, *Mark*, 520.
20   Pilgrims normally walked into the city. Later reflection on this scene will make use of the prophecy of Zech 9:9 to characterize Jesus' entry as humble. However, there is no trace of Zechariah 9 in the Markan episode, and we should not speculate that perhaps Mark had it in mind (as E. Schweizer, *The Good News According to Mark* [trans. D.H. Madvig; London: SPCK, 1971], 227; Harvey, *Jesus*, 121-22, and Hooker, *Mark*, 257, also insist). Jesus' entry on an ass is probably part of the pre-Markan tradition, exploited to create a misunderstood episode of humble entry on an ass rather than a war-horse. See Taylor, *St Mark*, 452. Most commentators, however, find the use of *pōlos* (in both Mark 11:2, 4, 7 and Zech 9:9) as enough to develop a formative influence of the Zechariah text upon the Markan tradition. See, for example, Lohmeyer, *Markus*, 229. It is impossible to be sure about a pre-Markan stage of the narrative. For example, Gnilka's reconstruction of a pre-Markan passage, on the basis of Zech 9:9 and Gen 49:10-11 is pure speculation (*Markus*, 2:116-17). As with most who read the passage in a messianic sense, W. Grundmann, *Das Evangelium nach Markus* (THKNT 2; Berlin: Evangelische Verlagsanstalt, 1973 6th ed.), 224-226, uses Zech 9:9; Gen 49:10-11 and late Rabbinic material to support his messianic interpretation of the passage. See also Lane, *Mark*, 395-96.
21   The above reading of Mark 11:1-11 is at variance with the majority of interpreters who read the passage as a correct, if veiled, confession of Jesus' messianic status. See, for example, Lagrange, *Saint Marc*, 273-74; Nineham, *St Mark*, 291-94 (stressing, however, the ambiguity of the passage); Hooker, *St Mark*, 259-60; Gnilka, *Markus*, 2:120 (with reference back to Bartimaeus' confession of Jesus as the Son of David [10:47-48] as immediate preparation for this messianic acclamation); Lohmeyer, *Markus*, 232-33 (strongly aware of the ambiguity of the passage); LaVerdiere, *The Beginning*, 142-50 (who makes everything, 'the Lord', the ass [via Zech 9:9], the clothing, the branches on the road, and the acclamation, a correct recognition of Jesus' messianic status); Lane, *Mark*, 397-98; Schweizer, *Mark*, 229 (but stressing the lack of understanding); R.E. Watts, *Isaiah's New Exodus and Mark* (WUNT 2.88; Tübingen: J. C. B. Mohr [Paul Siebeck], 1997), 296-310.
22   Kelber, *Mark's Story*, 58. See also Idem, *The Kingdom*, 92-97. For a different reading, see Frank J. Matera, *The Kingship of Jesus. Composition and Theology in Mark 15* (SBLDS 66: Chico: Scholars Press, 1982), 70-74, who argues that there is a deliberate ambiguity in Jesus' entry. At one level Mark wishes to present Jesus as a royal figure, but the Markan readership is aware that his royalty will be exercised on the cross.
23   Schweizer, *Mark*, 227, suggests that the entry may have taken place in Bethany, and that Jesus went on to Jerusalem and the Temple the following day.

AN ENDING AND A NEW BEGINNING

crowd and the acclamation of vv. 7b-10, there is an ominous silence and even a note of threat sounded as Jesus, alone, enters Jerusalem and goes into the Temple. No word is said as Jesus looked around at everything that can be seen there (*periblepsamenos panta*).[24] Silence falls upon the acclamations, as Jesus surveys the Temple. At least two responses are generated by v. 11.

1. The silence and the disappearance of the crowd and the acclamations are signs that Jesus does not accept what has been said and done.[25] Nothing is explicit, but the reader is sufficiently aware of the reasons for Jesus' first and only presence in Jerusalem to understand the rejection of the acclaim involved in this lonely entry into the city and the Temple.
2. A tension is generated in the narrative. Why does Jesus go directly to the Temple? Why does he look around at everything? The text records no judgment of what he sees. He leaves the city, going outside its precincts to the neighboring village of Bethany with his disciples.

Jesus' departure marks the end of the first episode in Jerusalem. It has recorded Jesus' acceptance of God's agenda for his presence in Jerusalem (vv. 1-7a), but it has also recorded the failure of the disciples and many others to do so (vv. 7b-10). It closes, ominously, with Jesus' entry into Jerusalem and his surveying the scene at the Temple (v. 11). He will return there in the next episode (vv. 12-25).

> Jesus' first entry into Jerusalem is aimed at the temple (11:11). The temple, not the city as such, is of interest to him. [...] The Twelve are made to witness his solitary inspection of the temple. What they observe is hardly a triumphal entry. Jesus is neither recognized in the streets of Jerusalem nor installed in the temple as the Davidic Messiah. [...] The temple will not be 'his place', let alone the site of universal salvation.[26]

The end of Temple worship (vv. 12-25)

a) The cursing of the fig tree (vv. 12-14)

A journey from Bethany, the next day, separates the episodes which follow (vv. 12-19) from those surrounding Jesus' entry into Jerusalem (vv. 1-11). Another morning journey, apparently along the

---

24 See Taylor, *St Mark*, 457-58. Mark's intentions are not simply 'compatible with the view that this is his first excursion to the Temple' (Marcus, *Mark*, 2.776). For something of the 'tension' generated by v. 11, see Collins, *Mark*, 521. See P.G. Bolt, *Jesus' Defeat of Death. Persuading Mark's Early Readers* (SNTSMS 125; Cambridge, Cambridge University Press, 2003), 245, who correctly writes: 'His arrival in the temple creates an expectation of action (11.11), and since nothing occurs, suspense: what had he seen? and what will be do?'.

25 Commentators who read 11:1-11 as Jesus' messianic entry into Jerusalem devote little attention to the enigmatic v. 11. Hooker (*St Mark*, 260), for example, describes it as 'something of an anticlimax', and Lane (*Mark*, 398), claims that it is 'the quiet before the storm'. For Taylor, *St Mark*, 458, it is a sign of the basic historicity of the narrative: 'Presumably the crowds have melted away'. Nineham, *St Mark*, 294, suggests that v. 11 'seems to have been composed by St Mark in the interests of his time-scheme'. Grundmann, *Markus*, 232, catches the mood well: 'Es wird eine eigenartige Fremdheit zwischen Jesus und Jerusalem sichtbar'.

26 Kelber, *Mark's Story*, 58-59. P. Fredriksen, *Jesus of Nazareth, King of the Jews* (New York: Vintage Books, 2000), 241-59, rejects the widespread acceptance that the Temple episode and Jesus' prophecy of the future destruction of the Temple (Mark 13:2) caused his eventual arrest and execution. She suggests that the episode never happened, and that the messianic features of his entry into Jerusalem led to his death. See also Idem, 'The Historical Jesus, the Scene in the Temple, and the Gospel of John', in P.N. Anderson, F. Just, & T. Thatcher (eds.), *John, Jesus, and History, Volume I: Critical Appraisals of Critical Views*, (SBLSymS 44; Atlanta: SBL 2007), 269-71. She argues: 'A straight line connects the mood and acclamation of the triumphal entry to the *titulus* on the cross' (p. 291). For a denial of this possibility, see Collins, *Mark*, 513-14.

same route, will begin in v. 20. However, as we have already noted, vv. 12-14 and vv. 20-26 act as a frame around the account of Jesus' presence in the Temple (vv. 15-19). In vv. 12-14 a fig tree is cursed, and in vv. 20-26 the consequences of that curse, and the significance of the whole episode are reported.[27] The scene in the Temple (vv. 15-19) is 'sandwiched' between the cursing of the fig tree on one morning, and its being found withered on the next.[28]

The reader is told that Jesus was hungry (v. 12c), and saw a fig tree in leaf in the distance. He goes to the tree to find some fruit, to assuage his hunger, but on arrival at the tree, he finds only leaves.[29] For it was not the time for figs (v. 13: *ho gar kairos ouk ēn sukōn*). Jesus finds the external signs of good health, but no fruit. The comment from the narrator, explaining why there were only leaves and no fruit, makes Jesus' subsequent words extremely harsh. Jesus condemns the tree to fruitlessness: 'May no one ever eat fruit from you again'. The condemnation of the fruitless tree at a time of the year when there could not have been fruit seems unreasonable.[30] The expression *kairos* is a most unexpected word to use if the narrator's comment is to be taken on its face value. It does not mean 'season of the year', but is an expression used regularly in both the LXX and the New Testament to speak of an opportune moment, and to speak theologically of the moment for God's action.[31] It is the expression used in Jesus' initial announcement: 'The time (*ho kairos*) is fulfilled, and the kingdom is at hand' (1:15). The reader is left wondering about this strange condemnation of a fruit tree which has all the signs of life, but no fruit, because this was not its *kairos*. The cursing of the fig tree may be a symbolic condemnation of Israel (see Hos 9:10, 16-17; Micah 4:4; 7:1; Jer 8:13; 24:1-10; 29:17; Zech 3:10), but more of the story is required before the reader can be sure.[32] The episode comes to an end with a further remark from the narrator, important for the formation of the sandwich construction around Jesus' presence in the Temple (vv. 15-19). The disciples heard Jesus' punishing words against the fig tree (v. 14b), and they will recall it as they pass by the tree on the following day (vv. 20-21).

b) Jesus ends the cultic activity of the Temple (vv. 15-19)

Jesus comes to Jerusalem and enters the Temple, as he did on his first arrival (v. 15ab. See v. 11a). Earlier he gazed at everything there was to be seen (v. 11b). An ominous silence surrounded his first arrival, but on this occasion he moves into action. He began to drive out those who

---

27 For a history of the interpretation of 11:12-25, see Telford, *The Barren Temple*, 1-38.
28 See Marcus, *Mark*, 2:788-89, and Collins, *Mark*, 523-25, for suggestions concerning Mark's use of earlier traditions.
29 Mark uses Jesus' hunger to 'prepare the way for the story' (Taylor, *St Mark*, 459). For C.D. Marshall, *Faith as a Theme in Mark's Narrative* (SNTSMS 64; Cambridge: Cambridge University Press, 1989), 160, the hunger is a symbol of Jesus' demand for faith. Collins, *Mark*, 525, uses the hunger theme as an indication that what follows is a 'metaphorical narrative'.
30 Lohmeyer, *Markus*, 234, tries to overcome the harshness of Jesus' words by suggesting that the reference to the time of the year might be a gloss. See also Anderson, *Mark*, 265. Markus, *Mark*, 2:782, points out that the word *karpon* ('fruit') is used here, invoking 'the biblical notion of fruitfulness or fruitlessness as a symbol of spiritual health or disease'. See also Telford, *Barren Temple*, 261. For Collins, *Mark*, 525-26, the tree with leaves but no fruit symbolizes the fact that the leaders of Israel did not welcome Jesus.
31 See Kelber, *Mark's Story*, 60: 'It is not a botanical term indicating the season for figs but a religious term denoting the time of the Kingdom of God'. Gnilka, *Markus*, 2:124, comments on attempts to calculate what season of the year is indicated: 'Diese botanische Akribie entspräche kaum seinem Interesse'. On the use of the fig-tree as a symbol of good and bad people and institutions, see Marcus, *Mark*, 789-90.
32 Gnilka, *Markus*, 2:125, in the light of the prophetic use of the fig tree to refer to Israel, suggests that already in vv. 12-14 the message of Israel's failure to respond to the eschatological *kairos* is present. See also Marshall, *Faith as a Theme*, 160-61. Many have rightly suggested that the story is a 'legendary concretising' (Anderson, *Mark*, 263) of the parable in Luke 13:6-9, where the fig tree is clearly an image for Israel.

sold and bought, he overturned the tables of the money-changers and the stools of the sellers of pigeons (v. 15bcd).³³ This action strikes at functionaries whose tasks were essential to the right performance of the Temple cult. No other location other than the Temple itself (v. 15: *kai eiselthōn eis to hieron*) is given for this action. We are accustomed to supplying the entrance gate, or the open court of the Gentiles.³⁴ This is not in the text. Jesus enters the Temple, and within this sacred site of Israel the following actions and words take place. Money-changers were present at the Temple to ensure that the coinage used to pay the half-shekel Temple tax levied on Jews was acceptable within the Temple precincts. Coins carrying human effigies were changed into Tyrian coinage.³⁵ In this way the bearer's money was safe and available for the half-shekel tax, but so was the purity of the Temple area. Essential to the cultic life of the Temple were the sacrifices and offerings, great and small, that the faithful Jew made while in the Temple. This necessarily generated a buying and selling of goods which could be offered and sacrificed, including pigeons, the living thing sacrificed by the poorest and most humble (see Lev 12:8; 14:22; 15:14, 29).³⁶ Jesus' actions stop all supply of material for the cultic practices of the Temple, and make it impossible for people to change their coins to enter the precincts of the Temple without impurity.

The brief description of Jesus' further action in the Temple in v. 16 provides the key to the interpretation of his presence. Jesus takes control of everything that goes on in the Temple. He decides what will be allowed or not allowed there. He will not allow *hina tis dianegkēi skeuos dia tou hierou* (v. 16). The word *to skeuos* has many possible meanings. It can be a general indication of an object used for any purpose at all, thus a 'thing', widely used in English translations (e.g. 'he would not allow anyone to carry anything through the Temple' [RSV]). It also has the meaning of a vessel, or an instrument, and on the basis of some difficult New Testament texts (see 1 Thess 4:4) has come to be interpreted as a 'chosen vessel', one's own body, or the body of one's wife.³⁷ In v. 16 the word, set within the context of the Temple cult, can be given its basic meaning of a vessel or an implement, with the nuance, 'all that belongs to a complete outfit'.³⁸ The expression *to skeuos* in Mark 11:16 refers to the vessels and instruments that were used in the Temple as part of its traditional cultic practices. Jesus will not allow the use of any of the vessels or implements that form part of the day-to-day practices of the Temple. The processing, back and forth, with a variety of vessels and implements comes to a halt.³⁹ On his second day in Jerusalem, the Markan Jesus brings to an end practices essential for the purity of the Temple area (v. 15bc) and trades essential

---

33 The expression 'he began to drive out' (*ērxato ekballein*), although a common construction in the Gospel of Mark (*ērxato* + infinitive), creates the impression that Jesus' activity went on for some time.
34 See, for example, Taylor, *St Mark*, 462; Hooker, *St Mark*, 267; Gnilka, *Markus*, 2:128. They locate the incident in the Court of the Gentiles. The expression 'Court of the Gentiles' is a modern invention, never found in antiquity. Rev 11:2 is the closest one gets in the New Testament.
35 See I. Abrahams, *Studies in Pharisaism and the Gospels* (First Series; Cambridge: Cambridge University Press, 1917), 82-89; Hooker, *St Mark*, 267-68.
36 On both the money-changing and the animals, see E.P. Sanders, *Jesus and Judaism* (Philadelphia: Fortress, 1985), 61-76. As in all commercial activity, corruption was possible, and there was already a strain within pre-Christian Judaism that attacked such corruption. For Marcus, *Mark*, 2:782-83, whatever may have been the case historically, the Markan Jesus sees the activities as a sacrilege. For further *historical* reflection, see Moloney, 'Revisiting the Temple'.
37 On these meanings, see the discussion in BAGD, 754, s.v. *skeuos*.
38 LSJ, 1607, s.v. *skeuos*.
39 The usual explanation for v. 16 is that Jesus stops people taking short cuts through the Temple area, a practice prohibited in *m.Ber.* 9:5. See, for example, Lagrange, *Saint Marc*, 277; Grundmann, *Markus*, 231; Taylor, *St Mark*, 463; Hooker, *St Mark*, 268. This explanation trivializes Jesus' dominance of the Temple and its cult. Marcus, *Mark*, 2:783, includes sacred vessels in his review of the meaning of *skeuos*, but suggests it means a weapon. Collins, *Mark*, 530, accepts that the expression refers to vessels, but claims that Jesus is prohibiting the introduction of vessels from outside the Temple, thus profaning it.

for the provision of victims for sacrifice, even the most simple (v. 15d). He prohibits the use of all vessels and implements necessary for sacrifices and offerings (v. 16).[40] The effect of Jesus' actions, described in vv. 15-16, is that all activity in the cultic center of Israel comes to a stop! Summing up what this means, the story-teller succinctly states that Jesus takes command of the Temple area as such, deciding what is allowed and not allowed. In this highly symbolic narrative, Jesus is the master of the Temple. To suggest that the historical Jesus was able to drive out all who served Temple practice (v. 15), and then to determine what was allowed to happen or not happen within the entire Temple area, strains all imagination.[41] But *the Markan message* is clear. On his first full day in Jerusalem, Jesus brings to an end the cultic activity of the Jewish Temple.[42]

The teaching which follows is solemnly introduced (v. 17a: *edidasken kai elegen autois*). Jesus explains his actions in a fashion particularly eloquent to the Markan readers and listeners (v. 17). As with the actions of Jesus, the larger literary and theological design determines the meaning of Jesus' words. Citing LXX Isaiah 56:7, Jesus assumes the authority of Yhwh, speaking in the first person in the Psalm. The House of God, symbolized by the Temple, does not belong to the leaders of Israel. Metaphorical and symbolic language continues as Jesus insists that the Temple is 'my house'. The Scripture claiming that God's house, now the house of Jesus, will become a house of prayer for all the nations, must be fulfilled (v. 17b). The abominations now visible in the Temple of Jerusalem must be transformed. Jesus addresses an audience (*hymeis*), and accused them of having made God's Temple into a *spēleion lēistōn* (v. 17c).[43] The audience (v. 17c: *hymeis*) identifies itself in v. 18a: *kai ēkousan hoi archiereis kai hoi grammateis*. But the reference to the 'den of thieves' must not simply be read as an attack of Jesus upon the Jewish leadership *in the world of the story*. It must be read at two levels, as it has an association with *the world of the readers*.

At one level Mark records the memory of the historical Jesus' dissatisfaction with the abuse of the Temple by the Jewish practices of his time. This memory, probably already existing as a pre-Markan tradition,[44] is reported in vv. 15-19. However, the words that record his accusation must be

---

40 See Lührmann, *Markusevangelium*, 193. As Kelber, *Kingdom*, 101 n. 43, points out, over one-third of the references to *skeuos* in the LXX refer to sacred cult objects of the tabernacles, altar or Temple. Ernst, *Markus*, 329, doubts the connection with the sacred vessels. He regards Jesus' actions as putting into question Jewish Temple cult. *For Mark, Jesus' actions are more radical than 'putting into question'*.

41 See Grundmann, *Markus*, 230. As Sanders, *Jesus and Judaism*, 70, remarks: 'Any real effort to stop the trade necessary to the temple service would have required an army, and there is no evidence of a substantial martial conflict'. See also Lohmeyer, *Markus*, 237; M. Hengel, *Was Jesus a Revolutionist?* (Philadelphia: Fortress Press, 1971), 16-17. See the unacceptable efforts of Taylor, *St Mark*, 463, to overcome this difficulty. However, the 'historicity' of the incident is widely accepted. See, for example, Lane, *Mark*, 403-405; Gnilka, *Markus*, 2:130-31. It appears to me that this question should be broadened. Was Jesus' presence in Jerusalem and the Temple a problem *on only one occasion* (thus accepting the Markan scheme)? Perhaps Mark 11:15-19 is a blend of pre-Markan and Markan traditions which reflect Jesus' regular presence in Jerusalem and its Temple (as in the Fourth Gospel). See the following note.

42 See Kelber, *Kingdom*, 97-102. See Kelber, *Mark's Story*, 60: 'Jesus' two actions are tantamount to the shutting down of the business and the religious functions of the temple'. Kelber's assessment of 'endings' in Jerusalem is correct. However, his major case, that Jerusalem is being condemned, in favor of Galilee, as the 'place' of the kingdom (see *Kingdom*, 105-107), following the Lohmeyer-Marxsen geographical reading of Mark, goes beyond the evidence. For a more balanced assessment, see Marshall, *Faith as a Theme*, 161, and Gnilka, *Markus*, 2:129. The terse indications of vv. 15-16 are highly charged symbolic actions. A great deal of time and effort has been devoted to this question, especially in the light of Sanders, *Jesus and Judaism*, 61-76. Sanders suggests that Jesus' actions are a symbol of the Temple's future destruction, and not a cleansing. For a detailed discussion of this historical question, see the as yet unpublished paper (see n. 1), Moloney, 'Revisiting the Temple'.

43 The expression 'den of robbers' is rendered as in LXX Jer 7:11. This does not exclude the possibility of a Markan reading of the expression in terms of the Jewish revolt (see below). But for Collins, *Mark*, 530-32, Mark wishes to contrast the fact that the leaders did not welcome Jesus, God's Messiah, yet they continue ritual worship of God in the Temple

44 See Gnilka, *Markus*, 2:127-28.

linked with the violence in the Temple area which marked the final period of the Jewish war in 70 CE. The expression used for 'robbers' (*lēistēs*) is the term favored by Josephus to describe (always negatively) the Zealots, whom he blamed for the disasters that fell upon Israel and Jerusalem.[45] It is not a word used for those involved in sharp business practices. In the final days of the war, as the Roman armies encircled the city of Jerusalem and broke through the walls, the leaders of the revolt drew back into the Temple area and used it as a fortress (see Josephus, *J.W.* 6:68-80).[46] These events, fresh in the minds of the readers of the Gospel of Mark who are hearing of wars and rumors of wars (see 13:7), provide contemporary meaning to Jesus' accusation. In the immediate post-war period, Mark's readers and listeners are aware that the Temple, reduced to a *spēlaion lēistōn* by the leaders of Israel in revolt, has been destroyed by the Roman armies.[47] There is need for a new way for Israel and all the nations to turn to God in prayer. Symbolically, however, before the physical destruction of the Temple, Jesus has already brought its practices to a close (vv. 15-16), and indicated to the Jewish leadership that their administration of God's house had frustrated its purpose (v. 17).[48] In Jesus' later discussion with the disciples he will tell them how the prophecy of Isaiah 56:7 will be fulfilled (see vv. 22-25). Despite the attempts of Israel to frustrate God's designs, Jesus' house will become a house of prayer for all the nations. A memory from the story of Jesus speaks eloquently to the experience of the Christian community.

The leaders of Israel, hearing Jesus' words, renew the earlier decision of the Pharisees and the Herodians to plan the death of Jesus (v. 18a. See 3:6). Their plan lies dormant for the moment, due to the extreme wonder and amazement of the crowds at Jesus' teaching (v. 18b). It will be hatched in due course, as the plot of the chief priests and the scribes, still aware that they must work carefully to avoid a revolt among the people, draws in Judas (14:1-2, 10-11). As the passion of Jesus unfolds, they manage to avoid the opinion of the people.

Paradoxically, as the reader and the disciples (!) already know from the passion predictions (8:31; 9:31; 10:33-34), the success of their plan to destroy Jesus leads to his resurrection. The reader, the disciples and the leaders of the Jews will soon be told that the rejected corner stone will become the foundation of a new Temple (see 12:10-11; 14:57-58).[49] The house of Jesus cannot be the Temple of Jerusalem, now destroyed, but it will provide access to God for all the nations. The

---

45 See M. Hengel, *The Zealots. Investigations into the Jewish Freedom Movement in the Period from Herod I to 70 A.D.* (Edinburgh: T. & T. Clark, 1989), 41-46. Hengel remarks: 'Josephus used the word *lēistai* to brand the Zealots as lawless rebels and criminals in the Roman sense and as men who in the end received the punishment they deserved'. See also K.H. Rengstorf, 'lēistēs', *TDNT* 4:257-62.

46 This section of Josephus' *Jewish War* is written with considerable passion, and little objectivity. At one point, refugees from the Temple area appeal to those inside to save the nation by surrendering the Temple to the (noble) Romans. Josephus describes the response from inside the Temple: 'These appeals only excited fiercer opposition, and retorting by heaping abuse on the deserters, they ranged their quick-firers, catapults, and *ballistae* above the city gates, so that the surrounding temple-court from the multitude of dead resembled a common burial ground and the temple itself a fortress' (*J. W.* 6.121).

47 See G.W. Buchanan, 'Mark 11:15-19: Brigands in the Temple', *HUCA* 30 (1959), 169-77; C.K. Barrett, 'The House of Prayer and the Den of Thieves', in E.E. Ellis & E. Grässer (eds.), *Jesus und Paulus. Festschrift für Werner Georg Kümmel zum 70. Geburtstag* (Göttingen: Vandenhoeck & Ruprecht, 1975), 13-20; Lührmann, *Markusevangelium*, 193, Collins, *Mark*, 531-32, and especially Markus, *Mark*, 2:784.

48 Marcus, *Mark*, 2:790-93, argues forcefully for a 'symbolic' meaning for the gesture. It is not the 'end' of the Temple, but its 'purging' of evil people and practices. For Collins, *Mark*, 532, the gesture indicates 'a symbolic condemnation of the leaders of the people, not a rejection of the temple or the people as a whole'.

49 See Gnilka, *Markus*, 2:129-30.

second day of Jesus' presence closes as the evening comes. Jesus and the disciples leave the city.[50] Jesus has brought worship in the Jewish Temple to an end, and has promised that his house would be a house of prayer for all the nations (v. 19. See v. 17b).

a¹) The withered fig tree, and a new way to God (vv. 20-25).

The following day Jesus and the disciples return to Jerusalem (see v. 27), passing the fig tree on their way. They all see the fig tree, now withered away to its roots. It is completely destroyed (v. 20). Jesus' words have come true; no one will eat of the fruit of this tree (see v. 14a). The reader is aware of a *reprise*. The second part of the sandwich construction is under way.[51] The link with the earlier passage continues as Peter, in the name of all the disciples who heard what Jesus had said on the previous day, remembers and speaks (v. 21a. See v. 14b). Addressing Jesus as 'Rabbi' he points out that the curse has had its effect (v. 21b). The fig tree as a symbol of Israel and its Temple (see Hos 9:10, 16-17; Micah 4:4; 7:1; Jer 8:13; 24:1-10; 29:17; Joel 1:7, 12; Zech 14; Ezek 17; 47; Psalms) is obvious.[52] Traditional access to God through Israel's Temple cult and worship had the external splendour (see v. 13 and v. 17). But Mark's story of Jesus is now nearing its end. He has been in Israel, preaching and demonstrating the advent of the Kingdom of God (see 1:14-15). He has met only resistance and rejection (see 2:1-3:6; 3:20-35; 6:1-6a, 14-29; 7:1-23; 8:11-13; 10:2). The time of Jesus among them, the *kairos*, the time of his bringing the Kingdom of God to them, is drawing to an end. *Never* has Israel shown receptivity to Jesus' person and words. The offer of the Kingdom has been steadily rejected. Even his chosen disciples are struggling to comprehend and accept all it involves. Jesus has begun a series of encounters with Israel's traditional ways to God, bringing them to an end. The fig tree, a symbol of Israel and its Temple, has rejected the possibility of Jesus' presence as the coming of the Kingdom (see 1:14-15), and will thus be forever unfruitful. The coming of Jesus is not the *kairos* of Israel and its Temple.[53] Jesus' deeds in vv. 15-16 symbolically brought to an end the cultic practices of the Jerusalem Temple. As the Markan community was aware, the house of God had become a den of thieves, and has been destroyed.[54]

Jesus does not explain the link between the withered fig tree and the now defunct Temple. He moves directly to explain how the prophecy of Isaiah 56:7 used in v. 17 will be fulfilled. No longer does one look to a defunct Temple and cult, destroyed both symbolically in Jesus' deeds and concretely in the actions of the Romans in 70 CE, but to faith (vv. 22-23), prayer (v. 24), and forgiveness (v. 25). Jesus' house will be a house of prayer for the nations (see v. 17b). A radical commitment to faith in God is called for (v. 22).[55] The hyperbolic example of the workings of such faith indicates its unconditional

---

50 Reading the plural *exeporouonto* in v. 19, rather than the strongly supported (e.g. Sinaiticus, Ephraim Rescript, Bezae, Koridethi) singular *exeporeueto*. It is difficult to be certain, as v. 18 makes the plural in v. 19 the *lectio difficilior*, however it may have been introduced to create a smooth passage to the plural of v. 20. The weight of the external evidence (e.g. Alexandrinus, Vaticanus, Paris, Freer Gospels) tips the balance in support of the plural. See Metzger, *A Textual Commentary*, 92. For a contrary position, see Taylor, *St Mark*, 465.
51 For suggestions concerning Mark's use of prior traditions, see Collins, *Mark*, 532-33.
52 See Gnilka, *Markus*, 2:124, and especially Telford, *The Barren Temple*, 128-63. On pp. 176-204, Telford draws upon later Jewish material that further supports this association.
53 See Telford, *The Barren Temple*, 237-38; Gnilka, *Markus*, 2:134. For Lührmann, *Markusevangelium*, 191, the question of the time of the year and the fruitfulness of the tree is not the issue. The reader must be made aware that what Jesus says will happen, does happen.
54 For Collins, *Mark*, 533-34, the withering of the fig-tree continues the theme of the failure of the Jewish leaders.
55 Some important witnesses (e.g. Sinaiticus, Bezae, Koridethi) make Jesus words conditional, 'If you have faith in God'. This reading, however, is probably the result of an assimilation to Luke 17:6; Matt 21:21. See Marshall, *Faith as a Theme*, 164-65; Marcus, *Mark*, 2:785.

and profoundly internal nature. It also hints that the wonder of the fig tree's withering is the result of Jesus' faith in God.[56] Believers are to ask the impossible: a mountain is to be taken up and cast into the sea, already symbolized in Jesus' bringing to an end the cult on the Temple mount.[57] Jesus' earlier words on the fundamental importance of what comes out of a person, rather than what goes in (see 7:14-15, 18-23), also uttered within a context of conflict with Israel, come to mind. The impossible becomes possible for the one who does not doubt in his heart (*en tēi kardiai autou*), but believes what he says (v. 23). The issue is not whether mountains move, but Jesus' insistence that prayers coming from the unquestioning and believing heart will, unlike the now defunct Temple, bear fruit. Such teaching shifts easily into the theme of prayer, catching up, initially, what was said in v. 23 about faith. In v. 23 the issue was asking with unconditional faith, while in v. 24 Jesus stresses more the actions of a believing supplicant. Union with God, established by faith in God (see v. 22), leads the believer into a situation where, in faith, whatever is asked for is already granted (v. 24). None of this can be proved, or fixed into a formula or a cult.[58] It demands an unconditional openness to the ways of God, and establishes a oneness between the praying believer, and the God who grants the request.[59] Jesus' instruction on prayer, however, is not only about the relationship between the believer and God. Matching the articulation of this teaching in Q (see Matt 6:12, 14-15; Luke 11:4),[60] Jesus insists that the relationship between the believer and God will be fruitless unless there is forgiveness between the believer and his or her neighbor. The first action in prayer is to forgive, so that the Father in heaven, father of both the one praying and the one forgiven, can forgive the sins of the one praying (v. 25).[61] One cannot pray to God, the Father in heaven, with hate in one's heart.[62]

---

56 On the history of the tradition, and the Markan literary and theological activity in linking vv. 22-25 to the cursing of the fig-tree, see Telford, *The Barren Temple*, 49-59. The expression *pistis theou* is rare in the New Testament (see Rom 3:3; 1 Thess 1:8; Heb 6:1; John 14:1). Here the genitive is objective, i.e. 'faith in God. See Gnilka, *Markus*, 2:134. Nowhere else in the Gospels are the disciples commanded to believe in God. For an attempt to include a subjective dimension in this faith (a faith that equals the faith of God), see LaVerdiere, *The Beginning*, 2:160-61.

57 Most suggest that the following sayings were collected from a variety of sources on the basis of catchwords: believe, pray. See, for example, Lohmeyer, *Markus*, 238-39; Taylor, *St Mark*, 465; Nineham, *St Mark*, 300; Grundmann, *Markus*, 233; Gnilka, *Markus*, 2:133; Painter, *Mark's Gospel*, 160. It is sometimes suggested (e.g. Grundmann, *Markus*, 234; Hooker, *St Mark*, 269-70; Marcus, *Mark*, 2:785-87) that 'this mountain' may refer to the Temple mount (or the Mount of Olives), and thus an extension of the destruction of the fig tree as an action against the Temple. An association with the Temple mount is part of the Markan message. It was a traditional saying (see Matt 17:20; Luke 17:6; 1 Cor 13:2; *Gos. Thom.* 48, 106), elaborated and inserted into this context by Mark to make this point. For a detailed discussion also coming to this conclusion, see Telford, *The Barren Temple*, 95-119. See also Marshall, *Faith as a Theme*, 165-69; Watts, *New Exodus*, 332-37; Marcus, *Mark*, 2:794. For long-standing links between moving mountains as evidence of faith, see S.E. Dowd, *Prayer, Power and the Problem of Suffering. Mark 11:22-25 in the Context of Markan Theology* (SBLDS 105; Atlanta: Scholars Press, 1988), 69-94.

58 On the relationship between prayer and the Temple, see Dowd, *Prayer*, 45-55.

59 Dowd, *Prayer*, 95-122, shows the intimate relationship between prayer, faith and power. The community addressed by vv. 22-25 is called to believe that nothing is impossible for God (see 10:27).

60 This aspect of Jesus' teaching on prayer reaches back to the teaching of the historical Jesus, but there is no need to claim, as does Taylor, *St Mark*, 467, that v. 25 'reflects a knowledge of the Lord's Prayer'.

61 The universal rejection of v. 26 as original has led to the suggestion that v. 25 may also be a gloss. It is to be retained. See the discussion in Lane, *Mark*, 410-11; Marshall, *Faith as a Theme*, 172-74, Collins, *Mark*, 537, and especially Dowd, *Prayer*, 38-45.

62 On the function of forgiveness in the newly constituted Temple of the Markan community, see Dowd, *Prayer*, 123-29. For an eloquent reflection of this aspect of vv. 23-25, see Marcus, *Mark*, 2:795-96. Marcus situates the passage in a community experiencing doubt, despair, war and persecution. Forgiveness, and not revenge, is called for. See also Bolt, *Jesus' Defeat of Death*, 245-46. Collins, *Mark*, 534-36, traces exhortations of vv. 22-25 and other moments of Jesus' instruction of his disciples in the Gospel of Mark. This is the only place in the Gospel of Mark where God is called 'your Father in heaven'. Prayer seems to be the place where disciples had to understand their relationship to God as Father (see Matt 6:9; Luke 11:2).

Conclusion

The way to God expressed in the cultic practices of the Jerusalem Temple has been brought to an end (vv. 13-14, 15-16, 20-21). There is another way to God: a way of life marked by faith, prayer and forgiveness (vv. 20-25).[63] Within the house of Jesus one finds a house of prayer for all the nations (see v. 17b). The reader is being led to accept that there will be another Temple, and within that Temple faith, prayer and forgiveness, not the cultic practices of Israel, will unite the believer with God.[64] These are not easy practices. They demand an unconditional commitment which comes from the depths of one's heart, and the prior forgiveness of one's neighbor before one turns to address the Father in prayer (vv. 22-25). The theme of the new Temple, a new way to God hinted at in vv. 12-15 will emerge more strongly in the conflicts which follow immediately between Jesus and the leaders of Israel (11:27-12:44. See 12:10-11), and will culminate in the passion narrative (see 14:58; 15:37-39).

Francis J. Moloney
Catholic Theological College, University of Divinity

---

[63] 'Mark employs the material positively to give content to the new "house of prayer" destined to supplant the old "den of robbers"', Marshall, *Faith as a Theme*, 163. See also Ernst, *Markus*, 334-35.

[64] On the praying community in vv. 24-25 as the expression of the faith (see vv. 22-23) of the eschatological community, see Marshall, *Faith as a Theme*, 170-72.

A Note on The Gospels' Jesus Tradition, Memory, and Issues Raised by Bart Ehrman

DARRELL L. BOCK

Anyone paying attention to Gospel studies will know that the issue of memory and its role in the Gospel tradition has becomes a major topic of discussion in Jesus studies. The topic was broached by Kenneth E. Bailey years ago when he used the context of Middle Eastern Bedouins to suggest a middle way between the claims of Bultmann and others, that oral tradition was unreliable because it was passed on in informal and uncontrolled ways, and the opposite claims of the Scandinavian school, arguing for a more controlled and formal tradition by appealing to rabbinic examples.[1] Bailey's informal but controlled model argued that it was not as free as Bultmann suggested, nor as precise as the rabbinic model. More recently, Robert McIver devoted a monograph to the topic.[2] Both these authors argued for a model of gist and variation when it comes to memory and tradition with the result that the tradition was assessed to be far more stable than had been suggested.

This approach has not gone without challenges. Theodore Weeden has argued against approaches like that of Bailey and McIver.[3] Bart Ehrman has also questioned this approach and has utilized recent study of the Watergate scandal and the White House lawyer John Dean's memory to make his point.[4] Dean was Richard Nixon's in house lawyer from 1970-73. It is his use of this study that this note is designed to review. Ehrman appeals to work done by Ulric Neisser.[5] Ulric compared Dean's testimony, which had elicited claims of him having a fantastic memory, with the Nixon tapes which had emerged after Dean had given that testimony. The issue was to see how well the famous eyewitness to the events had recalled what had taken place. Ehrman

---

1. Bailey's article 'Informal Controlled Oral Tradition and the Synoptic Gospels', can be found in two places: *Asia Journal of Theology* 5 (1991), 34–54 and *Themelios* 20.2 (Jan, 1995), 4–11.
2. Robert McIver, *Memory, Jesus, and the Synoptic Gospels* (Resources for Biblical Study, 59; Atlanta: Society of Biblical Literature, 2011).
3. 'Kenneth Bailey's Theory of Oral Tradition: A Theory Contested by Its Evidence', *Journal for the Study of the Historical Jesus* 7 (2009), 3–43.
4. Bart Ehrman, *Jesus before the Gospels: How the Earliest Christians Remembered, Changed and Invented Their Stories of the Savior* (New York: HarperCollins, 2016), 125–31.
5. U. Neisser, 'John Dean's Memory: A Case Study', *Cognition* 9 (1981), 1–22.

used Neisser's study to challenge the 'gist but variation' model that Bailey had argued for as common among the Bedouins he knew. Ehrman was seeking to undercut the claim that such an understanding of oral tradition and memory might provide a model for what we see in the Gospels. Bailey had argued that key stories of community history were told with variation but that the gist was maintained by elders who oversaw how the stories were being passed on.[6] This note will first observe Ehrman's summary and use of Neisser's study, before examining more closely all Neisser said.

Ehrman's Look at Neisser and Neisser's Look at John Dean's Memory

Ehrman sets up this discussion by claiming that memory is always constructed and prone to error.[7] He accepts that often memory is good in broad outline and even says fundamental things can often be right.[8] Despite this recognition of the 'gist', he goes on to say that when, where, with whom and how can get messed up and that a lot of details and whole episodes can get messed up. So much of the gist is correct, but there are many mistakes as well.

In reviewing Neisser's study, he cites this portion to justify what he had argued:

> Comparison with the transcript shows that hardly a word of Dean's account is true. Nixon did not say *any* of the things attributed to him here [...] Nor had Dean himself said the things he later describes himself as saying [...] His account is plausible but entirely incorrect [...] Dean cannot be said to have reported the 'gist' of the opening remarks; no count of unit ideas or comparison of structure would produce a score much above zero.[9]

This citation is about the conversation on September 15, not a summary of the whole study. Earlier Neisser said this about Dean's memory in general: 'We shall see later that Dean recalls the "gist" of some conversations and not of others; the determinants of memory are more complicated than he believes them to be. In particular, he did *not* remember what the President said in their first prolonged and momentous meeting. But there is no doubt about his confidence in his own testimony'.[10] Ehrman notes two more critical citations by Neisser of Dean's look at this event.[11] In the first example, Neisser calls Dean's testimony a 'fantasy of the meeting' and in the second Neisser summarizes and says that Dean's testimony about September 15, 'is wrong both as to the words used and the gist'. So it appears Ehrman has this right initially. Ehrman summarizes this way:

> whether Dean had a decent gist memory probably depends on how broadly one defines "gist". He knew he had a conversation with Nixon. He knew what the topics were. Nonetheless, he appears not to have known what was actually said, either by Nixon or himself.[12]

But we should read on. There are portions of Neisser's study Ehrman ignores. For example,

---

6   In the article Bailey also made a point to observe that different genre had different rules and were watched over with different levels of concern about accuracy.
7   Ehrman, *Jesus*, 126.
8   Ehrman, *Jesus*, 127.
9   Ehrman, *Jesus*, 129, citing 'John Dean's Memory', *Cognition*, 9. Italics are Ulric's. This article was accessed in http://people.whitman.edu/~herbrawt/classes/110/Neisser.pdf, 102–15. My citations will be from that version of the article. The citation Ehrman has is on p. 107 and is taken from the accessed, reprinted article. All subsequent references are to this accessed version with its page numbers.
10 Neisser, 'John Dean's Memory', 105.
11 'John Dean's Memory', 10, 13 (= pp.108 and 110 of the reprint edition).
12 Ehrman, *Jesus*, 129.

a few sentences right after the wrong and not the gist summary of the September meeting, Neisser says this:

> His testimony had much truth in it, but not at the level of "gist". It was true at a deeper level. Nixon was the kind of man Dean described, he had the knowledge Dean attributed to him, there was a cover up. Dean remembered all of that; he just didn't recall the actual conversation he was testifying about.[13]

Neisser goes on to discuss the March 21 meeting. In commenting on the first hour of that meeting, Neisser says Dean's memory 'was quite accurate. Comparison of the transcript with Dean's subsequent memory shows clear recall of the gist of what was said'.[14] Neisser notes in part it was because Dean gave a prepared report at this meeting. He also notes emphases Dean had about telling Nixon about the cancer on the presidency that were not 'faithful to any of these occasions'.[15] Neisser also notes that details about the million dollar statement were made but placed in the wrong conversation.[16] Neisser suggests Dean's ambition and effort to emphasize his own role led to 'reorganizing his recollections'.[17]

This is a fascinating study. Its actual results appear to be more mixed than the impression given by Ehrman's remarks. Let's cite Neisser's conclusions once he had completed his survey. He says, 'We are hardly surprised to find that memory is constructive, or that confident witnesses may be wrong'.[18] Later he adds,

> I believe John Dean's testimony can do more than remind us of their work [referring to earlier memory studies by W. Stern (1908) and F. C. Bartlett (1932)]. For one thing, his constructed memories were not altogether wrong. On the contrary, there is a sense in which he was altogether right; a level at which he was telling the truth about the Nixon White House. And sometimes – as in his testimony about March 21 – he was more specifically right as well. These islands of accuracy deserve special consideration.[19]

This sounds very different from the conclusions Ehrman drew. It is a major and important qualifier on how memory works and makes the case that the thrust of an event is often recalled well. Neisser goes on to discuss the difference between episodic memory and semantic memory and notes episodic errors in Dean but then goes on to say that there is *repisodic* memory that represents a repetition.[20] In effect, Neisser is arguing for a kind of compression and composite presentation that conflates conversations especially when they involve repeated themes. Neisser concludes this observation with this statement:

> What he says about these "repisodes" is essentially correct, even though it is not literally faithful to any one occasion. He is not remembering the "gist" of a single episode by itself, but the common characteristics of a whole series of events.[21]

He continues to contend that this might 'help us to interpret the paradoxical sense in which Dean was accurate throughout his testimony'.[22] He argues John Dean 'did not misrepresent this theme in his testimony'.[23] Neisser is referring to the cover-up here and notes gists can often be summarized in different words. So the transcripts did not undercut Dean's testimony because his overall portrait was on track. Neisser ends with this:

13 Neisser, 'John Dean's Memory', 110.
14 'John Dean's Memory', 111.
15 'John Dean's Memory', 112.
16 'John Dean's Memory', 113.
17 'John Dean's Memory', 114.
18 'John Dean's Memory', 113.
19 'John Dean's Memory', 113–14.
20 'John Dean's Memory', 114.
21 'John Dean's Memory', 114.
22 'John Dean's Memory', 114.
23 'John Dean's Memory', 114.

Except where the significance of his own role was at stake, Dean was right about what had really been going on in the White House. What he later told the Senators was fairly close to the mark: his mind was not a tape recorder, but it certainly received the message that was being given.[24]

Concluding Observations on Ehrman's Use of Neisser's Study, Memory, and the Jesus Tradition

So where does this survey of the Neisser article, and Ehrman's use of it, leave us? Four points can be made.

First, Ehrman has not fairly represented the article on John Dean's memory, or the points Neisser made about memory from it. Ehrman left out important dimensions and claims that Neisser made, including the key category the article contended for that is relevant to the Jesus discussion (*repisodic*). The result is that the issue of memory and Jesus is left in a more complicated frame than Ehrman suggests. In addition, that frame is far more favorable to the Bailey argument than Ehrman contends.

Second, the Neisser article wrestles with the issue of gist. It makes a distinction between gist of wording and gist of sense. Now anyone who has worked with historical Jesus studies will immediately recognize the difference as very much like the distinction between *ipsissima verba* (the very words of Jesus) and *ipsissima vox* (the very voice of Jesus). Most have long recognized that the Jesus tradition is more about *vox* versus *verba*. The tradition is likely to be summarizing Jesus on many occasions. The variations in similar scenes between the Gospels say as much. So this is not a perspective being read into how the Gospels handle scenes, but one that emerges as one works in the details of the Gospels.[25] Gist, as it appears to be used here by Bailey and others, has less to do with the exact words (which is why variation can occur in the first place) and more to do with the force of the whole event. On this standard, Neisser appears to give Dean enough credit that he could say the tapes did not really undercut the portrait he gave about what happened in Watergate. The presence of compression and repetition of themes as well as concerns about his own role in the events contributed to these variations.

Third, Neisser's study shows that we have to cope with issues of gist and compression especially for repeated events. This is especially relevant in the case of Jesus where as an itinerant preacher he would have covered themes on multiple occasions and in distinct kinds of settings. So the tradition may well reflect the *repisodic* character Neisser sees in Dean's testimony. Conflation and compression become more likely when one is trying to talk about multiple events in a short space. Again looking at parallels can help us here. One can simply compare the healing of Jairus's daughter in Matthew 9:18-26 and Luke 8:40-56 to see the kind of compression that is possible with an account. Matthew has reduced and conflated the account here. There is variation and gist. The core of the account, delivering two healings, is the same. This is a good example of gist and variation that is a product in this case of simple literary compression.

Fourth, there are factors that are distinct

---

24 'John Dean's Memory', 114.

25 My own initial look at his topic can be found in 'The Word of Jesus: Live, Jive, or Memorex', in M. Wilkens & J.Moreland (eds.), *Jesus Under Fire* (Grand Rapids: Zondervan, 1995), 74–99. This was followed up by my study that went beyond sayings to events that included actions in 'Precision and Accuracy: Making Distinctions in the Cultural Context That Gives Us Pause in Pitting the Gospels Against Each Other', in J.K. Hoffmeier & D.R. Magary (eds.), *Do Historical Matters Matter to Faith?* (Grand Rapids; Crossway, 2012), 367–381.

between Dean and the tradition that are important for our consideration. The apostles do not have self interest in these memories as Dean did. Neither is the memory a matter of just an individual's recall. We are dealing with corporate memory here and the likelihood of repetition in retelling from early on once these memories were deemed to be significant. Both of these elements would serve to reinforce the gist of the event. Another element of the corporate nature of this is that the materials were circulating officially through the churches. The materials that circulated through the hub churches in a region are likely to have been overseen and not handled as random recall. Before this material would have been used and reused in church, some type of reception would be in place to underscore the source and trustworthiness of what was being passed on. These are not random sources handled on a street corner somewhere, but corporate memory with oversight.

So considered on its whole, the study of Neisser gives support to the idea of gist when seen in this holistic and *repisodic* light. Neisser's study does not undercut the Jesus tradition in the manner Ehrman claimed. Ehrman's reporting selectively on Neisser's study has resulted in a skewed framing of the issue of memory and its dynamics. The case for a trustworthy core in such recollections, where much is at stake and many people are participating, is strong. The many variations within the parallels in many of the accounts do not look as if they seriously undercut the gist of what is shared between those accounts, at least in most cases. The model of Bailey is not as flawed as Ehrman's treatment suggests. As a result, the Jesus tradition may be far more trustworthy in pointing to root events than Ehrman suggests.

Darrell L. Bock
Dallas Theological Seminary

Preparing Israel for the Arrival of the Son of Man
Jesus' Kingship Parable (Luke 19:11-28) in its Historical and Literary Context

PETER G. BOLT

1. Would Jesus—or Luke—have owned the common interpretation of the 'Parable of the Pounds'?

In long-standing interpretation, by allegorically applying the nobleman's departure and return, Luke's 'Parable of the Pounds' (Luke 19:11-28) speaks of Christ's ascension and second coming, assumes 'Jesus himself predicted the delay of the parousia',[1] and moralizes that Christian readers ought to be faithful in the delay.

While questioning whether this common interpretation reflects the parable's original meaning on the lips of Jesus, recent scholarship nevertheless assumes that it reflects the parable's meaning within the Gospel of Luke. This article aims to take the historical critique one step further, to question whether even Luke would recognise it as his own, and to suggest an alternative.

The principle that a parable is not an allegory needs to be applied with rigour and consistency.[2] The parables of Jesus need to be interpreted non-allegorically, viewing all their elements together with integrity, in the context of Jesus ministry to first century Israel. But the parables also need to be interpreted as 'embedded texts', for they only exist in Gospel narratives. This article argues that 'the Pounds' is not an allegory, but a parable, both on Jesus' lips and in Luke's narrative portrayal, and, for both, its point is Christocentric and eschatological, urging hearers to see Jesus as the Son of Man, who is bringing in the Kingdom of God, and to find salvation and certainty in him.

2. The Parable In its Details and Drift

2.1 The context (verse 11)

Although the authenticity issue will be addressed below, for now it should be noted that Luke provides a clear context for the parable, and a clear reason for its delivery. Looking behind, the

---

1   Johnson, 'The Lukan Kingship Parable (Lk. 19:11-27)', *NovT* 24.2 (1982), 140 nn.6-8, who critiques the view, lists commentators who expressed this 'consistent view'. More could be added since 1982.
2   For the issue, see J. Jeremias, *The Parables of Jesus* (S.H. Hooke, transl.; London: SCM, ³1972 [ET: 1963, Original: 1954]; German: ⁸1970]), 66-89.

genitive absolute opening verse 11 shows that Jesus told the parable as a supplementary saying to those who heard his statement about Zacchaeus (19:10): Ἀκουόντων δὲ αὐτῶν ταῦτα προσθεὶς εἶπεν παραβολήν, 'while they were hearing these things, he spoke, adding [to these things] a parable'.[3] Looking ahead, the reason he told the parable is related to his proximity to Jerusalem and the consequential expectations of his hearers: διὰ τὸ ἐγγὺς εἶναι Ἰερουσαλὴμ αὐτὸν καὶ δοκεῖν αὐτοὺς ὅτι παραχρῆμα μέλλει ἡ βασιλεία τοῦ θεοῦ ἀναφαίνεσθαι, 'because he was near to Jerusalem and they thought that the Kingdom of God was immediately about to show up'.[4]

As the parable proper commences (v.12), the syntax ties it further to this situation by the consequential conjunction: εἶπεν οὖν, 'so he said, ...'. However, contrary to the common interpretation, nothing in this contextual statement demands that the parable be a *correction* to the stated expectations.[5]

2.2 The set up (19:12-14)

Setting the scene for later action, the parable opens by introducing 'a certain nobleman' who 'goes into a far country' (v.12). His purpose in doing so is simple, λαβεῖν ἑαυτῷ βασιλείαν καὶ ὑποστρέψαι, 'to receive for himself a kingdom and to return', that is, to be authorized to rule and then to exercise that rule.

Rather than focusing on his time away (as in the common interpretation), this introduction already throws the hearer's attention forward to what might happen after the nobleman receives the kingdom. Two sets of events occur prior to his journey. Firstly, 'after calling ten of his own slaves, he gave to them ten *mnas*,[6] and he said to them, "trade, while I am coming"' (v.13). Perhaps overly-confident that he will return as king,[7] he wants his servants to keep his money working in the meantime.

Secondly, because 'his citizens hated (ἐμίσουν) him', a delegation (πρεσβείαν)[8] follows to block his kingship bid (v.14).

2.3 The outcome (19:15-27)

The real action of the parable occurs after the master returns, having received the kingdom (v. 15, λαβόντα τὴν βασιλείαν). He calls the servants, to ascertain his profits (v.15). The first two report enormous returns on their money (vv.16-17; 18-19), but the third, who had wrapped it in a cloth fearing the master's severity, simply returns the *mna* with no increase. The master rewards the first two with authority over cities, but takes away the *mna* from the third.

Having dealt with his monetary matters, he then orders those he calls 'my enemies' (τοὺς ἐχθρούς μου), that is, the citizens who did not want him as their king, to be slaughtered in front of him (v.27, κατασφάξατε).

---

3   This is preferable to 'spoke an additional parable' (L.T. Johnson, *The Gospel of Luke* [Sacra Pagina 3; Collegeville, Minnesota: Liturgical Press, 1991], 289), because Jesus did not speak a parable in the Zacchaeus account.
4   ἀναφαίνεσθαι is rendered with the picture in mind of an island suddenly looming over the horizon (Acts 21:3).
5   For a critique, see Johnson, 'Lukan Kingship Parable', 146-149; *Luke*, 289, 292.
6   Simply called 'silver/money' (τὸ ἀργύριον) later in the parable, the Aramaic loan word μνᾶ is an indicator of the parable's overall Jewishness, and so its authenticity. See C.A. Evans, 'Reconstructing Jesus' Teaching: Problems and Possibilities', in J.H. Charlesworth & L.L. Johns (eds.), *Hillel and Jesus: Comparative Studies Of Two Major Religious Leaders* (Minneapolis: Fortress Press, 1997), 419 [397-426].
7   With Archelaus in mind (see below), it is easy to imagine Jesus' hearers smirking in delight at this detail, knowing that this privilege was refused, due to the petition of the Jewish embassy.
8   In the NT, πρεσβεία only occurs here and Luke 14:32. In 4 Macc. 4:11 it is used for another trip to Rome, as it is also for the Alexandrian Jews' appeal to Caligula, as reported in Philo's *Embassy to Gaius*.

2.4 The Concluding Setting

In the concluding narrative setting (v.28), Jesus continues the journey that has occupied Luke's attention since reporting Jesus' transfiguration (9:31, 51): 'And after saying these things, he went off before them, climbing up to Jerusalem' (v.28, ἐπορεύετο ἔμπροσθεν ἀναβαίνων εἰς Ἱεροσόλυμα). The point of view is that of the traveller, setting out from Jericho, now moving up the long climb towards Bethany (v.29), situated on the eastern slope of the Mount of Olives (v.29), from whence Jesus would soon descend (19:37) into the city (19:41).

2.5 'The Point'

The 'point', or 'application', or 'meaning' of the parable suggested here will emerge after the interpretive issues are worked through. However, discerning 'the point' raises issues of method, since a parable is not an allegory, and the two genres communicate differently. The internal details of an allegory correspond to external details in the situation of the presumed hearer, and interpretation consists in revealing these connections to extract 'application'. For a parable, however, these details are merely *the matrix from which the rhetorical impact of the parable emerges*. The 'point' of a parable is not the same as an intellectual summary of its 'teaching', or even its 'meaning'— understood in terms of content—, but it ought to be conceived as *a movement in life*. To be effective, a parable (like all communication) strives not to leave its hearers the same as it finds them. It is a rhetorical vehicle constructed to move its hearers 'from point A to point B', by means of making a profound impact upon them, often through proposing some kind of puzzle, or surprise, so that the hearers' minds are 'teased into active thought'.[9] To do so, the details of the parable may, or —perhaps even better— *will*, make multiple connections with the hearers, exposing their world, to draw them into the parable, but this is in order to move them through its relentless direction forward towards its *life outcome*, its point.

At this stage of the argument, it is sufficient to observe the overall direction of the parable. For the nobleman, the action moves from him taking steps to acquire kingship, to him exercising that kingship. For the other characters, the movement is from an articulation of their several relations to the nobleman, to their being called to account as the nobleman begins his reign. By domesticating the details to the direction, and in contrast to the common view, this bird's-eye view of the parable already suggests 'the point' is not found in the nobleman's initial journey or time spent away, but in the consequences of his kingship once confirmed.

As a rhetorical instrument, a parable is told to evoke a certain response in its hearers and its rhetorical point will be discerned therefore from the context (audience and setting) in which it is told. But since the parables of Jesus always come to us embedded in a Gospel, the Parable of the Pounds needs to be considered in two different (but related) contexts: the literary context of Luke's Gospel in which it is now packaged, and the original context of the life and ministry of the historical Jesus. This then raises the additional question, as to whether the function of the parable in Luke is in harmony with its function on the lips of the historical Jesus, or in opposition to it. And, in both cases, does the common interpretation prove to be adequate, or does it need correction?

---

9 C.H. Dodd, *The Parables of the Kingdom* (London: Collins, ⁵1967 [1935, rev. 1961]), 16: 'At its simplest the parable is a metaphor or simile drawn from nature or common life, arresting the hearer by its vividness or strangeness, and leaving the mind in sufficient doubt about its precise application to tease it into active thought'.

3. The Parable in its Literary Context

In 1982, L.T. Johnson's literary reading challenged the common interpretation. When understood in the flow of Luke's narrative, rather than referring to the delay of the Parousia, the parable 'illustrate[s] and interpret[s] the next section of Luke's story'. This 'kingship parable' warns not to refuse the king.[10]

Johnson found little in the parable itself suggesting 'an allegorical tale about the ascension-parousia', or indicating 'a temporal delay'.[11] Because of this lack, the common interpretation places considerable weight on the narrative setting (v.11) and reads the parable as a refutation of the crowd's expectation of the kingdom of God's imminent arrival. However, nothing indicates the crowd has a false view in need of correction.[12]

Emphatically denying that ἀναφαίνεσθαι is 'part of the technical language connected to the parousia',[13] and noting that Jesus' kingship is a feature of Luke's portrayal of Jesus in Jerusalem (22:29; 23:2; 23:37, 38, 42, 43),[14] Johnson concludes that 'Luke intended his parable to *confirm* 19:11, for the progress of Luke's story after the parable shows us in fact a "manifestation" of God's Kingdom "immediately"' (in 19:38).[15]

Despite explicitly rejecting allegory, interpreters often fail to rid themselves of its poison in one form or another.[16] Reflecting common practice, Johnson assigns correspondences between characters in the story and those in its embedding Gospel context: the nobleman is Jesus; the first two servants are the Twelve through whom the risen Lord continues to exercise authority; and the protesting fellow citizens are the leaders of Israel who reject Jesus and find themselves 'cut off from the people' (Acts 3:23; cf. 7:37 and Deut. 18:15-19).[17]

Because Jesus' parables always come embedded in the Gospels, literary analysis is essential and Johnson's insight that the parable acts as 'authorial commentary' on the wider narrative is helpful.[18] Nevertheless the historical question still begs an answer: how is Luke's narrative presentation of the Parable of the Pounds connected to the parable as spoken by Jesus of Nazareth?

4. The Parable in its Original Context

Just like parables in general are anchored in Jesus' authentic teaching,[19] a strong case can be made for the basic authenticity of this parable.

---

10 Johnson, 'Lukan Kingship Parable', 158-159. Johnson noted (p.141) earlier hints, both his own (*The Literary Function of Possessions in Luke-Acts* [SBLDS 39; Missoula: Scholars Press, 1977], 168-170) and those of David Tiede, *Prophecy and History in Luke-Acts* (Philadelphia: Fortress, 1980), 79. He later published the same view in *Luke*, 288-294.
11 Johnson, 'Lukan Kingship Parable', 143-144; *Luke*, 289, 292, 293-294.
12 Johnson, 'Lukan Kingship Parable', 146-149; *Luke*, 289, 292.
13 Johnson, 'Lukan Kingship Parable', 149.
14 Johnson, 'Lukan Kingship Parable', 150, see also 152-153; *Literary Function*, 170; *Luke*, 289, 293.
15 Johnson, 'Lukan Kingship Parable', 152.
16 Such as using allegorical assumptions to critique other views. E.g., Jeremias, *Parables*, 59-60: 'it is hardly conceivable that Jesus would have compared himself, either with a man "who drew out where he had not paid in, and reaped where he had not sown" (Luke 19:21), that is, a rapacious man, heedlessly intent on his own profit; or with a brutal oriental despot, gloating over the sight of his enemies slaughtered before his eyes'; Johnson, *Luke*, 294: 'the conventional interpretation can find no place for the installation of the slaves as participants in ruling within the kingdom, or the fact that the unreliable slave is not punished, only kept from ruling'.
17 Johnson, 'Lukan Kingship Parable', 158.
18 Johnson, *Luke*, 294.
19 Cf. Evans, 'Reconstructing Jesus' Teaching', 401: 'the parables are widely regarded as the most reliable part of the dominical tradition', see his n.11 for references.

4.1 The Parable in its Sociological Context

Beginning with Rohrbaugh in 1993, several studies utilizing social science models critique the prevailing interpretation by highlighting features of the parable that place Jesus' story in first-century Mediterranean peasant culture.[20] The master, with his voracious desire for power and wealth, and his two compliant and profitable servants, can only be viewed positively, and the third 'unproductive' servant negatively, from an élite perspective. Although this élite reading stretches from Chrystostom through to Calvin, it is particularly amenable to interpreters inured to the values of Western capitalism.[21] But for the Galilean peasants in Jesus' audience, it would be a frightening story, reflecting the oppressive world in which they were already struggling to survive, where 'the strong trample the weak and are rewarded for doing so'.[22] With notions of 'limited good' and production for use not exchange, peasants 'lived at the subsistence level and viewed traders as evil exploiters'.[23] Jesus' parable (not allegory) introduces a hated (v.14), and presumably already exploitative, master who receives even more power (vv.12, 15), which he ruthlessly exercises by calling his servants to account (vv.15-26), before slaughtering those he declares enemies (v.27). Although it is common to trivialize the amount of money involved,[24] it is more to the point to notice the inordinate profits turned in by the first two servants (1000% and 500%, compared to a Jewish predilection against any kind of usury, and a legal interest rate, even in Roman sources, of 12%).[25] The extremity of the results of their operation shows them to have been complicit in the master's exploitation of others, probably through loan-sharking deliberately designed to produce debts that necessitate land forfeiture.[26] They are rewarded for their efforts by being given authority over cities (vv.17, 19), which rather than being a share in political rule,[27] most likely refers to being given tax-gathering authority,[28] which will enable further exploitation for their own profit and that of the new king. Far from being damned as 'unfaithful', as in the common—and élite—reading, the third servant takes the role of the peasant hero, acting honorably by preserving the master's seed-funding, while refusing to participate in the exploitation of others through profiteering.[29] If the prevailing power structures are so corrupt that even legitimate and properly regulated opposition (v.14, οἱ δὲ πολῖται αὐτοῦ ... ἀπέστειλαν πρεσβείαν) can lead to wanton slaughter (v.27), then such passive resistance is not only wise, but it is the only course of action left open to the

---

20   R. Rohrbaugh, 'A Peasant Reading of the Parable of the Talents/pounds: A Text of Terror?', *BTB* 23.1 (1993), 32-39; E. van Eck, 'Do not question my honour: A social-scientific reading of the parable of the minas (Lk 19:12b-24, 27)', *HTS Teologiese Studies / Theological Studies* 67.3 (2011), Art#199, 1-11. www.hts.org.za, doi:10.4102/hts.v67i3.977; A.F. Braun, 'Reframing the Parable of the Pounds in Lukan Narrative and Economic Context: Luke 19:11-28', *CurrMTh* 39.6 (2012), 442-448. See also Evans, 'Reconstructing Jesus' Teaching', 420-423.
21   Rohrbaugh, 'A Peasant Reading', 33.
22   Rohrbaugh, 'A Peasant Reading', 35.
23   Rohrbaugh, 'A Peasant Reading', 33-34.
24   This evaluation is partly due to the master's in v.17, that his servant has been 'reliable in a tiny thing', although it is also influenced by the comparative value of Luke's *mna* (100 drachma/denarii) to Matthew's talent (=60 *mnas*). However, it is difficult to imagine a peasant dismissing 100 days wages (=one *mna*) as an inconsiderable amount; so also, Evans, 'Reconstructing Jesus' Teaching', 419.
25   Rohrbaugh, 'A Peasant Reading', 35-37. Johnson, *Luke*, 290.
26   Van Eck, 'Do not question my honour', 5, 7.
27   Contra Johnson, 'Lukan Kingship Parable', 155; *Luke*, 290, 291. This also damages his argument that in the wider narrative of Luke-Acts this refers to the apostles sharing in the rule of the risen Christ.
28   See Van Eck, 'Do not question my honour', 7-8.
29   Whereas the third servant is usually read as a negative example, in climactic third position he delivers the surprise of the parable, and is therefore a key to the parable's point. Cf. van Eck, 'Do not question my honour', 9-10; Rohrbaugh, 'A Peasant Reading', 35-37.

powerless.[30] Still alive, even if rejected by the corrupt system as unsuitable to be its instrument, the third servant has successfully written a 'hidden transcript' of protest.[31]

Reading the parable of the pounds 'with peasant eyes'—a strategy Rohrbaugh calls 'the environmental criterion' —shows that it comes from the earliest layer of the Jesus' tradition.[32] This judgement is reinforced by the many other features of the parable that place it securely in Jesus' Palestinian setting.[33]

However, although social science perspectives are useful for fitting the parable into a general social context,[34] they lack the specificity required for a properly *historical* inquiry.[35] This lack of historical specificity is matched by a tendency to speak of the 'meaning' of the parable in fairly general terms—reminiscent of Jülicher's famous reduction of the parables to general moral maxims, even if the new maxims are perhaps more social. So, for example, in Rohrbaugh's view, 'leaving the hearers to reflect on the possibilities the story holds for their own situations',[36] Jesus issues a 'warning to the rich about their exploitation of the weak'.[37]

But such generalisations don't give 'the crux'[38] of the parable and, as with Jülicher's moral maxims, they leave Jesus as a bland teacher simply reflecting the norms of peasant culture, hardly worth remembering, let alone crucifying. The point of the parable will not come from inserting Jesus into his social context, but from understanding what Jesus then inserted into that social context with his message of the kingdom of God and by his actions to bring it about.

For, although sociological models can assist in showing the suitability of a parable (or other item) for Jesus' first-century environment, they cannot reveal why Jesus *stood out* from that first-century environment. All models need to be rigorously examined for their adequacy,[39] and they also need to be subject to the 'empiricist critique', which pays attention to 'the richness, variety and irreducible uniqueness of individuals, institutions, and states in the ancient world'.[40]

Fortunately, the Parable of the Pounds is one part of Jesus' teaching that can be read with a great deal of historical precision.

---

30 Van Eck, 'Do not question my honour', 9-10.
31 Van Eck, 'Do not question my honour', 10, drawing on J.C. Scott, 'Protest and Profanation', *Theory and Society* 4 (1977), 1-21.
32 Rohrbaugh, 'A Peasant Reading', 37; Van Eck, 'Do not question my honour', 10.
33 See Evans, 'Reconstructing Jesus' Teaching', 419-420, who examines the parable's diction, generic parallels, and details that point to a setting in Jesus' ministry. He also shows that features of the common interpretation 'make little sense' in this setting, such as regarding the first two servants as heroes and the third as a poor model, as well as the lesson 'to be profitable at all costs'. He concludes that, 'the traditional interpretation ignores the biblical principles and economic realities by which the majority of Palestinians in Jesus' day lived' (p.420).
34 E.g. Van Eck, 'Do not question my honour', 9.
35 P.W. Barnett, *Jesus and the Logic of History* (NSBT 3; Leicester: IVP, 1997, 2001), esp. Chapter 1.
36 Rohrbaugh, 'A Peasant Reading', 32-33. Similarly, for Van Eck, 'Do not question my honour', 9-10, the parable has two 'points': 1. 'the élite are exploiting the non-élite', 'this is what the kingdom of Caesar looks like'; and, in the surprise, 2. The correct way to protest is not the political game contesting honour, but the political game without legitimizing the élite, using 'the weapons of the weak', the 'hidden transcript' of resistance, 'the way to protest'. Braun, 'Reframing', in turn, takes it as part of Luke's 'critique of wealth and consumption' (p. 442), reminding his readers that 'the Divine Dominion does not come in the lording over of others nor in the profit margins of successful investments' (p.448).
37 Rohrbaugh, 'A Peasant Reading', 38.
38 Contra Van Eck, 'Do not question my honour', 7.
39 M. Chancey, 'Disputed Issues in the Study of Cities, Villages, and the Economy in Jesus' Galilee', in C.A. Evans (ed.), *The World of Jesus and the Early Church. Identity and Interpretation in Early Communities of Faith* (Peabody, MA: Hendrickson, 2011), 67 [53-67]; his statements can be applied more broadly than economic models.
40 Chancey, 'Disputed Issues', 58.

4.2 The Parable in its Historical Context

It has long been recognised that the motif of the 'throne claimant' (19:12, 14-15a, 27) is an historical allusion to Archelaus.[41] On the death of Herod the Great (Spring, 4 BC), Archelaus journeyed to Rome to acquire his father's kingdom, but when a fifty person embassy followed him to protest, Caesar gave him the title Ethnarch, withholding the title king until he earned it, which he never did.[42]

The fact that this motif refers to historical events has not often been given due interpretive weight and—given the tendency to favour general, rather than particular, interpretations—sometimes it has even been dismissed as unimportant.[43] In 2007, however, Schultz revisited the parable in the light of the archaeological evidence relating to Archelaus's connections with Jericho, showing that this is an essential detail, enabling historical precision about the parable's setting in place and time. These conclusions can now be reinforced, since the final reports of the excavations have been published after Schultz's article.

After being appointed Ethnarch, Archelaus rebuilt Herod the Great's palaces in Jericho (*AJ* 17:340), situated on the southern extremity of the city.[44] He restored the Third Palace, 'the most complex in plan and grand in scale, [which] also presents the most elaborate assemblage of architectural decoration', with great emphasis on 'the diversity and richness of the decoration'.[45]

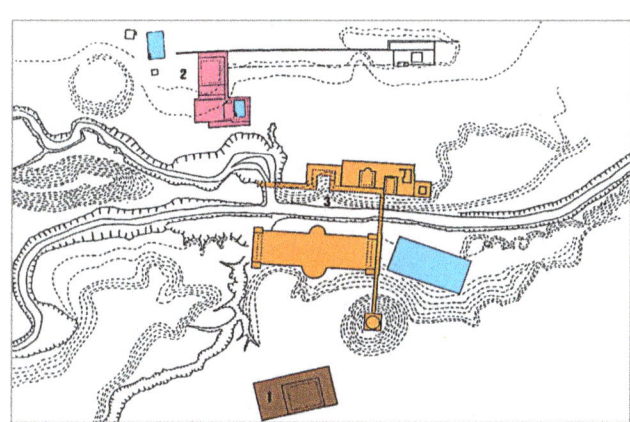

Plan of Herod's three palaces at Jericho. (Netzer, *Palaces*, fig. 42). The Jerusalem road ascended the southern ridge of the Wadi Qelt (bottom left of the diagram).

As Jewish travellers left Jericho and crossed the plain westward towards Jerusalem, they would see the two halves of the Third Palace complex on either side of, and joined by a bridge over, the Wadi Qelt, sitting on the lower ends of two ridges that then dramatically stretch upwards towards the horizon. After taking them around the southern section of the palace, with Herod's artificially constructed viewing mound rising high above, the road to Jerusalem

---

41 B. Schultz, 'Jesus as Archelaus in the Parable of the Pounds (Lk. 19:11-27)', *NovT* 49.2 (2007), 109 [105-127]: it is 'almost unanimously agreed that this motif is based on the life of Herod Archelaus'.

42 Josephus, *BJ* 2.14-39, 80-100 (2.2.1-2; 2.6.1-3); *AJ* 17:299-314 (17.11.1-2). Herod the Great had made a similar journey in 40 BC, *AJ* 14:370-389 (14.14.1-5); Antipas also went to Rome to press for the title, *BJ* 2.20-21 (2.2.3), *AJ* 17:224-227 (17.9.4).

43 Van Eck, 'Do not question my honour', 8-9. Note the stark contrast with F. Schleiermacher, *A Critical Essay on the Gospel of St Luke* (London: John Taylor, ET: 1825), 250: 'every hearer according to the occasion communicated by Luke, would have retained in his memory the main feature, that of the hostile citizens who would not that the should rule [...] and have forgotten the secondary feature of the servants'. For Schleiermacher, therefore, 'fidelity to the master cannot be the subject of the parable' (p.249).

44 Schultz, 'Jesus as Archelaus', 114.

45 O. Peleg-Barkat, 'The Architectural Decoration from the Hasmonean and Herodian Palaces at Jericho and Cypros', in R. Bar-Nathan & J. Gärtner (eds.), *Hasmonean and Herodian Palaces at Jericho: Final Reports of the 1973-1987 Excavations. 5: The Finds from Jericho and Cypros* (Jerusalem: Israel Exploration Society, 2013), 261 [235-269]. For the third palace, see S. Rozenberg & E. Netzer, *Hasmonean and Herodian Palaces at Jericho: Final Reports of the 1973-1987 Excavations. 4, The Decoration of Herod's Third Palace at Jericho* (Jerusalem: Israel Exploration Society, 2008). For a summary report of the complex, with diagrams, see E. Netzer, *The Palaces of the Hasmoneans and Herod the Great* (Jerusalem: Yad Ben-Zvi Press & Israel Exploration Society, 2001 [Heb: 1999]).

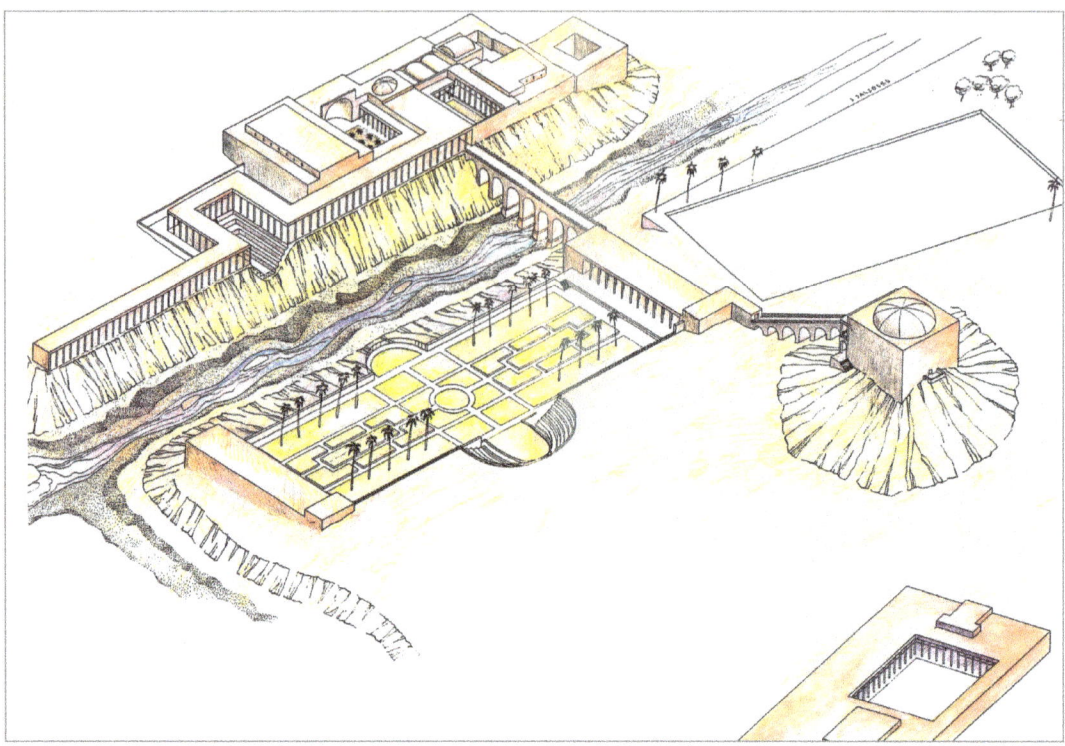

Reconstruction of Herod's Third Palace, with the First Palace in the foreground. (Netzer, *Palaces*, fig. 77). This would be the view from the Jerusalem road as it ascends the southern ridge of Wadi Qelt.

Bird's eye view of Wadi Qelt and the excavations of the North Wing of the Third Palace. (Netzer, *Palaces*, fig. 76).

rises steeply up the southern ridge, along the 'ascent of Adumin' (see Josh. 15:7; 18:17), from Jericho's 258 metres below sea level, towards Jerusalem's 754 metres above. Once on the ridge, they could look back on 'an impressive view' of some 2.83 hectares [7 acres] of palatial buildings, courtyards, gardens, and pools, restored by Archelaus, to be 'reminded of their last non-Roman ruler over Judea'.[46]

Schultz makes the point that the inclusion of this motif does not make sense at any stage of the parable's transmission, except at its original delivery.[47] Since Archelaus was no fondly remembered hero, and since the palace complex was abandoned after it was destroyed by earthquake in AD 48, it makes absolutely no sense that this motif would be inserted later by a Christian redactor or Luke himself.[48] It is:

> integral to the historical context in which it is framed, a context which was *en vigeur* only during the ministry of Jesus and accurately preserved in Luke's Gospel.[49]

Once the originality of the Archelaus motif is established, the parable's narrative introduction (v.11) cannot be easily dismissed as Luke's creation, for it also takes on the ring of authenticity.

> if we are to allow the Herodian Palaces to be the motivation behind an Archelaus motif, a possibility which Lk. 19:11 allows us to entertain, it fits best, if not only, when it is attributed to Jesus, precisely as he is leaving Jericho.[50]

As Jesus' followers walked out of Jericho upwards towards Jerusalem (cf. v.28), with his words to Zacchaeus fresh in their ears (19:10, cf. 11), it makes perfect sense that the sight of the palace would have evoked memories of Archelaus,[51] and consequently hopes that the Messianic kingdom that would put an end to such brutal and oppressive human rulers. Just like Jesus customarily used in his parables 'the "stuff" of every day life', drawn from agriculture or business, here he seizes on the sight of Archelaus' palaces and the memories evoked of his brutality, to address the crowd now expecting the sudden coming of the Kingdom of God with an extra parable. Thus, 'the brutality of Archelaus would no longer be a part of some allegory on the character of the Messiah, but merely part of the circumstantial setting which Jesus used in crafting his parable to more effectively communicate his message'.[52]

But was the parable designed to correct or confirm their expectation? The answer must come from the inter-relation between the two, understood within the eschatological framework(s) in which both Jesus and Luke were operating.

4.3 The Parable in its Proper Eschatological Context

The 'point' of the parable will not be properly discerned merely by placing it within a certain political, cultural, or economic framework. For sure, the parable needs to be read as part of the

---

46 Schultz, 'Jesus as Archelaus', 115.
47 Schultz, 'Jesus as Archelaus', 116-117, 119.
48 Schultz, 'Jesus as Archelaus', 115.
49 Schultz, 'Jesus as Archelaus', 126-127. This is counter to the regular, almost automatic, dismissal of v.11 as an inauthentic creation of Luke. E.g. Rohrbaugh, 'A Peasant Reading', 33, declares it 'cannot be original'; cf. Evans, 'Reconstructing Jesus' Teaching', 398, 424.
50 Schultz, 'Jesus as Archelaus', 117.
51 Since 'this corresponds exactly with where Luke has Jesus sharing the Parable of the Pounds', Schultz, 'Jesus as Archelaus', 115, asks pointedly, 'Could it be that this Herodian palace complex, last renovated and used by Archelaus but still standing in Jesus' day, triggered the Archelaus motif we find in the Parable of the Pounds?'.
52 Schultz, 'Jesus as Archelaus', 115.

'critique of wealth and consumption' shared by both Jesus and Luke, and so within 'the larger context of [their] economic vision'.[53] But both the parable and Jesus' 'economic vision' will be wrested from the framework that gives their proper meaning, if not understood within the larger framework of his *eschatological vision*. Scholars readily acknowledge that the Pounds, like his other parables, needs to be read in the light of Jesus' message about the in-breaking kingdom, but nevertheless debate whether Jesus' view of the future restoration was apocalyptic.

4.3.1 General apocalyptic context of Jesus (and Luke)

Although apocalypticism was a cultural phenomenon wider than Israel,[54] it was also a general feature of mainstream Judaism, not just the product of one of the various sects.[55] Exemplifying the long-standing scholarly 'intense aversion' to apocalyptic elements,[56] social science interpretations tend to assume Jesus' parables fit better in his 'real world context' if Jesus is viewed as a 'non-eschatological prophet'.[57] However, the weight of evidence from ongoing discoveries now requires the 'proxy data' of such non-eschatological assumptions to be firmly rejected.[58] The 'environmental criterion' must now factor in that the time at which Jesus lived was such 'an age of apocalypticism' that 'there can no longer be any doubt that Jesus was profoundly influenced by apocalypticism'.[59]

This apocalyptic spirit was demonstrably part of Jesus' own social relations. Jesus' own family held their own apocalyptic views, including a view that a Davidic Messiah from the non-royal line would bring the final stage of history, not just for Israel but for the world (see Luke 1–3).[60] His cousin and forerunner, John the Baptist' was renowned as an apocalyptic preacher.[61] Even if Jesus was 'clearly *not* an apocalypticist in the narrowest sense',[62] all the elements are there, from an expectation of a Messiah and an imminent kingdom; an imminent end of the world, associated with the coming of the Son of Man; through a pessimism, or even hostility, towards the present social order and those empowered by it; to a belief in the two ages, and the periodization of history as it moved relentlessly towards its conclusion whenever the evil powers would be overthrown and the Kingdom of God would break in.[63]

---

53 Braun, 'Reframing', 442; Van Eck, 'Do not question my honour', 9.
54 G. Boccaccini, 'Jewish Apocalyptic Tradition: The Contribution of Italian Scholarship', in J.H. Charlesworth & J.J. Collins (eds.), *Mysteries and Revelations: Apocalyptic Studies Since the Uppsala Colloquium* (Sheffield: Sheffield Academic Press, 1991, 35, as cited by S.E. Robinson, 'Apocalypticism in the Time of Hillel and Jesus', in Charlesworth & Johns, *Hillel and Jesus*, 129 [121-136].
55 Robinson, 'Apocalypticism', 131.
56 Robinson, 'Apocalypticism', 122, cf. 123-124.
57 Van Eck, 'Do not question my honour', 3, 6.
58 Such an inordinate amount of confidence can be placed in a model that it becomes 'proxy data', leading to 'constructing hypothetical scenarios not supplied by the ancient evidence but by "likelihood, analogy, or comparison"'. The problems are multiplied when the 'proxy data' then become a foundation for a superstructure of further deduction; D.A. Fiensey, 'Assessing the Economy of Galilee in the Late Second Temple Period: Five Considerations', in R. Hawkins & D.A. Fiensey (eds.), *The Galilean Economy in the Time of Jesus* (Atlanta: SBL, 2013), 178 [165-186], citing J. Andreau, 'Twenty Years after Moses I. Finley's *Ancient Economy*', in W. Scheidel & S. von Reden (eds.), *The Ancient Economy* (New York: Routledge, 2002), 33-49.
59 Robinson, 'Apocalypticism', 126-128, who discusses Josephus, Qumran, the Pseudepigrapha, and the New Testament.
60 R. Bauckham, *Jude and the Relatives of Jesus in the Early Church* (London: Bloomsbury, 2015 [1990, 2004]). With the family of Jesus amongst his sources, it is unsurprising that such views have found their way into Luke's Gospel, both directly, through the publication of the family genealogy (Luke 3, see Chapter 7), and indirectly in places such as the schematization of time to suit the eschatological timetable (e.g. 13:33).
61 Robinson, 'Apocalypticism', 125.
62 Robinson, 'Apocalypticism', 127-128.
63 Robinson, 'Apocalypticism', 123, 127-128.

4.3.2 A Sober View of the World

Jesus' Parable of the Pounds engages the real world of first century Israel, not simply in a general socio-cultural sense, but in the particular and pointed context of Rome dominating Israel with complicity from their own leadership. No structure spoke louder of the splendour of Herodian power than the palaces of Jericho— nor of the complicity of Israel's aristocracy in it.[64] Bedecked by Roman architectural novelties and probably even built with the assistance of a team of Roman architects and builders working together with Herod's own,[65] these magnificent buildings also spoke of the greater power of Rome with which he was in league.

If the memory of Archelaus' attempt at kingship, foiled by the protests of the Jewish embassy, brought a wry smile when Jesus introduced his over-confident nobleman attempting the same thing (v.12),[66] it would be wiped away by Jesus' casual detail, 'having received the kingdom' (v.15, λαβόντα τὴν βασιλείαν). The actual history was awful enough, but Jesus' parable proposes a horrifying 'what if' scenario: imagine how much worse it would be if he had actually received the title from Rome![67]

In the dealings of the nobleman with servant and 'enemy' alike, the real life situation of Jesus' hearers' was painfully exposed. Israel's leaders, both political and religious, were complicit in the people's exploitation. Even the partial success of their opposition to Archelaus had not prevented further arbitrary bloodshed and economic profiteering at their expense, through loan-sharks and tax-gatherers like Zaccheus, raking in unbearable profits.[68] Through such oppression, the irresistible force of Rome was now dominating the ancient people of God, who, in order to survive, either had to capitulate and become part of the evil system, or resist and face the risk of obliteration: 'the kings of the nations lord it over them, and those in authority over them call themselves "Benefactors"!' (Luke 22:25, εὐεργέται καλοῦνται).

But from Jesus' apocalyptic perspective, such human displays of wealth that trumpeted exploitation and oppression, testified to an even greater power beyond the veil. Since his testing at the start of his ministry (4:1-13) took place in the wilderness in the same area, these magnificent buildings could have been the concrete basis for the vision of 'all the kingdoms of the world in a moment of time' (4:5). On his last journey on the Jericho road, as Jesus once again saw the palaces evoking both Herod and his dynasty, other puppet kings like him, and the supreme Lord Caesar whom they served, he would have his own memory of when the devil promised that he would give Jesus 'all this authority and their glory' (4:6). By the devil's own admission, he is the power behind all the kings of the earth, those depicted in Daniel as a succession of beasts killing and devouring each other (Dan 7:1-12; cf. Luke 21:10). This is the harsh reality evoked by the rule of master of the

---

64 Herod's palace was known to the wider world (Strabo 16.2.41; Pliny, *H.N.* 5.70). Due to its pleasant winter climate, 'Jericho had long been a resort for the aristocracy', D.W. Roller, *The Building Program of Herod the Great* (Oakland, CA: University of California, 1998), 171. Whereas the smaller cities retained simpler, Hellenistic styles, and the Doric continued popular, at Jericho, as in other larger cities, Herod introduced innovations with local artisans copying 'Roman novelties' that were so readily 'embraced by the well-to-do citizens of these cities', Peleg-Barkat, 'Architectural Decoration', 261-262.
65 Reflecting on his 14 years of excavating the site, and, given that such Roman features are only found in three Herodian structures in the land of Israel, it was Netzer's considered opinion, admittedly with no documentary proof, that they were built with the assistance of a team of architects and builders sent from Italy as a reward and encouragement to Herod following Marcus Agrippa's visit to Judea in 15 BC; Netzer, *Palaces*, 48.
66 See n.7 above.
67 Cf. Salome's son Antipater, in his speech in Rome opposing Archelaus' bid for kingship, after rehearsing Archelaus' failings already, 'What sort of a king will this man be, when he hath obtained the government from Caesar, who hath slain so many before he hath obtained it?'; *BJ* 2.32 (2.2.5).
68 The embassy opposing Archelaus complained that their estates were in danger of being taken by him (*AJ* 17.305, 307 [17.11.2]) and that he used his slaves as tax gatherers (*AJ* 17.308 [17.11.2]).

parable (vv.12, 15) and his minions (vv.17, 19).[69]

Luke also clearly shares this apocalyptic view, for it is the framework in which he sets Jesus' ministry, from the devil's initial testing (4:1-13), through Jesus' vision of his fall (10:18), to his re-entry in the drama by entering Judas (22:3, cf. 4:13), before the final testing of both disciple and master (22:31-32, 39-46; cf. 4:1-13). In Luke's account, Jesus' arrest signals the apparent victory of Israel's corrupt leadership, who are cast as instruments of Satan himself through apocalyptic imagery: 'this is your hour and the authority of darkness' (22:53). Yet the true victory occurs behind the scenes, allowing Jesus to be confident of the arrival of his kingdom, even while hanging on the cross (23:43).

Both in Jesus' mouth and in Luke's presentation, the Pounds is not an allegory, it is a contrast. Daniel's vision looked ahead to when the Son of Man would come to the Ancient of Days, and the destructive, beastly power of human kingdoms would be stripped away, to be entirely replaced by the glorious Kingdom of God. At the beginning of the journey Jesus looked ahead to his death as Satan's fall from heaven (10:18-20), proleptically signaled in the success of the seventy(two). Now, in Jericho and as the last event before he reaches his goal, the Son of Man dramatically saved the lost (19:10). As Jesus' words and deeds provoke his followers to expect that the Kingdom of God was about to arrive (v.11), then the implication is clear: there is no future for those caught up in the rule of the beasts, for the future belongs to the Son of Man. But, when he comes, will the Son of Man find faith in the land of Israel (18:8)?

The Parable of the Pounds exposes the harsh world of Jesus' hearers and provokes them to a decision. If the Kingdom of God will sweep away the human rule they now chafe under, and if it is just about to arrive, are they ready to meet their king?

4.3.3 Jesus' Role in his Apocalyptic Eschatology

When Jesus challenged Israel to understand the times (12:54-56), this was tantamount to asking them to understand who had arrived in the midst of 'this generation' (cf. 11:29-32).

Certainly Jesus' apocalypticism made him stand out from his non-apocalyptic contemporaries, who collaborated with the political and economic 'realities' in order to survive. The non-eschatological, non-messianic views of Hillel, for example, probably mark him out as someone who adapted with the changing political situation in order to survive.[70] But Jesus did not adapt and was crushed by being delivered 'into human hands' (9:44). He also stood out from the non-eschatological peasant culture of social-science models, for, although well attuned to this outlook, part of his distinctiveness came from his astute ability to see this world in the light of the coming Kingdom of God, which therefore critiqued the structures of this world that eventually had their 'hour of darkness' (22:53).

But Jesus did not stand out from his contemporaries simply because he shared their apocalyptic eschatology with greater intensity and focus, but because he claimed to fulfill it. His presence within Israel brought the end of the ages, and provoked a crisis for the people of Israel and, beyond them, the nations. The question of apocalyptic timing now became a question of Christology. When the Pharisees asked him when the Kingdom of God would come (17:20), he said, 'the Kingdom of God is in your midst' (17:21), because he is the one who is pivotal to its arrival, for he is the Son of Man who will come to the Ancient of Days (Dan 7:13-14).

---

69 Cf. Josephus, *AJ* 17.309, where the embassy to Caesar opposing Archelaus pictured him as worse than a wild beast on the throne.

70 Showing 'little influence from apocalypticism' and silent on Messianism, Hillel 'shares neither Jesus' interest in the coming age and the eschatological kingdom of God nor his concern for the coming messiah'; Robinson, 'Apocalypticism', 129. For Hillel's adaptation to the changing times, see pp.129-136.

Evans has observed, that in their quest to separate out the authentic Jesus' tradition, Form Critics regarded too much as the secondary additions of the early church, because 'the interpretation the early church gave to Jesus' teachings was frequently and often uncritically assumed to be the original point of the teachings'.[71] This criticism should be pushed further, for it is also common to assume that the Gospel writers themselves reflect the interpretation that the early church gave to Jesus' teachings.

A case in point is Jesus' teaching on the 'coming of the Son of Man', which, according to the usual interpretation across the ages, refers to Christ's Second Coming. The Evangelists' supposed Parousia perspective is then said to lie behind them turning Jesus' parables into allegories.[72] More recently, however, this common view has been questioned, with an alternative proposal that it makes better sense of the original prophecy in Daniel and the use of it on Jesus' lips, and in the Gospels themselves, if the 'coming of the Son of Man' refers not to Christ's future return *to earth* (the Parousia), but to Christ's *resurrection and ascension to the right hand of the Father* to enter into his reign as Lord.[73]

This latter view can be confirmed as correct by Luke's two volume work. Acts shows that Stephen looked back on the coming of the Son of Man as a completed event (Acts 7:56) and even though the Book refers to the Second Coming, it never does so in terms of the coming of the Son of Man (e.g. 1:11; 3:21; 17:31; 24:25)—and neither does the rest of the New Testament.[74] By the criterion of dissimilarity, this is a clear demonstration that neither Jesus, nor Luke, shared the common interpretation. The flow of Luke's narrative coalesces the expectations of Jesus' 'lifting up' (9:51), with the Son of Man's resurrection (9:22; 18:33), and subsequent entry into his glory by way of the ascension (24:26; Acts 1:2). This was 'the coming of the Son of Man' according to Luke, looking back, and this was what Jesus, looking forward (22:69; Ps 110),[75] had as his goal.

When set within the context of Jesus' apocalyptic view of the future, instead of simply asking the audience to reflect on their situation and leaving them with a model of 'protest', the Parable of the Pounds challenges them to recognise the champion in their midst, who has come to seek and save the lost into the everlasting kingdom of God, which is just about to burst in on human history in an unmistakeable way.

Far from speaking at loggerheads with Jesus, this this is exactly what Luke reports.

5. The Parable In Luke's Account of Jesus' Ministry

Having established that the narrative linkage (19:11) reflects the original historical situation, and noting again that its language clearly forges a close link between the Zacchaeus incident (19:1-10) and the Parable of the Pounds (see Section 2.1 above), it is worthwhile to examine more closely the relationship between event and parable as part of Luke's 'orderly account' of Jesus' apocalyptic preparation of Israel for what was about to take place in Jerusalem.

---

71 Evans, 'Reconstructing Jesus' Teaching', 400.
72 E.g. Jeremias, *Parables*, 48-66; Rohrbaugh, 'A Peasant Reading', 33-34; Evans, 'Reconstructing Jesus' Teaching', 404.
73 See, amongst others, T.F. Glasson, *The Second Advent. The Origin of the New Testament Doctrine* (London: Epworth, 1945); J.A.T. Robinson, *Jesus and His Coming. The Emergence of a Doctrine* (London: SCM, 1957); Dodd, *Parables*, 81 (in part); P.G. Bolt, 'Mark 13: An Apocalyptic Precursor to the Passion Narrative', *RefThR* 54.1 (1995), 10-32.
74 This is true also of the book of Revelation (1:13; 14:14), where the references to the Son of Man can likewise be interpreted of Christ's ascension.
75 Even his 'apocalyptic discourse' can be read with the ascension in view (21:27; 21:36, cf. 9:26-28), but this cannot be argued here. For a similar argument for Mark's Gospel, see Bolt, 'Mark 13'; and P.G. Bolt, *The Cross from a Distance. Atonement in Mark's Gospel* (NSBT 18; Leicester: IVP, 2004), Chapter 3.

5.1 Looking Behind the Parable

Luke reports Jesus' arrival in Jericho with a participle, subordinated to the main verb: he was 'passing through' the city (v.1 Καὶ εἰσελθὼν διήρχετο τὴν Ἰεριχώ). Thus, the event is cast as a brief interlude on Jesus' journey towards Jerusalem —even if, in hindsight, of immense significance. The Zacchaeus account falls into two scenes (vv.2-6, 8-10) unfolding around a reported saying (v.7). The initial scene (vv.2-6) serves to bring the two men together and to the point at which Jesus invites himself to the house of this wealthy chief tax collector (see v.2), and Zacchaeus warmly supplies hospitality (vv.5-6). In wider perspective, this is thoroughly consistent with Jesus' previous actions (e.g. 5:27-32; 7:31-35).

Jesus partaking of Zacchaeus' hospitality evokes a response from the crowds, which, given Luke's story so far (see 5:30, 33; 7:33-34, 39; 15:2), is also thoroughly predictable, and, given the political and economic realities that prevailed in first-century Israel at the time, thoroughly authentic to Jesus' social context: 'seeing this, everyone grumbled, saying "with a sinful man he went in as a guest"' (v.7).

This saying then becomes the background for the second scene. Zacchaeus had earned the label 'sinner' because of his exploitative economic activities (cf. 7:31). Israel's leadership now served the Roman emperor, in a land far away, and the privileges Rome accorded Israel's élite classes were maintained through ordinary Israelites being exploited by those like Zacchaeus. Consistent with the economic nature of his 'sin', the coming of salvation to his house is marked by economic actions, reversing his previous crimes, and thus displaying his profound repentance evoked by the Saviour's presence. Presumably his exploitative practices in collaboration with, and as an instrument of, the corrupt systems of prevailing power, were now brought to a decisive end. Jesus takes Zacchaeus' voluntary almsgiving and excessive repayment (v.8) as a sign that salvation has arrived in his house (v.9). At this point Jesus, using his preferred self-designation, delivered a key statement about his own mission—which, given the rich theme of salvation in the Gospel, becomes *the* key statement in Luke's account of his ministry (19:10). Cast as an explanation of what they have just witnessed (γάρ), Jesus declared 'for the Son of Man came to seek and to save the lost'.

It is exactly 'while the people were hearing these things' (Ἀκουόντων δὲ αὐτῶν ταῦτα)—that is, Jesus' reflections on Zacchaeus' economic repentance (v.9) and his statement tying this in to his own mission (v.10)—, that Jesus 'spoke, adding in a parable (προσθεὶς εἶπεν παραβολήν).[76]

The details of the Parable of the Pounds are entirely fitting for this setting. Once the master is seen 'through peasant eyes' for what he is, 'apparently an oppressive gouger and a thief',[77] many of the details of the parable need to be viewed, not positively—as they must be in the common view—, but extremely negatively, as part of a text that ought to frighten anyone who lives in such a world! The master is politically ambitious, and arrogantly confident that he will succeed in his bid for kingship (vv.12, 13). He is greedily focused upon the money, making arrangements so that his profiteering will continue while he is away through others continuing to act on his behalf, and on his return, immediately calling them to see what increase has been made (v.15). Before he left he ordered them to put his money to work (πραγματεύσασθε), that is, profiteering (v.13), and on return demanded his profits (v.15, ἵνα γνοῖ τί διεπραγματεύσαντο). Because he rebukes the third servant for not even putting his *mna* on the banker's table so he could return it 'with interest' (v.23, σὺν τόκῳ), the work he expected from him and received from the first two servants, was not

---

76 This rendering reads Luke's construction as high Greek, with παραβολήν the object of the participle.
77 Evans, 'Reconstructing Jesus' Teaching', 422.

banker's interest, but some other higher return, probably loans at exorbitant interest levels in the hope of acquiring further land forfeiture from the inevitable loan default.

This negative picture of the master is reinforced by the explicit emotional content in the parable. His citizens oppose him because 'they hated him' (v.14, ἐμίσουν αὐτόν)[78] and the third servant fears him for his austerity (v.21, ἐφοβούμην σε, ὅτι ἄνθρωπος αὐστηρὸς εἶ), which, instead of denying, the master reinforces with an exactly corresponding statement (v.22, ὅτι ἐγὼ ἄνθρωπος αὐστηρός εἰμι). This picture of the master is then reinforced by the 'anti-proverb'—again perfectly agreed upon by both parties—that he is the kind of thief and exploiter who 'takes what he did not set in place, and reaps what he did not sow' (v.21, αἴρεις ὃ οὐκ ἔθηκας καὶ θερίζεις ὃ οὐκ ἔσπειρας; v.22, αἴρων ὃ οὐκ ἔθηκα καὶ θερίζων ὃ οὐκ ἔσπειρα).[79] This is not a positive description in any sense at all, and, in terms of the role of emotions in the dynamics of reading,[80] the negative emotions, both explicitly labelled and implicitly pictured, draw the hearers/readers sympathetically towards the servant, while opening distance between them and the master. The combined effect is clear: this master is categorically not a role model for anything at all for the hearer/reader. The dynamics of the parable are constructed so that they would be absolutely repelled by him, and they would even sit on judgement on him as a man completely devoid of humanity.

These dynamics also cause the hearer to read the other features of the master's activity negatively. His praise of the first compliant servant (v.17), 'well done!, good servant' for being 'faithful in a little' (by turning it into a lot!), cannot be a positive statement through which faithfulness is commended, neither for Jesus', nor Luke's audience. To be faithful to such a master in such a task is to be complicit in exploitation of ordinary people by a corrupt power system. The reward given to the two toadies just makes the picture worse, because their 'faithfulness in a little' earns them the privilege of being further engrafted into that corrupt system by wielding the authority to exploit a great many more people, probably as tax-harvesters (vv.17, 19).

The picture only gets worse as the master deals with the other characters. When the third servant reports that he has preserved the master's money safely (v.20)—the honourable thing to do, according to Jewish peasant economy[81]—the master 'judges' him, calling him 'evil' (v.22, κρινῶ σε, πονηρὲ δοῦλε) simply because he refused to do business with his master's money,[82] and then gloats over him further with yet another anti-proverb (v.26), for in his mouth this 'wisdom' is twisted and sick.[83] The damning of the master reaches its nadir when he turns to those citizens (v.14, οἱ πολῖται—not rebels!) who opposed him by means of the proper legal channels (a delegation to Caesar), labelling them 'enemies' (v.27), before mercilessly slaughtering them in front of him. All of this merely reinforces the hearer's repulsion. None of his labels can be taken positively in any sense that might link with any kind of moralistic 'application' in the life of Jesus' hearers.

But we must press even further. Once the details of the parable are thus properly understood in their appropriate context, given the Gospel's presentation on poverty and wealth, it seems

---

78 Archelaus was hated by his subjects and his relatives; Josephus, BJ 2.15, 22, 33, 82 (2.2.1, 3, 6; 2.6.1); AJ 17.227, 302 (17.9.4; 17.11.1)

79 The proverbial nature of the saying (Plato, Laws 913C; Josephus, Against Apion 2:216) suggests 'one who is so "hard" that he ignores conventional piety in his quest for power and possessions'; Johnson, Luke, 291.

80 See W.C. Booth, 'Distance and Point of View: An Essay in Clarification', in P. Stevick (ed.), Theory of the Novel (New York: Free Press, 1967), 87-107; P.G. Bolt, 'Touching the Emotions. Preaching the Gospels for Divine Effects', in M.P. Jensen (ed.), True Feelings (Leicester: IVP, 2012), 206-234.

81 Van Eck, 'Do not question my honour', 5.

82 Johnson, Luke, 291.

83 The saying here is best taken as that of the master, and its resemblance to Jesus' own teaching (8:18) simply reinforces the horror at wicked men being able to self-justify their wickedness as wisdom!

impossible to imagine that Luke would have not been in entire sympathy with this reading. Or, to make the case empirically, what evidence is there in the Gospel that Luke read Jesus' parable as a commendation for his readers to faithful service? It seems that there is absolutely no evidential basis for the proposal that Luke so completely distorted Jesus' parable, that he read it along the lines of the (much later) common interpretation. This scenario is not only foreign to Jesus' program it is also so far from Luke's own clear interests that it is astounding that interpreters still insist on dividing Luke from Jesus at this point. Quite simply, in his use of the Parable of the Pounds, Luke speaks with the same voice as Jesus.

To put it in other words, if not obvious already: careful attention to the detail of the parable, both in Jesus' original social setting and in that of the Gospel is absolutely fatal for the common, allegorically derived, interpretation of this parable. Instead, repelled by the master, his compliant servants, and the corruption that rejects the man doing the honourable thing and even takes away what little he has, the audience is disconnected from the entire exploitative system. If this is how the Gentiles rule with their Benefaction (cf. 22:25), then who wants it? Thus Jesus' Parable of the Pounds disconnects his hearers from the human kingdoms under the gift of Satan (4:5-6), in order to be ready for the glorious Kingdom of God, to arrive when the Son of Man comes to the Ancient of Days to take his throne.

5.2 Looking Ahead of the Parable

Luke's report of the authentic setting for the parable (v.11), not only ties it to the context from which it arose (the Zacchaeus event), but it also looks ahead by reporting the apocalyptic expectations aroused by that event concerning what might happen when Jesus' journey finally reaches its predicted destination in Jerusalem. As the parable concludes, Jesus re-enters his journey to that goal (19:28), with the crowd holding high hopes for the sudden appearance of the Kingdom of God.

Luke's infancy stories articulate the great expectations resting on Jesus' shoulders from before he was born, in fulfilment of the scriptural promises across the centuries (Luke 1–2). The words of Simeon and Anna (2:25-38) caused Jesus' parents to marvel (2:33), but Jesus' family also had their own sense that Jesus was fulfilling prophetic hopes.[84] According to Luke's portrayal, in the early stages of Jesus' ministry, he used the term 'Son of Man' to refer to his authority to heal and over the Sabbath (5:24; 6:5), and of himself in relation to his disciples (6:22), and to his critics (7:34). In the latter saying, he spoke of the Son of Man having come (ἐλήλυθεν; cf. 19:10) in the context of the forerunner, John, thus situating himself as a key player in God's plan unfolding within Israel's history, as described and promised in the Scriptures.

But it is in the Travel Narrative that these apocalyptic expectations gain greater weight, as the various strands of scriptural expectation come together in Jesus' person, and momentum, as the apocalyptic division of time becomes even more foreshortened and the end of the final stage of world history comes closer by metres (cf. 13:33).

Just before Jesus begins his final journey to Jerusalem, he predicts that, according to God's plan (implied by δεῖ, 'it is necessary'), he must suffer many things, be rejected by Israel's leadership, killed, and then rise on the third day (9:22). As he spelled out the serious implications of his coming death for his followers, he looked to the future judgement day, showing clearly that his use of this self-designation was influenced by the enigmatic figure in Daniel's central vision

---

84 Bauckham, *Jude and the Relatives*.

(9:26; Dan. 7:13-14). Here he brings 'Son of Man' into conjunction with the prophecies relating to Isaiah's Suffering Servant (especially Isaiah 52:13–53:12; see 22:37), who suffers before being lifted up, vindicated, to share his victory with others. By inserting the reference to the future 'coming' of the Son of Man, Jesus overlays his journey to Jerusalem with the eschatological expectations associated with Daniel's key figure, whose 'coming' is to the Ancient of Days, in order to receive the authority to reign over all peoples for all time, as the beast-like, death-dealing, human kingdoms were completely stripped of their power to be replaced by the glorious Kingdom of God. Showing his sense that he has brought the end stage of human history, Jesus concluded this remarkable conversation with the dramatic statement that (the coming of the Son of Man and so) the arrival of the Kingdom of God will be before his hearers taste death (9:27). In Luke's account, whereas he has spoken of the Kingdom before, this is the first time he announced that its arrival was imminent and this imminence is further reinforced from this moment on (9:62; 10:9, 11; 11:2, 20; 16:16; 17:20-21). As expected from Daniel, the arrival of the Kingdom is clearly associated with 'the coming of the Son of Man'.[85]

Immediately after, his transfiguration on the mountain (9:28-36) gave a glimpse of the glory of the future Kingdom (9:31, ἐν δόξῃ). Luke reports that the topic of conversation with his heavenly visitors was his 'exodus, which he was about to bring to fulfilment in Jerusalem' (9:31, τὴν ἔξοδον αὐτοῦ, τὴν ἔξοδον αὐτοῦ, ἣν ἤμελλεν πληροῦν ἐν Ἰερουσαλήμ). This description links Jesus' death, not only to God's great act of redemption by which he established the people of Israel as his own, but also to Israel's future deliverance, promised through the death of Isaiah's Servant of the Lord.

Once down from the mountain, and on the cusp of his last journey (9:51), Jesus again predicted his death in the same terms (9:44), ensuring that the expectations generated by his own predictions of his coming death and resurrection are overlaid with those generated by the prophets about two key messianic figures: Isaiah's Servant, who dies and is then lifted up; and Daniel's Son of Man, who comes to the Ancient of Days to receive the Kingdom of God.

Luke's introduction to his 'travel narrative' —a key structuring device of the second half of his 'orderly account' (cf. 1:1-4)— strongly reinforces these prophetic expectations overlaid on Jesus' own predictions. With vivid detail suggesting a source amongst those who had been there, Luke reports that Jesus 'set his face to go to Jerusalem' (9:51, αὐτὸς τὸ πρόσωπον ἐστήρισεν τοῦ πορεύεσθαι εἰς Ἰερουσαλήμ), and sets his resolute decision against an apocalyptic timetable: 'it came about when the days for his lifting up were fulfilled' (Ἐγένετο δὲ ἐν τῷ συμπληροῦσθαι τὰς ἡμέρας τῆς ἀναλήμψεως αὐτοῦ). Although the vocabulary differs, at a conceptual level Jesus' ἀνάλημψις is evocative of the 'lifting up' of the Servant of the Lord (Isa. 52:13), and the 'coming of the Son of Man' (Dan. 7:13-14).[86] Now Luke's readers, like Jesus' hearers, are expecting, as the goal of his journey to Jerusalem, the coming of the Son of Man and the arrival of the Kingdom God.

As the journey proceeds, the expectation is both sustained and intensified. Just like in Daniel's vision, once the Son of Man receives the Kingdom from the Ancient of Days he shares it with God's people (Dan 7:18), so now Jesus instructs his followers to seek the Kingdom of God, knowing that the Father has given it to them already (12:31-32). As he does so, he adds the

---

85 'Luke does more than intensify the number of references to the kingdom in this section. He associates the Kingdom explicitly with the words and work of Jesus, and he pictures the Kingdom as imminent'; Johnson, 'Lukan Kingship Parable', 154.

86 This is true despite the paucity of vocabulary shared between the three passages. They are, however, tied together by the vocabulary of glory (Isa. 53:12; Dan. 7:14; cf. Luke 24:26). There is evidence that Daniel's vision was a reflection on and extension of the lifting up of Isaiah's servant; see H.C. Cavallin, 'Tod und Auferstehung der Weisheitslehrer. Ein Beitrag zur Zeichnung des frame of reference Jesu', *SNTU* (1980), 107-121.

parables of the Doorkeeper and the Burglar (12:35-38, 39-40), urging watchfulness, given that 'the Son of Man will come at an hour when you do not expect him' (v.40). In the light of the imminent end, with the hour of judgement descending upon them, he berates his hearers for not being able to interpret the times properly (12:54-59). As he drew closer to his destination, when a Pharisee asked him specifically, when the Kingdom of God would come (17:20), Jesus reiterated that it would come suddenly without warning, for it would come without any prior signs to be observed, because, in his person, it is already in their midst (17:20-21). He told his disciples that, as the days drew closer, they would long to see one of the days of the Son of Man (17:22), hinting that impending trouble would increase their expectancy. When the Son of Man comes, it won't be so unclear that it becomes a subject for debate or discussion, but it will be a sudden event, like the flash of lightning (17:23-24). But before the Son of Man and the Kingdom comes, he must fulfil his role as Servant, suffering many things and being rejected by 'this generation' (17:23-25). His sudden coming will interrupt the regular rhythms of ordinary life, just like the flood did for Noah and the fire from heaven did for Sodom (17:26, 30). For Jesus, there is no doubt that this is Israel's imminent future, the only question (as he put it in his parable of the Unjust Judge, 18:1-8) is, 'when the Son of Man comes, will he find faith in the land [of Israel]?' (18:8).[87] Thus the imminent expectation of the sudden coming of the Son of Man to receive the Kingdom of God raises the immediate implication: will Israel be ready?

Having asked the question, Jesus directs his attention to entering the Kingdom when it comes (18:9-14; 18:15-17; 18:18-30), for now is the time to be prepared. Having done so, he took the disciples aside and gave them the final and most detailed prediction of his death and resurrection. Reinforcing his previous predictions, he now clearly focuses on the importance of the coming of the Son of Man: 'behold we are going up to Jerusalem, and everything written through the prophets concerning the Son of Man will reach its goal' (18:31). The breadth of his statement indicates that more than just the Son of Man prophecy (Dan 7:13-14) is in view. Jesus saw himself as fulfilling the Scriptures in their entirety (see 24:25-27, 44-49), and, because they all point to him, he has drawn all Scriptural messianic expectations, especially those of the Servant, together under his most significant title, so that, whenever the Son of Man comes, 'everything written about him through the prophets will reach their goal' (τελεσθήσεται πάντα τὰ γεγραμμένα διὰ τῶν προφητῶν). The thing to notice here, is that he expects all this to happen in Jerusalem.

Thus, when salvation arrives in the house of such a sinner as Zaccheus and Jesus announces, 'the Son of Man has come to seek and to save the lost (19:10), he is not simply making a statement about his *modus operandi* in having come (like that of 7:34). Because of his predictions along the way, this expression is now pregnant with expectation of the coming of the Son of Man, along with the glorious Kingdom of God. Unsurprisingly, having heard Jesus' apocalyptic predictions of his destiny, the crowd pick up the eschatological fervour and expect it to all happen when they arrive in Jerusalem.

Because the Kingdom of God is about to arrive, Jesus tells the Parable of the Pounds to move them to the life outcome, that they will not be swept away as the kingdoms of the beasts are swept away, but they will, instead, be ready for the King when he begins to rule.

---

87 γῆ needs to be translated according to context, whether referring to some local topographical feature (5:3, 11; 6:49; 8:8, 15, 27; 13:7; 14:35; 22:44; 24:5), the surface of the world (11:31; cf. Acts 1:8; 21:35), the cosmos (10:21; 12:56; 16:17; 21:25, 33), or, as in this case, the land of Israel (2:14; 4:25; 5:24; 12:49, 51; 18:8; 21:23; 23:44)—even if events in the land have cosmic significance.

6. Conclusion

In incorporating Jesus' Kingship Parable into his 'narrative concerning the things fulfilled amongst us' (1:1, διήγησις περὶ τῶν πεπληροφορημένων ἐν ἡμῖν πραγμάτων) Luke spoke with the same voice as Jesus. The Gospel is a straight-forward narrative about Jesus, not some kind of coded message intended to address the problems and circumstances of his audience, by means of moralistic exhortation and exemplars, and allegorical puzzles. When properly understood against the Scriptural promises,[88] the facts of Jesus Christ held significance for the whole world. It was therefore not the foreground factors that determined his writing: he was propelled from behind.[89] Writing from a scientific empiricist perspective,[90] Luke carefully laid out the facts about Jesus, so that they might speak for themselves. Jesus' narration of this parable takes its place amongst those facts, serving Luke's stated purpose to bring ἀσφάλεια (certainty/security/assurance) for his readers (1:4).

Luke reports how, in Jericho when Jesus stood right next to the magnificent buildings which proclaimed the glory of the kingdom of the beasts, with the arrival of salvation to one such as Zacchaeus vividly in the crowd's minds, the Son of Man who had come to seek and to save the lost added another parable into the mix. The point of the parable was to prepare the Israelite crowd. In Jerusalem the Son of Man will come, ascend to the Ancient of Days, and receive the Kingdom of God. By separating them from the beastly oppressive human kingdoms, the parable gets them ready to embrace the king who seeks and saves the lost.

However, Luke's account goes on to show that, far from receiving him, through their official structures and leadership, Israel rejected their king, in concert with the official structures and leadership of the Gentiles, who also rejected *their* king. At the cross, the whole world had concretely expressed their rebellion against God and his Messiah (Acts 4:23-30; Psalm 2), proving themselves sinners. When Jesus rose from the dead to enter his glory (24:26), this was the long expected coming of the Son of Man to the Ancient of Days to receive the Kingdom of God. Once the Son of Man was installed as 'both Lord and Christ' (Acts 2:36), all that remains of God's plan to complete before the Kingdom of God arrives in all its fullness, is for forgiveness of sins to be proclaimed to the nations (Luke 24:47). And if the crucifixion of the Messiah registered the whole world as sinners, then this only makes everyone ripe for the news that that same tragic event means forgiveness for all who turn to Christ as their Saviour and Lord (Luke 24:45-47; Acts 2:38-39), knowing the certainty of 'the things fulfilled amongst us' (Luke 1:4; Acts 2:36).

With such a gracious king, when Luke's good news goes out amongst the nations, will they receive the king? Will he find faith on the earth?

Peter G. Bolt
Sydney College of Divinity

---

88 See R.J. Dillon, 'Previewing Luke's Project from his Prologue (Luke 1:1-4)', *CBQ* 43 (1981), 205-227.
89 R.J. Bauckham, 'For Whom were the Gospels Written?', in R.J. Bauckham (ed.), *The Gospel for All Christians. Rethinking the Gospel Audiences* (Grand Rapids: Eerdmans, 1998), 9-48; although, given the significance of their Subject, it is better to see the Gospels intended not simply for 'all Christians', but for all people. Luke stands in continuity with the Christ-centred, rather than audience-centred, earliest preaching of the apostles, samples of which he includes in his book of Acts. See P.G. Bolt, 'Mission and Witness', in D.G. Peterson & I.H. Marshall (eds.), *Witness to the Nations. The Theology of Acts* (Carlisle & Grand Rapids: Paternoster & Eerdmans, 1998), 191-214.
90 L. Alexander, 'Luke's Preface in the Context of Greek Preface-Writing', *NovT* 28 (1986), 48-74; The *Preface to Luke's Gospel. Literary Convention and Social Context in Luke 1.1-4 and Acts 1.1* (SNTSMS 78; Cambridge: Cambridge University Press, 1993).

Jesus and the Grace of the Cross
Luke 23:34a and the Politics of 'Forgiveness' in Antiquity

JAMES R. HARRISON

The historical authenticity of Jesus' prayer to God to forgive his enemies (Luke 23:34a: Πάτερ, ἄφες αὐτοῖς) is still debated by New Testament scholars. The disputed textual tradition underlying the verse and the ambiguous status of the internal arguments in favour of the logion have meant that a definitive answer to its authenticity remains elusive.[1] Where Luke 23:34 is accepted as an authentic Jesus logion,[2] scholarly discussion largely revolves around the identity of those whom Jesus forgives (Jews, Romans, or both?) and the 'ignorance' motif (Luke 23:34; cf. Acts 2:36; 3:17; 13:17; 17:30). Significant investigations of ἀφίημι and ἄφεσις have been undertaken,[3] but this discussion has not been brought into dialogue with the variegated understanding of forgiveness in antiquity and its dominant terminology (συγγνώμη; συγγιγνώσκω). The time is long overdue for a reappraisal of the authenticity and the import, socially and theologically, of the logion.

---

1 For recent discussions, see J.H. Petzer, 'Eclecticism and the Text of the New Testament', in P.J. Hartin and J.H. Petzer (eds.), *Text and Interpretation: New Approaches in the Criticism of the New Testament* (Leiden/New York/Kobenhaun/Köln: E.J. Brill, 1991), 47-62; G.P. Carras, 'A Pentateuchal Echo in Jesus' Prayer on the Cross: Intertextuality Between Numbers 15, 22-31 and Luke 23, 34a', in C.M. Tuckett (ed.), *The Scriptures in the Gospels* (Leuven: Leuven University Press/Peeters, 1997), 605-16; J. Delobel, 'Luke 23:43a: A Perpetual Text-Critical Crux?', in W.L. Petersen (ed.), *Sayings of Jesus: Canonical and Non-Canonical Essays in Honour of Tjitze Baarda* (Leiden/New York/Köln: E.J. Brill, 1997), 25-36; J.A. Whitlark and M.C. Parsons, 'The "Seven" Last Words: A Numerical Motivation for the Insertion of Luke 23.34a', *NTS* 52 (2006),: 188-204; J.M. Strachan, *The Limits of a Text: Luke 23:34a as a Case Study in Theological Interpretation* (Winona Lake: Eisenbrauns, 2012).

2 Among Lukan commentators supporting the authenticity of the saying, see M.-J. Lagrange (Paris: Gabalda, 1921), 587; G.B. Caird (New York: Seabury Press, 1963), 251; E. Schweizer (SPCK: London, 1964), 359-360; L. Morris (London: IVP, 1974), 326-327; I.H. Marshall (Grand Rapids: Eerdmans, 1978), 867-868; J. Nolland (Nashville: Thomas Nelson, 1993), 1144; D.L. Bock (Grand Rapids: Baker, 1996), 1848-1851, 1867-1868; F. Bovon (Genève: Labor et Fides, 2009), 368-369. C.F. Evans (London: SCM, 1993), 867-868 supports its inclusion in the text of Luke, though not necessarily as a saying of the historical Jesus. F.W. Danker (Philadelphia: Fortress, 1988), 373, argues that no conclusive judgement can be made regarding the 'ambivalent manuscript tradition'. J.M. Creed (London: Macmillan, 1930), 286, argues that the logion is inauthentic. J.A. Fitzmyer (Garden City, NY: Doubleday, 1981), 1500, 1503-1504, seems to adopt a position of historical 'agnosticism' regarding the authenticity of the logion.

3 E.g. R. Bultmann, 'ἀφίημι, ἄφεσις, παρίημι, πάρεσις', *TDNT* (G. Kittel, ed.; Grand Rapids: Eerdmans, 1964), 1.509-12; H. Leroy, 'ἀφίημι, ἄφεσις', *EDNT* (H. Balz and G. Schneider, eds.; Grand Rapids: Eerdmans, 1990), 181-83; C. Spicq, 'ἄφεσις', *TLNT* (Peabody: Hendrickson, 1994), 238-44; C. Breytenbach, 'ἀφίημι, ἄφεσις', *ThBLNT* (L. Coenen and K. Haacker, eds.; Witten: SCM/R. Brockhaus, 2010), 1737-42.

Luke is a third generation document, as the preface to the Gospel makes clear (Luke 1:1-4).[4] While some scholars assign the Gospel to a pre-70 date, the majority conclude that the work was written c. AD 80–90.[5] New Testament scholars have justifiably concentrated on the manuscript evidence in determining the authenticity of our logion, but the text-critical results of this debate, as we shall see, have been less than conclusive. Consequently, a more comprehensive approach that takes seriously the Jewish and Graeco-Roman understanding of forgiveness is required. Only then will we be able to address properly the historical status of the logion, both in its late twenties Palestinian oral context and its early eighties Graeco-Roman literary context. An investigation of *both* contexts of the logion is required if we are to determine the likelihood of whether

a) the logion is the theological invention of an unknown interpolator, whose motives for adding the logion to the text remain a matter of speculation and whose textual legacy was confined primarily to the Western witnesses;
b) the logion is the theological invention of Luke, designed for the pastoral and theological edification of his Graeco-Roman readers;
c) the logion is an authentic logion of the historical Jesus, but is now without a recoverable context in his ministry, due to the difficulties of our manuscript tradition;
d) the logion is an authentic saying of the historical Jesus, uttered in the context of his crucifixion, notwithstanding the difficulties of our manuscript tradition.

If it can be demonstrated that our logion does not fit comfortably with what we know of forgiveness in the Jewish and Graeco-Roman contexts, then (c) and (d) are most likely options because of the discontinuity of the logion with its late twenties and early eighties contexts. To determine whether the context of the logion is historically recoverable to Jesus' crucifixion—i.e. (d) as opposed to (c)—we have to consider the strength of the internal literary arguments.

At the outset, several brief comments need to be made on scholarship on the Jewish and the Graeco-Roman context of our logion. First, it is surprising that the Graeco-Roman context of forgiveness has not caught the attention of Lukan scholars in a Gospel designed for a Gentile audience. Even more remarkable is the fact that classical scholars and modern philosophers have only just begun to investigate the little studied motif of forgiveness in antiquity.[6] The evidence of the philosophers is instructive in this regard,[7] as well as the writings of the rhetoricians and the dramatists.[8]

Nor has the related concept of 'clemency' been brought into a sharp dialogue with Jesus' prayer

---

4 First generation: αὐτόπται καὶ ὑπηρέται γενόμενοι (Luke 1:2). Second generation: πολλοὶ ἐπεχείρησαν ἀνατάξασθαι διήγησιν (1:1). Third generation: ἡμῖν, i.e. Luke, Theophilus, and the church (1:3). See E. Scheffler, 'Compassionate Action: Living According to Luke's Gospel', in J.G. van der Watt (ed.), *Identity, Ethics, and Ethos in the New Testament* (Berlin/New York: Walter de Gruyter, 2006), 77-106, at 79.
5 Note the differing dates for the composition of Luke's Gospel suggested by scholars: the late sixties approaching AD 70 (e.g. I.H. Marshall, *Commentary on Luke* [Grand Rapids: Eerdmans, 1978], 33-35) or AD 80-85 (e.g. J.A. Fitzmyer, *The Gospel According to Luke I–IX* [Garden City, NY: Doubleday, 1981], 57).
6 C.L. Griswold, *Forgiveness: A Philosophical Exploration* (Cambridge: Cambridge University Press, 2007); D. Konstan, *Before Forgiveness: The Origins of a Moral Idea* (Cambridge: Cambridge University Press, 2010); C.L. Griswold and D. Konstan, *Ancient Forgiveness: Classical, Judaic, and Christian* (Cambridge: Cambridge University Press, 2011).
7 For discussion, see K. Metzler, *Der griechische Begriff des Verzeihens* (Tübingen: Mohr Siebeck, 1991), 137-81.
8 See D.A. Hester, 'To Help One's Friends and Harm One's Enemies: A Study in the *Oedipus at Colonus*', *Antichthon* 11 (1977), 22-41; Metzler, *Der griechische Begriff*, 121-27; M.W. Blundell, *Helping Friends and Harming Enemies: A Study in Sophocles and Greek Ethics* (Cambridge: Cambridge University Press, 1989), s.v. Index, 'Forgiveness'.

of forgiveness.[9] Danker has helpfully appealed to 'clemency' (*clementia*) of the imperial benefactors as background to our logion.[10] However, Danker has not sharply enough differentiated the Lukan understanding of 'forgiveness', with its different terminology, from its imperial counterparts, Augustan and Neronian. Moreover, Danker does not take into account the spread of Stoic opinion regarding *clementia* in the first century. We cannot assume that Luke's Gentile auditors would have necessarily agreed with the imperial propaganda regarding the Roman ruler's *clementia*, even though they would have been well aware of its ubiquity.

Second, in terms of the Jewish context, it is curious that most commentators have evinced no interest in Luke's use of ἀφίημι in Luke 23:34 against the backdrop of the LXX or the wider literature of Second Temple Judaism.[11] Consequently we have no way of discerning whether Jesus' prayer for his enemies on the cross (Luke 23:34; cf. 6:27-28, 35) is socially radical in its Jewish context or even distances itself from other notable Jewish approaches to forgiveness. Thus this article will first address the Jewish corpus of literature before proceeding to the Graeco-Roman understanding of forgiveness.

I will argue that Luke's Graeco-Roman auditors would have struggled to reconcile their cultural understanding of forgiveness with the forgiveness offered by the crucified Christ. The widespread maxim of 'helping friends and harming enemies' would have better expressed the social realities of the first-century world for Luke's auditors. Equally, Jewish auditors of Luke's Gospel—including those Palestinian auditors who originally heard and preserved Jesus' logion for posterity in the late 20's or early 30's—would have been initially disturbed by the theological and social implications of Jesus' prayer, if the Greek Jewish use of ἀφίημι is sufficiently representative. Alternatively, they may well have been attracted by Jesus' highly unconventional view of social relationships in God's counter-cultural Kingdom—an attraction that ensured that the logion became part of the oral and written dominical tradition. Jesus' logion, argued to be authentic in this article, radically undermined the ancient politics of hatred, irrespective of its religious and cultural context.

At the outset we turn briefly to the difficulties posed by the manuscript traditions and assess if we can determine, on text-critical and stylistic grounds, the authenticity of the logion.

1. Assessing the Manuscript Traditions of Luke 23:34a

The issue of the manuscript evidence is delicately poised.[12] The prayer logion (Luke 23:34a) is included in ancient authorities from the mid-second century AD onwards including Tatian, Hegesippus, and Marcion.[13] This does not seal the case for authenticity, however. The manuscript

---

9 On clemency in antiquity, see D. Konstan, *Pity Transformed* (London: Duckworth, 2001); F.B. Dowling, *Clemency and Cruelty in the Roman World* (Michigan: University of Michigan Press, 2006); S. Braund, *Seneca: De Clementia* (Oxford: Oxford University Press, 2009).

10 F.W. Danker, *Jesus and the New Age: A Commentary on St Luke's Gospel* (Philadelphia: Fortress, 1988), 373. See also S. Matthews, 'Clemency as Cruelty: Forgiveness and Force in the Dying Prayers of Jesus and Stephen', *BibInt* 17 (2009), 118-46. On patronage in Luke, see J. Marshall, *Jesus, Patrons and Benefactors* (Tübingen: Mohr Siebeck, 2008). For extra discussion, see J.P. Meier, *A Marginal Jew*. Volume IV: *Law and Love* (New Haven and London: Yale University Press, 2009), 478-646, esp. 528-51.

11 The only exception to this is D.L. Bock, *Luke 9:51—24:53* (Grand Rapids: Baker, 1996), 1849-50.

12 See Strachan, *The Limits of a Text*, 10-11, for a useful summary of the textual evidence.

13 Delobel, 'Luke 23:43a', 29, points out that the testimony of Tatian is the '*terminus ante quem* of Luke 23:34a as part of the third Gospel in the middle of the second century'. On the basis of this, he concludes: 'It would appear, therefore, that from the point of external criticism the attestation in favour of the original presence of the logion is stronger than is usually thought'.

evidence for the inclusion of the logion in its longer reading comes almost exclusively from the Western witnesses. Only after the fourth century do other witnesses start to appear.

By contrast, consistently early witnesses omit the logion, including the Codices Vaticanus and Bezae, as well as papyrus Bodmer XIV-XV, among others. Moreover, these witnesses belong to different textual families (Western, Alexandrian) and they exhibit geographical diversity.[14] Consequently, scholars have argued that the logion, interpolated after the composition of Luke, (a) disrupts the flow of the crucifixion pericope;[15] (b) did not belong to the earlier Markan passion narrative (i.e. Luke's source);[16] and (c) is modelled on Stephen's prayer in Acts 7:60 or on Isaiah 53:12.[17] Moreover, the 'ignorance' motif accompanying Jesus' prayer of forgiveness is found exclusively in Acts (3:17; 13:27; 17:30), as opposed to the Gospel of Luke (*pace*, Luke 12:48). This feature, it is claimed, is another pointer to the logion being a theological creation of the early church or of an unknown interpolator.[18]

In response, scholars upholding the authenticity of the logion as part of the original Lukan autograph have argued that the logion fits perfectly Luke's motifs of prayer for the enemy, forgiveness, and ignorance.[19] The close parallelism between Acts 7:60 and Luke 23:34a points to the dependence of the pericope of Stephen upon the Jesus prayer logion, not the other way around.[20] Various theories have also been posited for the logion being omitted by later scribes. Two examples will suffice.[21] First, since an anti-Judaic sentiment had penetrated certain quarters of early church life,[22] Jesus' logion was suppressed because those with anti-Judaic feelings found it inconceivable that God could forgive the Jews.[23] Second, since Jesus' prayer for forgiveness did not avert the destruction of Jerusalem in AD 70, the logion was omitted lest it appear that God did not hear Jesus' prayer.[24]

But such arguments are double-edged and are able to be turned back on their proponents. For example, with reference to the first theory outlined above, it could be argued that an anti-Judaic interpolator added the 'ignorance' motif to the logion in order to exculpate the Romans and thereby increase Jewish responsibility for Jesus' death. In other words, the same theory—i.e. the presence of anti-Judaic sentiment in the early church—can spawn contradictory text-critical

---

14 Whitlark and Parsons, '"Seven" Last Words', 189; Delobel, 'Luke 23:43a', 28.
15 Fitzmyer, *Luke*, 1503. C.F. Evans, *Saint Luke* (London: SPCK, 1990), 867, comments: 'Structurally it breaks the sequence, so that *And they cast lots*... as the action of the executioners follows awkwardly after it'.
16 Delobel, 'Luke 23:43a', 29.
17 Marshall, *Luke*, 868.
18 J.B. Green, *The Gospel of Luke* (Grand Rapids: Eerdmans, 1997), 821, observes that the 'ignorance' motif is presaged in Luke 12:48 and is also found in the Pentateuch (Lev 5:17-19; Num 15:25-31). Similarly, E.E. Ellis, *The Gospel of Luke* (London: Marshall, Morgan & Scott, 1974 rev.), 267-68; Carras, 'A Pentateuchal Echo', *passim*.
19 F.B. Craddock, *Luke* (Louisville: John Knox, 1990), 273, argues that the 'forgiveness' logion (Luke 23:34) is anticipated beforehand in Jesus' instructions to pray for the enemy, love him, and forgive him (6:27-28, 35; 17:4). Similarly, see Danker, *Jesus and the New Age*, 373.
20 Craddock, *Luke*, 273, states: 'In writing the Gospel, Luke Anticipated Acts, so that much in the Gospel has its fulfilment and clarity in Acts. To try to understand either without the other is a fruitless exercise in excessive rigidity'. Bock, *Luke*, 1868, observes: 'Luke frequently notes parallelism between events'.
21 In what follows, I am indebted to the discussion in Petzer, 'Eclecticism', 57.
22 A. von Harnack, *Studien zur Geschichte des Neuen Testaments und der alten Kirche* (Berlin and Leipzig: W. de Gruyter, 1931), 92-98.
23 G.B. Caird, *The Gospel of Luke* (New York: Seabury Press, 1963), 251; E. Schweitzer, *The Good News according to Luke* (London: SPCK, 1984), 359. The 'ignorance' motif (Luke 23:34a) was also dropped because of anti-Judaic sentiment within the later church (E.J. Epp, 'The "Ignorance Motif" in Acts and Anti-Judaic Tendencies in Codex Bezae', *HTR* 52 [1962]: 51-62).
24 See F. Bovon, *L'Évangile selon saint Luc* 19, 28-24, 53 (Genève: Labor et Fides, 2009), 369; Marshall, *Luke*, 868.

hypotheses. The different manuscript readings among our witnesses can be explained either as a scribal omission of an authentic Jesus logion or as an interpolator's addition of an inauthentic Jesus logion.[25] How do we determine which hypothesis will best account for the manuscript divergence at Luke 23:34a? The decision is, of course, entirely subjective. In sum, while some of these text-critical hypotheses are possible, their speculative nature and contradictory results mean that they are ultimately unprovable.[26]

The logion, of course, might belong to the fluid oral tradition of Jesus' logia and was inserted by a copyist at a later stage into the Western editions of Luke's Gospel, though not necessarily in the precise context in which it was originally articulated.[27] But the stylistic parallelism between the Jesus and Stephen tradition is too carefully constructed for this, presupposing the priority of the Jesus logion in the Lukan text.[28] In particular, Stephen's martyrdom is strongly modelled on the paradigm of Jesus' death, a good argument for Luke 23:34a having been originally uttered in the historical context of Jesus' crucifixion. Further, as Marshall points out,[29] each of the major subunits in Luke's passion narrative contain a logion (Luke 23:28-31, 43, 46), but this stylistic feature is interrupted if this particular saying in verse 34 did not belong to the Lukan autograph. Nonetheless, the reason for the omission of the logion in so many diverse authorities remains a mystery, notwithstanding the strong stylistic arguments for its inclusion.

Either way, there is no reason to doubt, as we will see, the historical authenticity of the logion as an oral tradition. The logion fits the criterion of coherence,[30] being congruent with what we know of Jesus' distinctive teaching in the Gospels regarding the enemy (Luke 6:27-36). But, significantly, it also meets the criterion of dissimilarity, as we will see, by virtue of its distinctiveness in its Jewish and Graeco-Roman context.[31]

2. The Jewish Understanding of Forgiveness: A Study of ἀφίημι and ἄφεσις

We have noted above that very few Lukan commentators have attempted to situate Luke 23:34a within the wider Jewish understanding of forgiveness. Further, no attempt has been made to situate the logion within a comprehensive study of ἀφίημι and its cognates in the Greek Jewish

---

25 One could even envisage a third hypothesis where a later interpolator relocated an authentic Jesus logion, uttered in a totally different context of Jesus' ministry, to the context of Jesus' crucifixion and then added the 'ignorance' motif to heighten anti-Jewish sentiment over Jesus' death. The increasing complexity of such hypotheses points to their ultimate weakness.
26 Petzer, 'Eclecticism', 57.
27 R.H. Stein, *Luke* (Nashville: Broadman & Holman, 1992), 589, airs this as a possibility, but also concedes that the logion might have been part of the original text of Luke ('it is impossible to be dogmatic').
28 See especially the arguments of Delobel, 'Luke 23:43a', 34-35.
29 Marshall, *Luke*, 868. Contra, Evans, *Saint Luke*, 867.
30 On the criterion of coherence and its limitations, see S.E. Porter, *The Criteria for Authenticity in Historical Jesus Research: Previous Discussions and New Proposals* (Sheffield: Sheffield Academic Press, 2000), 79-82. On the criterion of dissimilarity and its limitations, see G. Theissen and D. Winter, *The Quest for the Plausible Jesus: The Question of Criteria* (Westminster John Knox Press; Louisville/London, 2002), *passim*; Porter, *The Criteria for Authenticity*, 70-76.
31 See especially the recent defence of the historicity of Jesus' teaching on 'love of enemy' in Meier, *A Marginal Jew*. IV.478-646.

literature.[32] In this section we will examine the use of ἀφίημι and ἄφεσις in the LXX, the Greek Jewish pseudepigrapha, Philo and Josephus. The secular usage of each word will be bypassed, unless it has relevance for the social and economic relations of the covenantal people of God. We will also bring into discussion the attitude evinced towards the 'enemy' or 'outsider' in the Dead Sea Scrolls, as well as the strategies that the rabbis commended for handling insult or provocation. Hopefully, we will then be able to determine under what tradition of forgiveness the logion falls and whether it is distinctive in its cultural and religious context.

2.1 ἀφίημι and ἄφεσις in the LXX

Where divine forgiveness is mentioned in the Hebrew Old Testament writings, the verb ἀφίημι translates either *nasa* ('to release from guilt or punishment') or *sala* ('to forgive', 'to pardon'). The instances where ἀφίημι renders the Hebrew *nasa* are usually petitionary. God is addressed in heart-felt prayers for personal forgiveness (LXX Ps 24:18 [MT 25:18]; LXX Ps 31:1, 5 [MT 32:1, 5]) or for the forgiveness of others (ἀφίημι: Gen 18:26; Exod 32:32; Num 14:19). On occasion, the certainty of God's forgiveness (LXX Ps 84:2 [MT 85:2]) becomes the grounds for the petition for the restoration of Israel (Ps 84:4-9 [MT 85:4-9]). Other affirmations of God's forgiveness (Isa 33:24b) crown his promises of a restored Jerusalem (33:20-24a). Significantly, the occasional human transaction of forgiveness is also included under this terminology, including the reconciliation of Joseph with his brothers (Gen 52:17: ἀφίημι [Hebrew: *nasa*]).

In instances where ἀφίημι renders the Hebrew *sala*, the emphasis is more on the forgiveness mediated though the 'sin' and 'guilt' offerings of the Levitical cultic system (Lev 4:20, 35; 5:6; 19:22; Deut 15:2). Both 'intentional' and 'unintentional' sins are covered under divine forgiveness (Num 15:25, 26, 28). Thus we see how God has graciously set in place the cultus by which a right relationship with him, when ruptured by sin, can be restored though the appropriate sacrifice. This is further illustrated when ἀφίημι renders the Hebrew *kipper* ('to make atonement') in Isaiah 22:14.

By contrast, the noun ἄφεσις in the LXX focuses heavily on the social and economic relations of the people of God. First, ἄφεσις translates the Hebrew word *yobel*, or the 'Jubilee' year, during which the inhabitants of the land were freed (Lev 25:10, 11, 12, 28, 31, 33, 40, 41, 50, 52, 54; 27:17, 18, 21, 23, 24; Num 36:4). Second, ἄφεσις also translates the Hebrew *samat*, a word that referred to the 'release' from debts on the seventh year (Deut 15:1, 2, 3, 9; 31:10). Third, the sabbatical release of the land from cultivation each seventh year was rendered by ἄφεσις (Exod 23:11; Lev 25:2-7; Hebrew equivalent: *samam*). This 'release' motif is expanded metaphorically in Isaiah 58:6 and 61:1 where ἄφεσις begins to acquire the 'messianic' nuance of freeing the 'oppressed' and the 'captives'.[33] But only once in the LXX, as several scholars have

---

32 Forgiveness terminology abounds in the Gospel of Luke. The noun ἄφεσις ('forgiveness') and its verbal form ἀφίημι ('to forgive') are used 46 times (1:77; 3:3; 4:18 [bis]; 4:39; 5:11, 20, 23; 6:37; 7:47 [bis]; 8:51; 9:60; 10:30; 11:4 [bis]; 12:10 [bis], 39; 13:8, 35; 17:3, 34; 18:16, 28; 19:44; 21:6; 23:34; 24:47). See the helpful article, engaging the writings of N. T. Wright: J. Chatraw, 'Balancing out (W)Right: Jesus' Theology of Individual and Corporate Repentance and Forgiveness in the Gospel of Luke', *JETS* 55.2 (2012), 299-321. For an attempt to understand Jesus' forgiveness solely in prophetic terms, see T. Hägerland, *Jesus and the Forgiveness of Sins: An Aspect of His Prophetic Ministry* (Cambridge: Cambridge University Press, 2012). Inexplicably, Hägerland omits any discussion of Luke 23:34a.

33 Spicq, 'ἄφεσις', *TLNT*, 240-41. Isaiah 61:1-2 was an important messianic text for the writers of the Dead Scrolls (4Q521 1 ii 1-14), but Jesus claimed to be the text's messianic fulfilment in his sermon at the Nazareth synagogue (Luke 4:18-21; cf. 7:22). For discussion, see C.A. Evans, 'Jesus and the Messianic Texts from Qumran: A Preliminary Assessment of the Recently Published Materials', in, C.A. Evans, *Jesus and His Contemporaries: Comparative Studies* (Leiden, New York, and Köln: Brill, 1995), pp. 83-154, esp. 118-24, 128-29.

noted,³⁴ does ἄφεσις acquire the nuance of forgiveness in the release of the sin-bearing scapegoat into the desert (Lev 16:26), although there is no Hebrew equivalent in this particular case.³⁵

Finally, elsewhere in the LXX, an ethos of divine reciprocity is articulated in order to encourage human forgiveness with the covenantal community: 'Forgive the neighbour the wrong he has done, and then your sins will be pardoned when you pray' (ἀφίημι: Sir 28:2).³⁶ In sum, ἀφίημι and ἄφεσις are not widely used in the LXX for forgiveness. The cultus-centred aspect of forgiveness in the Old Testament meant that different semantic domains expressed the reality of divine mercy towards sinners (washing, cleansing, covering, etc.).³⁷

2.2 ἀφίημι and ἄφεσις in the Pseudepigrapha, Philo and Josephus

As far as the Jewish understanding of forgiveness in the Jewish pseudepigrapha, the offer of divine forgiveness was often predicated on the prior repentance of the offender (ἀφίημι: TGad 6:3; 7:5; PssSol 7:7; TAb 14:12, 14; cf. 3:8; PrMan 7, 13f; Sir 17:29; 1 En 50:2-4; Jub 41:23-25).³⁸ Occasionally, the practicality of dealing with the intransigence of the unrepentant forces a different strategy: 'But even if he is devoid of shame and persists in his wickedness, forgive him from the heart and leave vengeance to God' (ἀφίημι: TGad 6:7). In terms of background to the 'ignorance' motif in Luke 23:34a, there are traditions where petitioners invoke God for forgiveness due to the limitations arising from their own ignorance (ἀφίημι: Jub 41:25; cf. JosAsen 6:7; 17:10; TJud 19). Last, cultic sacrifice (ἀφίημι: TJob 42:8) and heart-felt prayer (ἀφίημι: 1 En 13:14, 6) also effects divine forgiveness.

By contrast, Philo (20 BC—AD 50) largely allegorises references to forgiveness in the LXX. In terms of ἀφίημι, Philo interprets Cain's lack of forgiveness in Genesis 4:14 as a reference to the danger of divine abandonment (ἀφίημι: Det 141-149, 150-155). The mention of forgiveness in Exodus 32:32 (ἀφίημι: Her 20-21) is allegorised as the wise man's freedom of speech. Philo adopts the same approach with ἄφεσις. Philo interprets Abraham's intercession for the forgiveness of Sodom (ἄφεσις: Gen 18:16ff) as an allegory about the prayers of those instructed in wisdom (*Mut* 228-229). Elsewhere, Philo uses ἄφεσις conventionally of the remission of sins through the sacrificial system (Mos 2.147; Spec 1.190, 215, 237), as well as the forgiveness for intentional and non-intentional murder (Leg 3.128). However, Philo also speaks in a Stoic manner about the emancipation of the human soul from the passions through prayer or by the exercise of humility (*Her* 273; *Congr* 108).

Last, in an intriguing sidelight to the public humiliation of Jesus' crucifixion, Philo refers to the (so-called) 'forgiveness' that the governor of Egypt extended to Jews who had rebelled in AD 38 against his decision to erect statues of Caligula in the synagogues of Alexandria. The Jewish rebels

---

34 Leroy, 'ἀφίημι, ἄφεσις', *EDNT*, 181-82; C. Brown, 'Forgiveness', 'ἀφίημι', *NIDNT* (C. Brown, ed.; Exeter: Paternoster Press, 1975), 698.

35 In sharp contrast, however, note what Spicq, 'ἄφεσις', *TLNT*, 242, says about the surprising use of ἄφεσις in the New Testament: 'It is remarkable that the NT writers use ἄφεσις thirty-six times, always meaning pardon from sins; there is never a secular meaning, as if this were a technical term reserved for religious use'.

36 On the emergence of more reciprocal understandings of divine grace in the LXX, see J. R. Harrison, *Paul's Language of Grace in Its Graeco-Roman Context* (Tübingen: Mohr Siebeck, 2003), 110-14.

37 Brown, *NIDNTT*, 698.

38 The later rabbinic literature also brings out this emphasis. The Midrash, for example, states the case unequivocally: 'Says the Holy One, even if they (your sins) should reach to Heaven, if you repent I will forgive' (Pes. Rab. 44:185a). Interestingly, the Tosefta, on the basis of Exodus 34:6-7, quantifies God's forgiveness as five hundred-fold that of His wrath (*t. Sot.* 4:1).

were crucified alive, after they had been publicly scourged, at the very same time as the festival honouring the emperor's birthday. As Philo ironically observes regarding the coincidence of the timing of their crucifixion (*Leg 84*) with the public festival,

> [Flaccus] commanded living men to be crucified, men to whom the very time itself gave, if not entire forgiveness, still, at all events, a brief and temporary respite from punishment; and he did this after they had been beaten by scourgings in the middle of the theatre; and after he had tortured them with fire and sword [...]

In the case of Josephus (AD 37/38—c. 100), the historian routinely employs ἀφίημι in contexts dealing with political acquittal or pardon (e.g. Joseph: *AJ* 2.146; Solomon: *AJ* 7.362; Herod the Great: *BJ* 1.455, 505; *AJ* 15.258; Herod Philip: *AJ* 18.107). However, Josephus does occasionally refer to the forgiveness of God (*AJ* 6.92; 11.144) and the release of the Jubilee year (*AJ* 3.282).

2.3 Jewish Understandings of Forgiveness in the Dead Sea Scrolls and Rabbinic Literature

a. Forgiveness in the Dead Sea Scrolls Literature

The literature of the Dead Sea Scrolls is particularly revealing for the attitude that it takes to the enemies of the community. While the writers of the Dead Sea Scrolls boldly highlight the reality of divine forgiveness and justification,[39] strong imprecations are brought against God's enemies that emphasise their exclusion from divine forgiveness. The enemy, in the view of the Qumran covenanters, was to be accorded no mercy (*1QS* 2.5-8),

> Be cursed in all the works of our guilty wickedness,
> May God make you an object of terror by the hands of all the avengers of vengeance [...]
> Be cursed, without mercy, according to the darkness of your works.
> Be damned in the place of everlasting fire.

The community rules of conduct are equally clear regarding the disobedient (*IQS* 10.20),

> I will bear no rancour
>   against them that turn from transgression,
> but will have no pity
>   on all who depart from the way.

Finally, in an anti-Samaritan writing possibly ante-dating the destruction of the rival temple on Mount Gerizim by John Hyrcanus (4Q372 fr.1. *ll.* 14-20),[40] the writer presents the Samaritans as inciting Joseph's brothers to hand Joseph over to the foreigners. In the revealing filial prayer of Joseph to God, God is invoked to judge Joseph's captors and to extend grace towards the covenantal community:

---

39 On divine forgiveness, see IQH IV Hymn 1; VI Hymn 5, XIV Hymn 14; XV Hymn 17; XVI Hymn 18; XVIII Hymn 19; XXI Hymn 24; IIQPsa XIX; IIQ13 *ll*.5ff. On the divine justification of sinners (especially in light of Genesis 15:6), see MMT C (= The Exhortation) 4Q39814-17 ii conflated 4Q399 II.25-26, 31-32; IQS XI. *ll*.5ff, *ll*.10ff; CD IV *ll*.5ff. The translation used is G. Vermes, *The Complete Dead Sea Scrolls in English* (London: Penguin Books, [4]1998).

40 4Q372 fr.1 *ll*. 12-13: 'They made for themselves a high place on an elevated mountain to excite the jealousy of Israel. They spoke wor[ds of ...] of the sons of Jacob and caused disgust with the words of their mouth, blaspheming against the Tent of Zion'.

> And for all of this, Joseph [was put] into the hands of strangers to consume his strength and break his bones until the time of his end [...] cried to the mighty God that he should save him from their hands. He said, 'My Father and my God, do not abandon me to the hands of the nations. Execute judgement for me so that the humble and the poor may not perish. Thou hast no need of any nation or people to help Thee. [Thy] fing[er] is greater and more powerful than anything in the world. For Thou optest for the truth, and in Thy hand there is no violence whatever. Also Thy mercies are many and Thy loving-kindness is great for all those who seek Thee. They are stronger than I and all my brothers have joined me.

The 'judgement' motifs in this text are just as rhetorically compelling as the 'mercy' motifs. Because the 'nations' have no power in comparison to Joseph's all-powerful God, the 'humble' and 'poor' of God's covenantal community will be exalted over their enemies. God would execute his judgement on behalf of Joseph with the 'signs and wonders' reminiscent of the later Exodus generation, as the writer's allusion to the 'finger of God' motif makes clear (Exod 8:19; cf. 3:20; 6:1, 6; 9:3; 13:3, 14; Luke 11:20).

b. Forgiveness and the Handling of Insult in the Rabbinic Corpus

The rabbinic corpus post-dates the New Testament and its traditions cannot be traced with certainty back to the New Testament era.[41] Notwithstanding, the voices of those who inherited and developed the oral and scriptural traditions of rabbinic Judaism post AD 70 repay careful attention for the light they throw on the continuities and discontinuities with the pre-70 Jewish traditions of forgiveness. In the rabbinic discussions of forgiveness, there is strong emphasis on how one reacts to injuries against oneself or to the intentional disgrace of one's neighbour. This provides an interesting point of comparison for Luke 23:34a, especially if the logion is considered the product of a later interpolator in the Western witnesses from the second century AD onwards. In each of the texts cited below, the rabbis characteristically cite Old Testament texts or point to the example of God in order to articulate the rationale for conciliatory behaviour in the face of personal provocation or insult. Consequently, they provide an interesting backdrop for assessing what might be distinctive about our prayer logion.

Meg. 28a brings out in a manner similar to Sirach 28:2, discussed above, the divine forgiveness of sins that occurs when forgiveness is willingly offered to others:

> Mar Zutra, when he went to bed, was wont to say: 'Forgiven be everybody who may have done me an injury' [...] Raba said: If a man passes by his rights, his sins shall be passed by. For it says, 'He pardons iniquity and passes by transgression' (Mic. 7.18). Of whom does he pardon the iniquity? Of him who passes by an offence [done to him].[42]

Similarly, according to T.Bab.K. 9.29.30, God reciprocates compassion to those who are compassionate to their unrepentant tormentors:

> If a man has received an injury, then, even if the wrongdoer has not asked his forgiveness, the receiver of the injury must nevertheless ask [God] to show the wrongdoer compassion, even as Abraham prayed to God for Abimelech (Gen. 20.17) and Job prayed for his friends.

---

41 G.W. Buchanan, 'The Use of Rabbinic Literature for New Testament Research', *BTB* 7 (1977), 111-22; P.S. Alexander, 'Rabbinic Judaism and the New Testament', *ZNW* 74 (1983), 237-46; S.T. Lachs, 'Rabbinic Sources for New Testament Studies—Use and Misuse', *JQR* 74.2 (1983), 159-73.
42 C.G. Montefiore and H. Loewe, *A Rabbinic Anthology* (New York: Schocken, 1974), §1510.

> R. Gamaliel said: Let this be a sign to you, that whenever you are compassionate, the Compassionate One will have compassion on you.[43]

Tanh.B., Hukkat, 63b cites Numbers 21.7 to highlight Moses how forgave and prayed for those who had spoken against his leadership of Israel during the wilderness wanderings. The text concludes by emphasising the centrality of prayer in the process of forgiveness:

> For one who pardons can never become cruel. And how do you know that if a man asks pardon of his neighbour whom he has offended, and that if the neighbour refuses to pardon him, he, the neighbour, and not the offender, is called a sinner? Because Samuel said, 'As for me, far be it from me to sin unto the Lord by refraining to pray for you' (1 Sam 12:23). When was this? When the people came and said, 'We have sinned'.[44]

Finally, the long-suffering of God towards the blaspheming nations is cited as another reason for forbearance of the offended towards those who revile them (Midr. Ps. on Ps.86:1 [186b, §1]),

> R. Abba said in the name of R. Alexandri: He who hears himself cursed, and has the opportunity to stop the man who curses him, and yet keeps silence, makes himself a partner with God, for God hears how the nations blaspheme him, and he is silent.[45]

2.4 The Historicity of the Luke 23:34a in Its Jewish Context

The logion of Luke 23:34a fits the genre of the LXX petitionary prayers of Abraham and Moses for the forgiveness of cities and the nation of Israel. Prayer for personal forgiveness, a marked feature of the Old Testament penitential Psalms and the Thanksgiving Hymns of Qumran, is glaringly absent from the Jesus' own prayer life with the Father. Further, the forgiveness requested for others is in no way linked to the cultus, as forgiveness often was in the LXX. There is no connection between the logion and the 'Jubilee' or 'release' traditions of the LXX, even though Jesus alludes to these traditions elsewhere as the rationale for his ministry (Luke 4:18-21; cf. 7:22). Nor is there any hint of the allegorising of forgiveness, as with Philo. There is probably implicit recognition on Jesus' part of the LXX distinction between 'intentional' and 'unintentional' sin in his reference to sin committed in ignorance (Luke 23:34a: οὐ γὰρ οἴδασιν τί ποιοῦσιν). But even here Jesus' approach is different to the Old Testament pseudepigraphic literature where the *petitioner's* ignorance is at the forefront.

What seems to be primary in Jesus' approach in petitioning forgiveness for others is his filial consciousness, a feature absent from the requests of Moses and Abraham. Significantly, Πάτερ is in the emphatic position in the Greek rendering of the prayer (Luke 23:34a). This filial consciousness is certainly present in the prayer of Joseph in 4Q472 fr.1. However, the writer of the Dead Sea Scroll also distances Joseph sufficiently in his intimacy with God so that there is no overestimation of Joseph's status: the prayer address is 'My Father and my God'. Nor is there any expectation in Jesus' logion that God will reciprocate forgiveness if forgiveness is extended to others, a feature that is present in Sirach and the later rabbinic traditions. Somehow, precisely because of Jesus' filial consciousness (Luke 23:34a, 46a: Πάτερ) and his dependence upon the

---

43 Montefiore and Loewe, *A Rabbinic Anthology*, §1282. Der.Er.Z. 7.3. *fin* (§1285) states: 'Let a man forgive the disgrace to which he has been subjected: let him seek no honour through the disgrace of his neighbour'.
44 Montefiore and Loewe, *A Rabbinic Anthology*, §1296.
45 Montefiore and Loewe, *A Rabbinic Anthology*, §1286.

Father (23:46a: εἰς χεῖράς σου παρατίθεμαι τὸ πνεῦμά μου), the fulfilment of the prayer—in Luke's view at least—bears its own momentum as far as God's soteriological plan (cf. Acts 3:17; 13:27; 17:30).

Also the prayer logion is marked by forgiveness towards the enemy in a way that differentiates Jesus from the traditions found in the LXX and Second Temple Judaism.[46] We have noted how the Dead Sea Scrolls writers extend no mercy to the outsider (*1QS* 2.5-8; *1QS* 10. *ll*.5ff). Only the 'humble 'and 'poor' of the covenantal community will be vindicated (4Q472 fr.1). Furthermore, unlike many of the imprecatory Psalms in the Old Testament (Pss 55:15; 58:6; 69:28; 109:9; 137:9), Jesus did not call for his vindication over his enemies and, concomitantly, their destruction. Nor did Jesus call down judgement against his persecutors, as did the Maccabean martyrs in 2 Macc 7:19, 34-35 and 4 Macc 9:15.

Perhaps the later rabbinic handling of insult perhaps comes the closest to Jesus' extension of forgiveness: but the level of provocation discussed is the routine collisions of every-day social relations. If the historical context of Jesus' prayer logion is indeed the cross, we have moved into new territory in terms of forgiveness of the enemy. Additionally, the rationale of the rabbinic prayers for forgiveness is founded on oral tradition, scriptural precedent, and the imitation of God. There is nothing comparable to the sense of filial consciousness that precedes Jesus' request for the forgiveness of others.

In sum, the prayer logion of Jesus does exhibit distinctiveness within the 'forgiveness' traditions of the LXX and Second Temple Judaism. While we might be hesitant to invoke the 'criterion of dissimilarity' in all its force for the prayer logion, given some of the continuities noted above, its distinctive features make its historicity in a Jewish context highly likely. The original late twenties to early thirties Palestinian auditors would have been as much surprised by the logion as Luke's auditors later in the century.

---

46 In saying this, I am not implying that love towards the enemy was absent from the LXX, Second Temple Judaism, and the later rabbinic corpus. Admittedly, in the Old Testament there is no explicit commandment to love the enemy. Indeed, to the contrary, strong nationalistic expressions of hatred towards the enemy occasionally emerge (e.g. Exod 23:22; Lev 16:7-8; Deut 6:19; 20:14; 21:4; Josh 10:13; Judg 5:31; 1 Sam 14:24; Esth 7:13; 9:1, 5, 16). Nevertheless, there is the Mosaic commandment to assist the enemy in the case of emergency (Exod 23:4-5). In Proverbs 25:21-22, a text cited by Paul (Rom 12:20), the writer urges beneficent treatment of the enemy, with the promise of divine reward to the merciful (Prov 25:22b) and, conversely, an intensification of the enemy's shame or punishment because of the beneficence (Prov 25:22a). On the history of interpretation of Proverbs 25:22a and Romans 12:20b, see Fitzmyer, *Romans*, 657-658. Gloating over the fall of an enemy is also inimical to God (Prov 24:17). More generally, retaliation in kind against one's neighbour is forbidden (Prov 24:29; cf. Lev 19:17-18), though the enemy is not in view here. In the apocryphal literature, 4 Maccabees 2:14 stipulates that beneficence should be exercised towards the enemy in particular circumstances. In the pseudepigraphic literature, *Joseph and Aseneth* (Jos. Asen. 23:9; 28:4, 14) emphasises the importance of not rendering evil for evil to the neighbour, though once again any application to the enemy is bypassed. By contrast, the Dead Sea Scrolls, Josephus and Philo are all silent regarding loving the enemy. As far as the rabbinic literature, it is stated in t. *Baba Metzia* 2.26 that helping the enemy should be the social priority before helping one's friends: 'Aid an enemy before you aid a friend, to subdue hatred'. Nor should there be any gloating over the demise of the enemy: 'Let not your heart be glad when your enemy falls lest the Lord see it and it displeases him' (Talmud, *Ethics of the Fathers* 4:24). Last, in *y. Ned.* 9.4, the writer, citing Leviticus 19:19, denies the right of vengeance towards the brother. In conclusion, although mercy might be exercised to the enemy in some situations for the sake of social cohesion, there is nothing like the open-ended nature of Jesus' command to love the enemy in Second Temple Judaism. Even the emphasis on non-retaliation in several Jewish writings is more focused on the 'brother' or 'neighbour' than on the 'enemy'. Above all, Jesus' radical coupling of the general 'love' command with beneficence towards (Luke 6:27b), prayer for (6:28b), and blessing and forgiveness of the enemy (6:28a; 23:34a), goes far beyond what was expected in social relations in first-century Judaism. For an excellent discussion of the issue, see Meier, *A Marginal Jew*, IV.532-51.

3. Graeco-Roman Understandings of Forgiveness

3.1. Introduction

In the eastern Mediterranean world forgiveness was not considered one of the Greek heroic virtues. The retributive ethos of helping one's friends and harming one's enemies was too securely established through the Homeric world of Achilles, Patroclus, Hector and Odysseus.[47] 'Forgiveness' terminology was used in a variety of stereotyped contexts. First, the language of 'forgiveness' was part of the diplomatic parlance used in negotiated or enforced surrenders of the defeated to the victorious in war.[48] Second, the language of 'forgiveness' was also used in the law-courts for the pleas of defendants in the legal process.[49] Third, there is sporadic mention of the forgiveness of the gods/god—or at least supplication for it—on the part of various dependents, or the forgiveness of their providentially appointed representatives in terms of the imperial ruler.[50] However, there is virtually no comment in the literary sources on what this forgiveness (cultic?) means in practice.[51]

Outside of these stereotyped conventions we gain little insight into the dynamics of ancient 'forgiveness'. Cicero's tortured comment in *Ep.* 2.16 demonstrates the complexities of enmity and forgiveness within the shifting alliances of the late republic:

> Now the fact of my finding it pleasantest to reside in my marine villa causes some to suspect me of an intention to embark on a voyage: and, after all, perhaps I should not have been unwilling to do so, had I been able to reach peace: for how could I consistently sail to war: especially against a man who, I hope, has forgiven me, on the side of a man who by this time cannot possibly forgive me?[52]

Occasionally we find evidence of the unexpected abandonment of status and honour, in the face of considerable provocation, by an act of forgiveness that goes against the agonistic culture of antiquity. Diodorus Siculus mentions how the poet Alcaeus, a confirmed enemy of Pittacus, had reviled him mercilessly in his poetry. However, Alcaeus fell into Pittacus' hands, but was unexpectedly freed by Pittacus with the maxim: 'Forgiveness is preferable to punishment'.[53] However, such magnanimity is rare.

3.2. Aristotle's Understanding of Forgiveness

In Aristotle, language of 'forgiveness' routinely appears in ethical contexts involving the ticklish question of human responsibility. συγγνώμη—and its cognates—is used in discussions relating

---

47 Hester, 'To Help One's Friends', 24-25, 29.
48 Appian, *BCiv.* 5.10.96; 5.13.124; *BPun.* 12.88; *BHisp.* 9.48; Diodorus Siculus 9.31.3; 10.27.2; 11.45.5; 16.20.1; 17.109.3. Pausanias 4.20.10; 7.15.2; Josephus, *BJ* 2.52, 301; 5.348; Polybius 23.16; Plato, *Menex.* 242C; Livy 6.26.
49 Demosthenes, *Or.* 23.132; 24.66, 126; 40.46; 45.82; Andocides, *Or.* 1.90; 3.21; Diodorus Siculus 11.26.1; Isocrates, *Plat.* 30; idem, *Big.* 12; Herodotus 8.140A.1; Lysias, *Or.* 19.56; 18.20; Dinarchus 1.11. Note the impressive array of terminology used in Lysias, *Or.* 14.40: 'Wherefore you ought now to condemn this man as one whom you have judged to be a hereditary enemy of the city, and to set neither pity (ἔλεον) nor forgiveness (συγγνώμην) nor any favour (χάριν) above the established laws and the oaths that you have sworn'.
50 Tacitus, *Hist.* 2.29; *Ann.* 11.6.
51 Pindar, *Pythian Odes*, 4; Cicero, *Deiot.* 7.21; Lucan, *Pharsalia*, 9.38, 117, 938; Livy, 1.31; 3.58; Aristophanes, *Vesp* 1.36.7; Pliny, *HN* 14.28; Euripides, *Ion.* 1437; Plautus, *Amph.* 3.21.
52 Note, too, the acerbic comment of Cicero in *Mur.* 31.65: 'Forgive nothing ... Say rather, forgive some things, but not everything'.
53 Epictetus, Frag. 63 reports the maxim more fully: 'Forgiveness is better than punishment; for one is the proof of a gentle, the other of a savage, nature'.

to (a) the extent to which succumbing to the passions is 'excusable' (EH 3.1.1: συγγνώμης; 7.6.2: συγγνώμη; 7.8.6: συγγνωμονική);[54] and (b) the degree to which 'ignorance' contributes to actions being deemed 'pardonable' or 'unpardonable' (EH 5.8.12: συγγνωμονικά, οὐ συγγνωμονικά).[55] While Aristotle's reference to 'ignorance' recalls the 'ignorance 'motif of Luke 23:34b, Luke's concern is more salvation-historical rather than the decidedly ethical emphasis of Aristotle. Apart from this insignificant thematic overlap, the concerns of each author are fundamentally different.

Of greater interest is Aristotle's discussion of 'consideration' (γνώμη). Somewhat artificially, Aristotle strains the meaning of γνώμη and its derivatives (συγγνώμη: 'forgiveness'; συγγνωμονικός: 'forgiving') in order to establish a link between the consideration for others and equitable judgement (ἐπιεικής).[56] In other words, the extension of 'forgiveness' in social relationships must not undermine fundamental issues of justice and equity in the allocation of 'consideration' to others. The text is important because it laid the ground for Seneca's discussion of *clementia* in Book 2 of *De Clementia*. Aristotle's text is rendered below (EH 6.11.1),

> The quality termed 'Consideration' (γνώμη), in virtue of which men are said to be considerate, or to show consideration for others (συγγνώμην), is the faculty of judging correctly what is equitable (ἐπιεικούς). This is indicated by our saying that the equitable man is specially considerate for others (forgiving: συγγνωμονοκόν), and that it is equitable (ἐπιεικές) to show consideration for others (forgiveness: συγγνώμην) in certain cases; but consideration for others (συγγνώμη) is that consideration (γνώμη) which judges rightly what is equitable (κριτική τοῦ ἐπιεικοῦς ὀρθή)—judging 'rightly' meaning judging what is 'truly' equitable.

In sum, we see how the Greek understanding of forgiveness, at least in Aristotle's rendering, could not easily be extended to those who had broken the just requirements of divine law. Behind Aristotle's understanding of 'forgiveness' lay an ethical meritocracy that would not have easily accommodated Jesus' prayer for the ungodly on the cross.

3.3. Traditional Stoic Understandings of Clemency

Before we explore Seneca's understanding of mercy, it is important to appreciate that in orthodox Stoicism *clementia* ('mercy') was dismissed because it was founded on an emotional impulse and was therefore undesirable. Precisely because *clementia* failed to impose a just and deserved penalty, the justice of its operations was held in question. A fragmentary source commenting on the Stoics says (SVF 3.640),

> They say that the good man is not lenient (ἐπιεικῆ), for the lenient man is critical of a punishment that is deserved; and they identify being lenient with assuming that the punishments fixed by law are too harsh for wrongdoers and with thinking that the law-giver is distributing punishments contrary to what is deserved.

Diogenes Laertius (7:13 = SVF 3.641) observes that Stoic wise men

> do not experience pity (συγγνώμην) or have forgiveness (τὸ εἴκειν) for anyone; they do not relax the penalties fixed by the laws, since indulgence (ὁ ἔλεος) and pity (ἐπιείκεια) and even

---

54   Epictetus 2.21.
55   For discussion of Aristotle's language of 'forgiveness', see Griswold, *Forgiveness*, 4-12; Metzler, *Der griechische Begriff*, 155-74.
56   On ἐπιεικής, see Metzler, *Der griechische Begriff*, 166-72.

leniency are psychological incapacity, pretending kindness in place of punishment.[57]

Cicero (*Tusc.* 3.20-21), too, denies that the wise man is animated by any compassion:

> The wise man, however, does not come to feel envy; therefore he does not come to feel compassion either (*ergo ne misereri quidem*). But if the wise man were accustomed to feel distress he would also be accustomed to feel compassion (*miseri etiam soleret*). Therefore distress keeps way from the wise man.

Finally, Stobaeus agues that the Stoics do not extend forgiveness because it the personal vices of the forgiven are inevitably whitewashed. Ultimately, forgiveness undermines moral accountability:

> They say that <the sensible man> forgives <no one; for it is characteristic of the same man to forgive> and to think that the man who has made a [moral] mistake did not do so because of himself, although [in fact] everyone who makes a [moral] mistake does so because of his own vice. And that is why it is quite proper for them to say that he does not even forgive those who make [moral] mistakes.[58]

Given this depreciation of *clementia* in traditional Stoic thought, Seneca's approach represents an ideological novelty in its first century context. How is Seneca different to other Stoics on the issue of clemency?

3.4. Seneca's Understanding of Clemency

Seneca's two-volumed (but incomplete) work, *De Clementia* ('Concerning Mercy') is datable to the year AD 55-56, given the clear allusion to the eighteenth year of Nero in *Clem.* 1.9.1.[59] For our purposes, the most interesting observations concerning *clementia* as a royal virtue occur in De Clementia II, a manuscript that has not come down to us intact.[60] There the king is to demonstrate a particular type of 'mercy': *clementia* ('mercy') over against *misericordia* ('pity').[61] According to Seneca, *clementia* ('mercy') restrains the mind from taking vengeance in cases where retribution is deserved,

---

57 Note Diogenes Laertius' comment (7.123) that the Stoic wise men 'are not pitiful and make no allowance for anyone; they never relax the penalties fixed by the laws, since indulgence and pity (ὁ ἔλεος) and even equitable consideration are marks of a weak mind, which affects kindness in place of chastising. Nor do they deem punishments too severe'. Gellius (*NA* 14.4) quotes Chrysippus' comment on Justice: 'He wished it to be understood that the judge, who is the priest of Justice, should be dignified holy, austere, incorruptible, proof against flattery, pitiless and inexorable towards the wicked and guilty, upright, lofty and powerful, terrifying thanks to the force and majesty of equity and truth. Stobaeus classifies the passions under appetite, pleasure, fear and distress (2.90, 19—91, 9 = SVF 3.394, part.: tr. A.A. Long and D.N. Sedley, *The Hellenistic Philosophers. Volume 1: Translations of the Principal Sources, with Philosophical Commentary* [Cambridge; Cambridge University Press, 1987], 412 §E). In the case of 'pity', it is categorised under distress (cf. Diogenes Laertius 7.111). Again, Diogenes Laertius (7.115) observes: 'And as in the body, there are certain predispositions [to disease], for example catarrh and diarrhoea, so too in the soul there are tendencies, such as proneness to grudging, proneness to pity (ἐλεημοσύνη), quarrelsomeness and the like'. See also Seneca, *De Ira* 2.10: 'That you may not be angry with individuals, you must forgive mankind at large (*universis ignoscendum est*), you must grant indulgence to the human race (*generi humano venia tribuenda est*)'.

58 Stobaeus 2.11d. Tr. B. Inwood and L.G. Pearson, *Hellenistic Philosophy: Introductory Readings* (Indianapolis/Cambridge: Hackett, 21997), 220-21.

59 On the dating of *De Clementia*, see B. Mortureux, 'Les idéaux stoïciens et les premières responsabilités politiques: le "De Clementia"', *ANRW* 2.36.3 (1989), 1641-45; Braund, *De Clementia*, 16-17.

60 It is beyond the bounds of this article to resolve the tension between *De Clementia* I, where pardon and forgiveness are virtues, and *De Clementia* II, where they are vices. For discussion, see Konstan, *Pity Transformed*, 103.

61 For discussion of the definitions of *venia* ('pardon'), *clementia*, and *misericordia*, see Dowling, *Clemency and Cruelty*, 6-8; Braund, *De Clementia*, 38-40.

or where one is tempted to be too lenient in fixing a punishment (Clem. 2.3.1-2). By contrast, *misericordia* ('pity') is a mental defect because, according to Stoic thinking, it succumbs with sorrow at the sight of people's ills (*Clem.* 2.4.4-5.1; 2.6.4).[62] As Seneca observes, 'Pity (*misericordia*) regards the plight, not the cause of it; mercy (*clementia*) is combined with reason' (*Clem.* 2.5.1).

By contrast, the wise man, guided by *clementia*, has a serene mind that is not clouded by the plight of others or by strong emotions such as sorrow (*Clem.* 2.5.4-5). Seneca argues that *clementia* serves the cause of justice by not succumbing to *misericordia* in pardoning crimes worthy of punishment (*Clem.* 2.7.1, 3),

> Pardon is given to a man who ought to be punished; but a wise man does nothing which he ought not to do, omits to do nothing which he ought to do; therefore he does not remit a punishment which he ought to exact [...]. Mercy (*clementia*) has freedom in decision; it sentences not only by the letter of the law, but in accordance with what is fair and good (*aequo et bono*); it may acquit and it may assess the damages at any value it pleases. It does none of these things as if it were doing less than is just, but as if the justest thing were that which it has resolved upon. But to pardon is to fail to punish one whom you judge worthy of punishment; pardon is the remission of punishment that is due. Mercy (*clementia*) is superior primarily in this, that it declares that those who are let off did not deserve any treatment; it is more complete than pardon, more creditable.

But, given that *clementia* as a virtue was the preserve of the Julio-Claudians, what ethical paradigms does Seneca advocate for handling routine breakdowns in human relationships?

3.5. Seneca and the Firmness of the Wise Man: Strategies in Dealing with Injury and Insult

According to Seneca, *clementia* is the preserve of his young charge, Nero. The ruler, as the head of the body of state, infuses the body politic with both justice and mercy when he exercises *clementia* properly in his rule. But how then does the 'wise man' respond to every-day provocations—with forgiveness, or with another strategy entirely?

Seneca's answer to this question is addressed in his treatise *De Constantia*. He argues in *De Const.* 3.2 that the wise man can receive no injury (*iniuria*) or insult (*contumelia*). This is because, as we will see, the wise man is invulnerable to injury because of his superior moral strength as opposed to the routine endurance of normal human beings (*De Const.* 3.2-3). As Seneca elucidates, 'the power of wisdom is better shown by a display of calmness in the midst of provocation'. After making a distinction between *iniuria* and *contumelia* (*De Const.* 5.1), Seneca asserts that the wise man can never be robbed of his virtue (5.3-5),

> Injury has as its aim to visit evil upon a man. But wisdom leaves no room for evil, for the only evil it knows is baseness, which cannot enter where where virtue and uprightness already abide. Consequently, if there can be no injury without evil, no evil without baseness, and if, moreover, baseness cannot reach a man already possessed by uprightness, then injury does not reach the wise man [...]. Virtue is free, inviolable, unmoved, unshaken, so steeled against the blows of chance that she cannot be bent, much less broken.

---

62 On the differing stances of Stoicism to *clementia*—one favourable, the other unfavourable—see Braund, *De Clementia*, 66-68.

In this imperturbability to any injury, Seneca proposes, the wise man becomes 'like a god in all save his mortality' (*De Const.* 8.2).[63] Thus the wise man casts 'all injuries far from him, and by his endurance (*patientiaque*) and his greatness of soul (*magnitudine animi*) protect himself from them' (*De Const.* 9.4; cf. 15:3: *animi magnitudinem*).

In regard to the handling of insults, 'magnanimity (*magnanimitatem*), the noblest of all the virtues' enables the wise man to scorn 'the puffed-up attitude' of the proud and the arrogant (*De Const.* 11.1). Seneca presents Cato as the supreme exemplar (*De Const.* 14.3-4; cf. 1.3; 7.1) in handling the provocation because he does not engage in forgiving his provocateurs but instead displays sublime indifference to the world:

> 'But,' you ask, 'if a wise man receives a blow, what shall he do?' What Cato did when he was struck in the face: he did not flare up, he did not avenge the wrong (*vindicavit iniuriam*), he did not even forgive it (*ne remisit quidem*), but he said no wrong had been done. He showed finer spirit in not acknowledging it than if he had pardoned it (*maiore animo non agnovit quam ignovisset*) [...]. He does not regard what men consider base or wretched; he does not walk with the crowd, but as the planets make their way against the whirl of heaven, so he proceeds contrary to the opinion of the world.[64]

Only in one place in *De Constantia* (19:3) does Seneca assign to prayer a positive role. In the midst of the heated battle, it enables the warrior to move towards the truth and the imperturbability of being a wise man. But, once the wise man has emerged from the crucible of injury and insult, he is self-sufficient and has no need for prayer.[65]

4. Luke's Graeco-Roman Auditors and Jesus' Logion in Luke 23:34a

We have already determined that the prayer logion reported in Luke 23.34a was historically distinctive in terms of the contemporary Jewish understandings of forgiveness. But what would the Mediterranean basin auditors of Luke's Gospel in the early eighties have made of Jesus' prayer to his Father to forgive his persecutors?

In terms of the Graeco-Roman context, Jesus' prayer for the forgiveness of his enemies, as he was nailed to the cross, would have repulsed traditional Stoics. Forgiveness and mercy, in their view, belonged to the unstable emotions as opposed to the rational faculties. While Luke's presentation of Jesus on the cross is more 'Stoic' and martyrological than his Markan counterpart, discussed below, the outburst of Jesus' emotional prayer entirely destroyed the credibility of Luke's portrait. Moreover, Jesus' inability to absorb injury without resorting to the desperate expedient of

---

63 Seneca, *De Const.* 8.3: 'The man who, relying on his reason, marches through mortal vicissitudes with the spirit of a god, has no vulnerable spot where he can receive an injury'.
64 Note the comment of the Loeb translator (J.W. Basore, *Seneca: Moral Essays. Volume 1* [London: W. Heinemann, 1963], 90) regarding Seneca's imagery: 'It was supposed that the sphere of heaven revolved about the earth from east to west, and that while the sun, moon, and planets were swept along in this revolution, they also moved in their own courses in the opposite direction'. As Seneca concludes about the wise man (*De Const.* 15.2-3), 'his virtue has placed him in another region of the universe'. Seneca also cites Socrates and Antisthenes (*De Const.* 18.5) as further exemplars of endurance (*quorum laudamus patientiam*).
65 Dio Chrysostom (*Or.* 8.15-16.) states that in facing hardships the wise man does not pray for relief: 'nor does he pray to draw another antagonist, but challenges them one after another, grappling with hunger and cold, withstanding thirst, and disclosing no weakness even though he must endure the lash or give his body to be cut or burned'.

prayer would have disqualified him as a man of virtue: he did not exhibit the sublime indifference and self-sufficiency required in the time of testing. As far as the Senecan model of 'clemency', Jesus did not show sufficient discrimination in his bestowal of forgiveness, offering it to malefactors who did not respond with gratitude and who had not displayed the requisite evidence that they would change for the better. Aristotle's concern for equity was similarly bypassed: true justice had been demeaned in this wasted demonstration of 'unjust' forgiveness. Above all, at the most basic level of ancient civic ethics, Jesus had not helped his friends at all by *loving* his enemy. The security of the state was predicated on helping friends and *hating* the enemy. We are facing here the appearance of a radical new ethic and paradigm of behaviour that would transform social relations in antiquity.

We might ask, in light of the incomprehensibility of Jesus' prayer for his enemies on the cross for Graeco-Roman auditors, what Lukan auditors might have gleaned that was positive in terms of their own cultural expectations and recognition. First, the benefaction context is important here. The three-fold taunt of the malefactors at the cross to save himself (v. 35: σωσάτω ἑαυτόν; v. 37: σῶσον σεαυτόν; v. 39: σῶσον σεαυτόν) might have posed the question about the kind of benefactor he was. A series of questions emerge here. Was Christ the 'endangered' benefactor who risked his life or resources on behalf of the city, celebrated in the honorific inscriptions?[66] Was he like Pittacus, noted above, who did not take advantage of those who had reviled him? Was he like those ancient heroes who died for their city and friends, as was the case with the Spartans and Athenians who had perished for Greece against the Persians at Thermoplylae (480 BC) and at Plataea (479 BC)?[67] Was he like those first Maccabean martyrs who were killed on the Sabbath, refusing to fight against the Seleucids on God's holy day and thereby dishonour their Lord (1 Macc 2:29-38)? Luke's salvific language could conceivably point in any one of these directions, recalling the illustrious exempla of their beneficent deaths. But somehow such suggestions do not embrace the depths of Christ's unsolicited forgiveness and his compassion for the spiritual blindness of his opponents. As Bock correctly observes,

> Jesus is interceding for his enemies because they have made an erroneous judgement about him. This should not be their last chance. More chances to respond were graciously given as the disciples preached to them often in Acts about the opportunity to receive forgiveness. There is is no vindictiveness in Jesus, only hope for a reversal.[68]

Christ's unusual act of beneficence had gone far beyond all contemporary expectations. To be sure, the endangered benefactor places himself in situations of serious risk and so identifies himself with the needs of his dependents that his own resources are genuinely imperilled. But, unlike Christ, he does not die for his dependents: only living 'endangered' benefactors are honoured. Further, in contrast to Pitticus, Christ had blessed his tormentors while he was still under their power. In the case of those who had died for their city and country, Christ had forgiven and died for his entirely ignorant persecutors and enemies, irrespective or whether they were Romans, Jews, or just the uncomprehending crowds watching his tortured fate on the cross. Nor had he died for the sanctuary of Zion and God's holy Law, as did Maccabean martyrs. Rather he died, as

---

66 On the 'endangered benefactor', see F.W. Danker, *Benefactor: Epigraphic Study of a Graeco-Roman and New Testament Semantic Field* (St Louis: Clayton Publishing House, 1982), 417-27.

67 See M. Hengel, *The Atonement: The Origins of the Doctrine in the New Testament* (London: SCM, 1981), 6-15, for examples.

68 D.L. Bock, *Jesus According to Scripture: Restoring the Portrait from the Gospels* (Leicester/Grand Rapids: Apollos/Baker Academic, 2002), 386.

the Gospels of Mark and Luke make clear, in the place of the 'many', a role divinely assigned to him who, as the Isaianic suffering Servant,[69] would inaugurate the new covenant (Mark 14:24; Luke 20:22b) that would supplant the old Mosaic covenant by establishing a new Exodus through the soteriological deliverance of his death (Luke 9:31: ἔλεγον τὴν ἔξοδον αὐτοῦ, ἣν ἤμελλεν πληροῦν ἐν Ἱεροσαλήμ).[70] Finally, ironically, as a crucified criminal, Christ experienced the full curse of the Law (Deut 21:23; cf. Gal 3:13; Luke 22:37: μετὰ ἀνόμων ἐλογίσθη), thereby establishing a sharp contrast between his ignominious (but covenant-renewing) death and the Law-affirming deaths of the righteous Maccabean martyrs.[71] Again, the contemporary paradigms of sacrificial beneficence were undergoing radical revision.

Second, in Luke's portrait, Christ called upon his Father, amidst his own desolation, to forgive his enemies (Luke 23:34a: Πάτερ) and then, again in total dependence upon the Father, handed his spirit back to the God in sublime calmness before dying (23:46b: Πάτερ). This would have spoken powerfully to Luke's contemporaries about the love of God amidst the vilest of humanity's acts in history, as well as the imperturbability of divine love in the face of the injuries perpetrated by one's enemies. At the deepest level, the Stoic quest for insulation from life's shocks had been met in the most profound and paradoxical way through the death of Christ on the cross and by virtue of his unbreakable filial relationship with the Father.

We now turn to a comparison of the account of Christ's crucifixion in the Gospels of Mark and Luke, with a view to seeing why Luke has adopted such a different approach to the death of Jesus.

5. Luke's Intention in Inserting the 'Forgiveness' Logion into the Crucifixion Narrative: Comparing the Markan and Lukan Accounts of Jesus' Death

5.1. The Mockery and Irony of the Cross: Speaking Authentically to the Late 60's Roman Audience of Mark's Gospel

Our investigation of Mark's account of the crucifixion will focus upon four pericopes: the crucifixion itself (Mark 15:22-27), the mockeries (15:29-32), the death of Jesus (15:33-37), and its consequences (15:15:38-41). Mark's masterly use of intertextual echoes and direct LXX citations

---

69 On πολλῶν, see LXX Isa 53:10, 12b: αὐτὸς ἁμαρτίας πολλῶν ἀνήνεγκε; cf. λύτρον ἀντὶ πολλῶν: Mark 10:45b; τὸ αἷμά μου τὸ ἐκχυννόμενον ὑπὲρ πολλῶν: 14:24: τὸ αἷμά μου τῆς διαθήκης τὸ ἐκχυννόμενον ὑπὲρ πολλῶν; cf. Luke 22:20b [τὸ ὑπὲρ ὑμῶν], 37 [Isa 53:12]; 23:33. See D.J. Moo, *The Old Testament in the Gospel Passion Narratives* (Sheffield: Almond, 1983), 122-138. Contra, see C.K. Barrett, 'Mark 10:45: A Ransom for Many', in *New Testament Essays* (London: SPCK, 1972), 20-26, who argues for a Maccabean background for Mark 10:45. Additionally, supporting the 'Servant' allusions, see V. Taylor, *Jesus and His Sacrifice: A Study of the Passion Sayings* (London: MacMillan, 1951), passim; S. McKnight, *Jesus and His Death: Historiography, the Historical Jesus, and Atonement Theory* (Waco: Baylor University Press, 2004), 207-24; contra J. D. G. Dunn, *Christianity in the Making Volume 1: Jesus Remembered* (Eerdmans: Grand Rapids, 2003), 809-18. Isaiah 53:12c—where the suffering Servant is reckoned among the transgressors—also coheres with features of Luke's passion narrative: Christ was led away with criminals (Luke 23:32), crucified with them (23:33), and placed under the same sentence (23:40b), even though he was innocent (23:41; cf. Isa 53:9b).
70 LXX Exod 24:8: τὸ αἷμά μου τῆς διαθήκης; Mark 14:24: τὸ αἷμά μου τῆς διαθήκης; Luke 22:20 (1 Cor 11:25), ἡ καινὴ διαθήκη ἐν τῷ αἵματί μου.
71 On Jesus' understanding of himself at the Last Supper as the eschatological Passover lamb (Luke 22:20) who would establish a new covenant community by means of his impending death, see B. Pitre, *Jesus and the Last Supper* (Grand Rapids: Eerdmans, 2015), 374-443.

of the Psalms, as well as the literary use of doublets and triplets, opens up important theological perspectives regarding the death of Jesus.

First, prior to the crucifixion, Mark has already established intertextually that Jesus was the Isaianic suffering Servant. As noted, there are the two πολλῶν references denoting the dependents benefiting from his death (Isa 53:12; Mark 10:45b [ἀντὶ πολλῶν]; 14:24 [ὑπὲρ πολλῶν]). Also, there are the sets of two references to Jesus's silence, one set occurring before the High Priest Caiaphas (14:60a; 14:61) and the other before Pontius Pilate (15:4a; 15:5), each recalling the silence of the Isaianic lamb led to its slaughter (Isa 53:7a, 7b. 7c).

Second, the relentless drive of Mark's narrative towards the eventual death of Jesus on the cross in Mark 15 is given increased momentum by

- the three divisions of time (Mark 15:25 [third hour], 33 [sixth hour], 34 [ninth hour]);
- three mockeries (15:17-20 [soldiers], 15:31 [chief priests and teachers of the law], 15:32 [the two crucified criminals flanking Jesus]);
- three reactions to Jesus' death (Mark 15:39 [centurion], 40-41 [Galilean women], 42 [women from Jerusalem and environs]).[72]

But an increased theological emphasis accompanies this increase in narrative momentum. The heavy emphasis upon 'time' points to the imminent fulfilment of eschatological time announced at the beginning of the Gospel (Mark 1:15a). Furthermore, the time references point forward 'to the hour of the consummation of God's final judgement (Dan 11:40, 45 LXX)'.[73] The Messianic Kingdom was about to appear, with the count-down near to conclusion in its progress, and paradoxically, its advent to be achieved through the death of the promised Messiah. The mockeries add further hues and pathos to the rejection suffered by Jesus as the suffering Servant (Isa 53:3 [cf. 50:6]; Mark 10:45; 14:24), the righteous Sufferer of the Psalms (Ps 22:6-8; Mark 15:34 [Ps 22:1]), and the stricken Shepherd of Zechariah (Mark 14:27 [Zech 13:7]; cf. the allusion to the Ezekiel 'shepherd' traditions in Luke 10:3; 19:10; 15:4-6 [Ezek 34:16, 23-24; 37:24]).[74] Christological issues, therefore, are at the forefront of the Markan narrative of human mockery.

Last, the reactions to Jesus' death pose the real question in terms of the reversal of expectation: a Roman centurion (Mark 15:38-39) responds to the crucified Christ and the women, largely absent from Mark's Gospel, demonstrate that they are the only faithful disciples remaining till the end with Christ as opposed to the conspicuously absent Twelve (15:40-41). Will the faithless male disciples ever make the grade? The sons of Zebedee, who had requested places at Jesus' right and left in glory (Mark 10:37), are nowhere to be seen, now that two robbers have been crucified at Jesus' right and left (15:27). The two disciples had failed to understand that the entry into glory for every believer was cruciform (Mark 8:34; Luke 9:23). But even the courageous women, if Mark 16:8 represents the unconventional ending to the Gospel,[75] cower in fear at the news of the resurrection

---

72 H. Wansbrough, *The Passion and Death of Jesus* (London: Dartman, Longman, and Todd, 2003), 102.
73 B. Witherington III, *The Gospel of Mark: A Socio-Rhetorical Commentary* (Grand Rapids: Eerdmans, 2001), 379.
74 See the masterly discussion of J. Marcus, *The Way of the Lord: Christological Exegesis of the Old Testament in the Gospel of Mark* (Louisville: Westminster/John Knox, 1992), 172-198. For the entire list of the Psalms of the Righteous Sufferer in Mark's passion narrative fron Ch. 14-15, see ibid., 174-75. Additionally, see C.A. Evans, 'Jesus and Zechariah's Messianic Hope', in B. Chilton and C.A. Evans (ed.), *Authenticating the Activities of Jesus* (Boston and Leiden: Brill, 2002), 373-88; W.H. Bellinger and W. R. Farmer (eds.), *Jesus and the Suffering Servant: Isaiah 53 and Christian Origins* (Harrisburg: Trinity Press International, 1998).
75 See the insightful discussion of D.J. Juel, *A Master of Surprise: Mark Interpreted* (Minneapolis: Fortress, 1994), 107-21, explaining the theological force of a verse 8 ending, traditionally conceived.

and remain silent, paralysed in disobedience to the angel's command (Mark 16:7). Humanly speaking, one could not imagine a worse start for early Christianity.

Third, deeply embedded in the Mark's narrative of the crucifixion are three sets of doublets: two drinks offered Jesus (Mark 15:23, 36), two mentions of the crucifixion (15:24, 25), and two loud cries of Jesus (15:34, 37). Mark's intertextual echoes and quotations of LXX Psalms tell us that the invisible hand of God is powerfully at work despite appearances to the contrary, bringing his long-prophesied soteriological plan to completion. The wine offered Jesus is mixed with myrrh, fulfilling Psalm 69:21b; the division of Jesus' clothes by casting lots fulfils Psalm 22:18. But most crucial of all is Jesus' intonation of Psalm 22:1 (Mark 15:34), significantly rendered in Greek and in Aramaic. Cullman rightly comments regarding the confronting logion that 'we dare not gloss it over',[76] especially when it is followed hard on the heels by another inarticulate cry (Mark 15:37). We are staring at death 'in all its frightful horror'.[77] Lane lends further insight by observing that 'Jesus' cry of dereliction is the inevitable sequel to the horror which he experienced in the Garden of Gethsemane' (Mark 14:33-34, 36).[78]

How, then, is Mark 15:34 to be understood? First, from God's side, it represents the wrathful sundering of the uninterrupted filial relationship between the Father and Son, notwithstanding the perfect submission of the Son up to and including the cross ($A\beta\beta\alpha\ O\ \Pi\alpha\tau\acute{\eta}\rho$: Mark 14:36;[79] $O\ \theta\varepsilon\acute{o}\varsigma\ \mu o\upsilon\ O\ \theta\varepsilon\acute{o}\varsigma\ \mu o\upsilon$: 15:34b; cf. $\Pi\acute{\alpha}\tau\varepsilon\rho$: Luke 23:34a, 46b). The Son, vicariously and representatively, had embraced his Isaianic Servant role of sin-bearing for the many (Isa 53:12b [cf. vv. 4-6, 8, 10b, 11b]; Mark 10:45; 14:24, 27; cf. 2 Cor 5:21; Gal 3:13), drinking the cup of God's wrath until it was empty (14:36a). But what of the inarticulate cry in Mark 15:37? Does this represent the triumphant cry of Christ handing back his shattered life to the Father for post-mortem vindication (cf. Luke 23:46)? Or is this the inconsolable cry of the bereft Christ who now faces cosmic emptiness, robbed of the Father's eternal loving presence because of his Messianic sin-bearing on behalf of many? Mark's ambiguity is impenetrable. The 'loudness' of each of Jesus' cries (Mark 15:34, 37) calls us to ponder which interpretation is the most apposite, but with no easy resolution provided. Mark's tension is agonisingly deliberate. Nevertheless, there are glimmers of the decisive eschatological victory to come. The whole context of Psalm 22 is intoned by Jesus, finding fulfilment in his experience of the cross (Mark 15:24 [Ps 22:18], 25 [Ps 22:16b], 29 [Ps 22:7-8], 34 [Ps 22:1]), but, more importantly, it speaks of the Lord's dominion over the nations that will be established by the divine reversal of the Psalmist's suffering (Ps 22:27-31).[80] So it will be for the crucified Christ three days after the Golgotha experience (Mark 8:31-32; 9:30-32; 10:32-34).

However, unbeknown to modern readers, further mockery ripples beneath the surface of Mark's narrative for its original audience. The gallows humour attached to crucifixion by the ancients is highly revealing in this regard.[81] A witty epigram of Lucillius, an unknown writer from the reign of Nero, lampoons the crucified by attributing to them exactly the same invidious drive

---

76 O. Cullmann, 'Immortality of the Soul or Resurrection from the Dead: The Witness of the New Testament', in K. Stendahl (ed.), *Immortality and Resurrection. Death in the Western World: Two Conflicting Currents of Thought* (New York: MacMillan, 1965), 17.
77 Cullmann, 'Immortality of the Soul', 17.
78 W.L. Lane, *Commentary on the Gospel of Mark* (Grand Rapids: Eerdmans, 1974), 572; Witherington, *The Gospel of Mark*, 398-99; R.H. Stein, *Mark* (Grand Rapids: Baker Academic, 2008), 715-16.
79 See Stein, *Mark*, 662-63.
80 See the close parallelism detected by Marcus, *Way of the Lord*, 182, between Psalm 22 and Mark 15:20b—16:7.
81 On the gallows-humour attached to crucifixion in antiquity, see Welborn, *Paul, the Fool of Christ*, 124-47.

for celebrity and social ascendancy at the moment of their death as the élites of antiquity.[82] The epigram, which acerbically highlights by implication the social envy characteristic of the élites, states that

> Envious Diophon, seeing another man near him crucified on a higher cross than himself, fell into a decline.[83]

While the envy of the crucified man may just be limited to his rival's 'more impressive cross', as Cook has argued,[84] it is more likely that the *higher position* of the cross, symbolic of social superiority in a world of grandiose élite monuments, also consumes the victim.

A joke from the *Philogelos* ('The Laughter-Lover'), an ancient joke book dateable to after AD 391, presents the continued competition of an athlete on the cross with this wry observation about his superior 'athletic' status:

> On seeing a runner who had been crucified, an Abderite remarked, 'By the Gods, now he does fly—literally!'[85]

Further, Gaius Maecenas—the famous Roman literary patron, writer and friend of Augustus—prays to live longer no matter what suffering still remained ahead of him. It is worth observing that the ancients did not baulk at linking the experience of the crucified on the cross to people suffering with physical disabilities. Both groups belonged, in the view of the ancient élites, to the contemptible 'no accounts' of society:

> Fashion me with a palsied hand,
> Weak of foot, and a cripple;
> Build upon me a crook-backed hump;
> Shake my teeth till they rattle;
> All is well, if my life remains.
> Save, oh, save it, I pray you,
> Though I sit on the piercing cross.[86]

In other words, the cross was seen by Mark's Graeco-Roman contemporaries as so antithetical to the ancient celebrity circuit of the political élites that they could devise jokes about the crucified competing for social status and ascendancy while pinioned to the cross and still get a humorous rise of recognition from their audience. The Gospels, too, reflect aspects of this grim cruciform humour when the two crucified rebels alongside Christ derisively heap insults upon him (Mark 15:27-32), rejecting this failed would-be Messiah and Prophet who could not save himself or fulfil any of his pathetic prophecies. Furthermore, the scene of the cross is prefaced by the mock-homage paid by the Roman soldiers to Christ as King of the Jews, spoofing a royal coronal investiture by offering him the purple robe and crown of thorns (Mark 15:16-19).

---

82 On the grandiose funeral monuments of the Roman élites and imperial rulers from the republic to the late Empire, see P.J.E. Davies, *Death and the Emperor: Roman Imperial Funerary Monuments from Augustus to Marcus Aurelius* (Austin: University of Texas Press, 2004), 1-48.
83 Lucillius, *Anthologia Graeca* 11.192.
84 J.G. Cook, *Crucifixion in the Mediterranean World* (Tübingen: Mohr Siebeck, 2014), 10.
85 B. Baldwin, *The Philogelos or Laughter-Lover* (Amsterdam: J.C. Gieben, 1982), §121.
86 Seneca, *Ep.* 101.11. For full discussion, see J.R. Harrison, 'Paul and the Social Relations of Death at Rome (Rom 5:14, 17, 21)', in S.E. Porter (ed.), *Paul and His Social Relations. Pauline Studies: Volume VII*, (Leiden: Brill, 2012), 85-123, at 122-23.

The cross of Jesus, therefore, is inherently social in its ideological outworking, precisely because it was inextricably enmeshed with the political power of the élites over the condemned in a first-century context, as much as it was soteriological in the eternal plan of the omnipotent God of the universe. Mark spoke adeptly into both contexts, social and theological, displaying the paradoxical triumph of Christ in abject weakness and foolishness for all to see. Despite the relentless mockery, gallows humour, and shame associated with the cross, the élites—Herod, the Temple priests, and Pilate—would not determine the final result of Christ's ministry, as the élites and their followers thought that they so decisively had: 'Let the Christ, the King of Israel, descend now from the cross, that we might see and believe' (Mark 15:22; cf. 14:63-65; 15:15). Rather, precisely by remaining on the cross as an abject figure of ridicule, Christ undid the power of his opponents and secured salvific freedom for his dependents.

The savagery of the mockery endured by Christ in his weakness would have had powerful resonance with the Roman audience of Mark's Gospel in the capital of the Empire,[87] especially if the work was written c. AD 69, as Hengel argues.[88] After the savagery of the Nero's persecution of believers in AD 64 and the terror aroused by the rumours abroad about the dead Nero returning *redivivus* at the head of the Parthian armies,[89] Mark's portrait of a shamed and reviled Christ, who was vindicated over the Herodian and Roman élites by his Father for the sake of his cowardly and faithless disciples, would have generated in them deep comfort and raised the expectation of Christ's resurrection renewal in their lives (Mark 16:7).

Why, then, does Luke diverge from this paradigm in his presentation of the crucifixion in Chapter 23, adding his own special 'L' tradition (Luke 23:34a), whereas Matthew, by contrast, remains much more conservative in handling the Markan tradition that he has inherited?[90]

5.2. Forgiving the Ignorant (Luke 23:34a), Moving Beyond the Imperturbability of the Graeco-Roman Sage to the Transformation of the Believer in Christ

At one level, it was the very success of Mark's portrait of Christ's crucifixion that demanded a more nuanced approach from Luke as he sought to commend the spread of the Gospel from Jerusalem to Rome to interested Graeco-Roman auditors in Luke-Acts. The cruciform horror of Christ's death in Mark's narrative may have posed a problem for some of his Graeco-Roman auditors in that the foolishness of the cross was such an object of ridicule that any consideration of its redemptive claims almost became an impossibility. Cullmann spotted the problem in his famous study on how Socrates and Christ faced death.[91] Socrates towered over his distraught disciples by virtue of his imperturbability just before his suicide, welcoming death as a liberating friend, whereas Christ trembled at the approach of his death, considered by him to be the disruptive enemy of God's creation, seeking on three occasions the comfort of his sleep-sodden disciples and praying that, if possible, he might be spared the impending tribulation.

---

87 For a Roman destination for Mark, with the capital of the Empire firmly in view, see Lane, *Mark*, 16–21.
88 See M. Hengel, *Studies in the Gospel of Mark* (SCM: London, 1985), 1–30.
89 Rev 13.3; 17:8-11; *Sib. Or.*, 4.119-124; 5.137-141; 5.361-396; Dio Chrysostom, *Or.* 21; Tacitus, *Hist.* 1.2; 2:8-9; Dio Cassius 46.19.3; Suetonius, *Nero* 40; *Dom.* 57.
90 On Matthew and the passion of Jesus, see Weber, *The Cross*, 110-17.
91 Cullmann, 'Immortality of the Soul'.

However, in the famous suicide scene of Nero's tutor at Rome (AD 65), contemporary with Mark's Gospel, the Stoic philosopher Seneca, clear limits to the Socratic paradigm of imperturbability emerge, notwithstanding its venerable tradition. However, Seneca's wife resisted his pleas, suiciding with him (Tacitus, *Ann.* 15.63). But, whereas Socrates dismissed the women and children just before his suicide and upbraided his disciples for their sorrow, Seneca treats his wife Paulina with tenderness:

> Seneca embraced his wife, and with a tenderness very different from his philosophical imperturbability, entreated her to moderate and set a term to her grief, and take just consolation, in her bereavement, from contemplating his well-spent life.[92]

Likewise, Luke presents Christ accepting his ignominious death with equinamity. He upbraids the distraught women following his processional route towards the cross, forbidding them to weep for himself, but, in his selfless concern for the weak in any time of crisis, counselling them to weep instead for themselves and their children as the impending judgement of Jerusalem drew ever closer (Luke 23:28-31). Symbolically the way to avoid judgement is acted out before them in the figure of Simon of Cyrene: he picks up Christ' cross and follows the Messiah to his death (Luke 23:26; cf. 9:23; 14:27).[93] The death of the Lukan Christ is martyr-like in its dignified nobility, characterised by a calm and prayerful engagement with his Father to the very end, and by a confident submission to the Father in handing back his πνεῦμα to him (Luke 23:46). The Markan cry of dereliction (Mark 15:34), also reproduced in Matthew 27:46, is tellingly omitted from Luke's account. The logion is replaced both by Christ's prayer of forgiveness for his unknowing tormentors (Luke 23:34a) and also by his final prayer of faith (Luke 23:46 [Ps 31:5a). The final quotation from another Psalm of lament, as Weber correctly concludes,[94] is inserted as a replacement for Mark 15:34 because the cry of Ps. 22:1 might be misinterpreted as 'a cry of despair'. But, ironically, in so doing, Luke included a new dominical tradition (Luke 23:34a) that was, as we have argued, equally confronting to Jewish and Graeco-Roman auditors.

Notwithstanding these Lukan rhetorical flourishes, it would be unwise to assume 'that Luke described the passion purely as the martyrdom of a righteous one, and thus replaced the theology of the cross by a theology of exaltation'.[95] The strategic placement of the Simon of Cyrene pericope symbolically endorses a cruciform discipleship, cohering with Christ's teaching elsewhere. Furthermore, Satan's 'opportune time' for the future testing of Christ (Luke 4:13) ultimately arrived with the defection of Judas (22:21-23, 47-48), the betrayal of Peter (22:31-34, 54-65), and the 'time of trial' at Gethsemane and Golgotha (22:46).[96]

Why, then, did Luke include this startling logion? Scholars have suggested several viable reasons. First, Strahan has argued that the logion of Luke 23:34a is coherent textually because it shows:

(a) the consistency between Christ's exemplum on the cross and his dominical teaching on forgiving and benefiting one's enemy (Luke 6:27-28);
(b) the connection between the ignorance of the Jewish and Romans persecutors, which is understood to involve their misperceptions regarding Jesus' messianic identity (cf. Luke 9:45; 18:34; 24:1-49; Acts 3:17; 13:27), and God's offer of Christ's grace and forgiveness to

---

92 Tacitus, *Ann.* 15.63.
93 Weber, *The Cross*, 123-24.
94 Weber, *The Cross*, 119.
95 Weber, *The Cross*, 121. See ibid., 121-24, for a rebuttal of this position.
96 Weber, *The Cross*, 121-22.

them through the apostolic preaching of the Resurrected One (e.g. Acts 6:7; 9:1-9; 10:1-8 [cf. Luke 23:47]; 13:12).[97]

Second, the pericope regarding the repentance of the thief on the cross (Luke 23:39-43; cf. 5:32; 18:13; 19:8) strategically follows the forgiveness logion (23:34a), demonstrating how the passion of Christ effected not only the radical experience of the divine forgiveness for the marginalised (e.g. Luke 4:18-19 [Isa 61:1-2a]; 5:12-26; 5:27-39; 7:36-50; 15:2; 19:1-10) but also provided entry into the Messianic kingdom in the present age (23:42-43).[98]

Thus the strategic placement of the forgiveness logion affords uninterrupted views of important soteriological vistas in Luke-Acts. It seems highly unlikely, therefore, that Luke 23:34a was a 'floating' logion in the Jesus tradition without any context and opportunistically seized by Luke for his own theological agenda. How Luke derived this historical tradition is unknown, though the authenticity of the logion is certainly secure within its Jewish and Graeco-Roman context, as demonstrated above. Was it one of the watching women at the foot of the cross who heard Jesus' quietly breathed prayer of forgiveness for the ignorant—reserved exclusively for the hearing of the Father but providentially overheard by her—and who understood much better than the male disciples its revolutionary content? Women are more prominent in the Gospel of Luke (1:26-28 [cf. 46-55], 39-45, 57-60; 2:36-38; 7:11-15, 36-50; 8:2-3, 40-56; 10:38-42; 11:27-28; 21:1-4; 23:27-31, 49; 24:1-12; cf. 15:8-10; 18:1-8) as opposed to the Gospel of Mark (5:24b-34; 7:24-30; 12:41-44; 14:3-9; 15:40, 47; 16:1).[99] Luke, therefore, was sensitive not only to their portrait but also presumably to the historical traditions regarding the historical Jesus that they alone possessed.

But more than contextual issues within the Gospel dictate Luke's inclusion of the logion. The ethical paradigm of the imperturbability of the Graeco-Roman sage in the face of hardships represented a challenge to the potential growth in godliness among the members of the early house churches in the Mediterranean basin.[100] Its seductive influence, if succumbed to, could stifle the ability of believers to act with compassion towards hostile outsiders and, indeed, sympathetically towards each other. Only the forgiveness of the cross, appropriated by believers and extended to others, could release people from the straightjackets of imperturbability. Self-control and self-protection, each quality summoned in response to the provocation of others and to personal tragedy, were important ethical values in Graeco-Roman social relations and were regularly articulated in popular philosophy. In seeking release from the imperturbable Self by means of Christ's transforming forgiveness, believers were freed to seek the very best for their enemies through prayer and beneficence, with a view to ushering them into the Kingdom of God by an encounter with the grace of the crucified Christ.

---

97 Strahan, *The Limits of a Text*, 61-87.
98 See the insightful discussion of R.C. Tannehill, *The Narrative Unity of Luke-Acts: A Literary Interpretation. Volume 1: The Gospel According to Luke* (Philadelphia: Fortress, 1986), 125-27.
99 See E.V. Dowling, *Women, Theology and the Parable of the Pounds in the Gospel of Luke* (London and New York: T&T Clark, 2007); S. Miller, *Women in Mark's Gospel* (London and New York: T&T Clark, 2004).
100 Thus Seneca writes: 'Know, therefore, Serenus, that this perfect man, full of virtues human and divine, can lose nothing... The walls which guard the wise man are safe from both flame and assault, they provide no means of entrance, are lofty, impregnable, godlike' (*Ep.* 1.6.8). On the intersection of early Christianity with the imagery of the wise man's high citadel of reason (cf. 2 Cor 10:3-6), see A.J. Malherbe, 'Antisthenes and Odysseus, and Paul at War', in *Paul and the Popular Philosophers* (Minneapolis: Fortress, 1989), 91-119, at 101-03.

6. Conclusion

This article has argued that Luke 23:34a is an authentic logion of the historical Jesus, inserted by Luke in its original context, as opposed to it being a case of the inclusion of a free-floating Jesus logion in a theologically convenient pericope. My speculation is that the history of the tradition originated with one of the nearby women disciples at the foot of the cross, who overhead Jesus' quietly intoned prayer for his tormentors.[101] Given Luke's close attention not only to traditions about women in his Gospel but also to their own eyewitness testimony about Jesus, it is not surprising that this logion belonged to Luke's own special tradition ('L') about the historical Jesus. The disputed status of the saying in the Lukan manuscript tradition remains an unresolved problem. Scholarly arguments regarding the reasons for the omission of the logion in some manuscripts reach diametrically opposite conclusions and, therefore, there is considerable subjectivity as to which hypothesis might be correct, if any. However, after an extensive investigation of ἀφίημι and συγγνώμη and their cognates in the Jewish and Graeco-Roman literature, as well as the wider forgiveness traditions of antiquity (including the role of *clementia*, the handling of insult, the strategy of imperturbability, etc.), the distinctive nature of Jesus' prayer in its ancient context ensured its historical authenticity.

The difficulties of the manuscript tradition have precluded New Testament scholars from considering in sufficient depth the theological implications of the logion's meaning in its exegetical context and in the Gospel of Luke more generally, though the suggestions of Strahan and Tannehill have shown the profit to be gained by such an analysis. This article has widened the parameters of the investigation by comparing the Markan and Lukan accounts of Jesus' passion. It has been argued that Mark's depiction of the shame, mockery, and divine forsakenness of the cross was so effective in its graphic portrayal that it potentially posed for auditors the question whether Jesus died with a cry of despair on his lips (Mk 15:34; Ps 22:1), as opposed to the Psalmist's uncompromising trust in God, no matter the gravity of the circumstances.

By contrast, Luke's powerful portrait of Jesus' martyr-like death—obedient to the Father until the very end and selflessly invoking divine grace towards the sinfully ignorant—would have captured the attention of Graeco-Roman auditors. It may have reminded them of the death of Socrates (Plato, *Apology* 30d; 41d),[102] or of the various martyrs who died for their cities. But the Graeco-Roman model of the imperturbable sage has distinct limitations as a paradigm for transforming social relations. The sage insulates himself from the vicissitudes of life through his self-control and indifference to personal insult and provocation, effectively isolating himself from social interaction as opposed to embracing his opponents relationally. Jesus, however, draws upon God's love for and mercy to his enemies (Luke 6:32-36; cf. Rom 5:6-8) and, by virtue of his

---

101 On the women at the cross and the tomb in Mark and Matthew being the sources of their own eyewitness stories, due to their being the only disciples present, see R. Bauckham, *Jesus and the Eyewitnesses: The Gospels as Eyewitness Testimony* (Grand Rapids: Eerdmans, 2006), 39–66.

102 Socrates (Plato, *Apology*, 39d) states: 'I am certainly not angry with those who convicted me, or with my accusers'. W. Klassen, *Love of Enemies: The Way to Peace* (Philadelphia: Fortress, 1984), 21-23, argues that Socrates was the first Greek thinker who did not accept 'the notion that it is best to harm your enemies and do good to your friends'. (p.21) But, as Klassen (p.23) notes, Socrates did not weep over Athens in the same way that Christ did over Jerusalem (Luke 19:41-44). Nowhere in the Greek tradition, adeptly set out by Klassen (pp. 12-26), is love towards, prayer for, beneficence to, and divine forgiveness of the enemy combined in such a comprehensive set of social relations as it is in Jesus' teaching (Luke 6:27, 28, 35; 7:36-50; 9:51-55; 10:25-37; 15:11-32; 14:7-14; 18:9-14; 19:1-10; 23:34a).

special status as the messianic and eternal Son, engages his Father to forgive them.[103] There is no impassivity on the part of either God or Jesus in this process of reconciliation. The Old Testament portrait of a suffering God and the depiction of Jesus' emotions in the Gospels speaks against divine impassibility.[104] Ultimately, Luke's 'Stoic' presentation of the cross, in comparison to the Gospel of Mark, undermined several central tenets of Stoic belief, opening up new possibilities for the transformation of the 'politics' of hatred through the experience of divine forgiveness.

James R. Harrison
Sydney College of Divinity

---

103 Klassen, *Love of Enemies*, 91, writes: 'Jesus does not forgive his enemies. To offer forgiveness to those who are not interested in it, is always to cheapen forgiveness. The triumph of his spirit of love is to request of God that in some way he may grant forgiveness'.
104 T.E. Fretheim, *The Suffering of God: An Old Testament Perspective* (Philadelphia: Fortress, 1984); S. Voorwinde, *Jesus' Emotions in the Gospels* (London and New York: T&T Clark, 2011).

Interpreting the Holy One of God in John 6:69
A Tradition-critical Analysis

DEBRA SNODDY

1. Introduction

There are three occurrences of the title ὁ ἅγιος τοῦ θεοῦ in the Christian Scriptures (John 6:69; Mark 1:24, par. Luke 4:34). The majority opinion favours the view that Luke's usage is dependent on Mark wherein the Gerasene demoniac identified Jesus as God's Holy One in the synagogue at Capernaum. Jesus duly silences the demon and expels him from the man, causing astonishment among the crowd.[1] But what of ὁ ἅγιος τοῦ θεοῦ in John 6:69? The context is very different: firstly, the title is spoken by Peter, in the context of the Bread of Life discourse; there is no expelling of demons; and no astonisheed crowds, but rather the opposite. Having spoken a 'hard word' many of Jesus'disciples leave and only the Twelve remain. Peter's confession is made in reponse to Jesus' question, 'Do you also wish to go away?' Then 'Simon Peter answered him, 'Lord, to whom can we go? You have the words of eternal life. We have come to believe and know that you are the Holy One of God'.[2] This study explores the possible influences on the fourth evangelist for the particular usage of the title ὁ ἅγιος τοῦ θεοῦ in this text.[3]

This study presupposes two fundamentals. Firstly, that the Gospel was written as a community document of faith rather than some kind of Christian resource on the life and work of Jesus of Nazareth, or as a missionary document to convert people to the way of the Nazarene.[4] Secondly, we deal with the text in its final form and, with G. Van Belle, we argue that the evidence from the Gospel itself ably demonstrates that one and the same author penned the text.[5]

With so little written exclusively on the Johannine Holy One of God (6:69),[6] primary research is required to establish its origins and possible influence. Our previous analysis of the scholarship on ὁ ἅγιος τοῦ θεοῦ in John 6:69 demonstrated that there is no consensus on the meaning of the title

---

1 See Mark 1:21-28 par. Luke 4:31-37.
2 See John 6:60-71.
3 The question of the meaning of this ambiguous title was the subject for my PhD STD disseration at the Katholieke Universiteit Leuven which was successfully defended in November 2014. Publication forthcoming in 2018.
4 See section 1.1 of my unpublished PhD STD dissertation and also J. L. Martyn, *History and Theology in the Fourth Gospel* (NTL; Louisville, Ken.: Westminster John Knox Press, 2003, 3rd ed.), 150, among others.
5 See section 1.1 below and G. Van Belle, *The Signs Source in the Fourth Gospel: Historical Survey and Critical Evaluation of the Semeia Hypothesis* (BETL 116; Leuven: Leuven University Press, Peeters, 1994).
6 Apart from two solitary articles by W. Domeris and H. L. Joubert (see below).

in its Johannine context, with commentators suggesting it is messianic,[7] prophetic,[8] or connected with the Wisdom literature,[9] with a minority opinion seeing the adjective ἅγιος as important.[10]

The focus for this particular study is to seek all possible and probable avenues for determining a clear, informed and balanced opinion on the form and content of the enigmatic title ὁ ἅγιος τοῦ θεοῦ. Therefore, in order to understanding something about ὁ ἅγιος τοῦ θεοῦ this study begins with an examination of how John makes use of other similar Christological titles, ὁ υἱὸς τοῦ θεοῦ,[11] ὁ υἱὸς τοῦ ἀνθρώπου,[12] and the absolute, ὁ υἱός,[13] to determine their possible correlation, or otherwise, with ὁ ἅγιος τοῦ θεοῦ. From thence, we will explore possible corollaries with titles from the Jewish Scriptures and the documents of Nag Hammadi and Qumran to determine other possible avenues of investigation for our study of ὁ ἅγιος τοῦ θεοῦ, based on the probability that John may have had exposure to these ideas and constructs, though not the documents themselves. Our reasoning for doing these researches is that the titles *within* the fourth Gospel may not be the only titles that may afford some insight into the mindset of the fourth evangelist. The three similar titles are used to reference the priest, Aaron, the prophet, Elisha and the Nazirite, Samson. Furthermore, the Aaronite title of Ps. 106:16[14] would, on the face of it, seem closest to ours and as such may hold some promise for our study.

We have previously asserted that ὁ ἅγιος τοῦ θεοῦ provides the crescendo for John 6 when Peter, serving as spokesperson for the Twelve, makes the astounding profession of faith. Clearly then Peter's confession does not stand as an isolated event but is drenched in the theological discussion of the chapter; a discussion that had taken up messianic, eschatological, Christological, and soteriological themes that relate to Jesus as God's emissary, bringing eternal life to the world. So the questions we need to give attention to are: from whence does John receive his tradition? Is this tradition strictly Jewish in background? And which strands of Jewish thought have informed

---

7   For the messianic interpretation see B. Lindars, *The Gospel of John* (London: Oliphants, 1972), 275f. and J.N. Sanders and B. A. Mastin (eds.), *A Commentary on the Gospel according to St John* (London: Black, 1968), 199f., for John 6:69; D.E. Nineham, *The Gospel of St. Mark* (Middlesex: Pelican, 1963), 79, for Mark; E.E. Ellis, *The Gospel of Luke* (London: Oliphants), 99-100, for Luke. Elsewhere in the Christian Scriptures Jesus is called 'the Holy One'—Acts 3:14 (*cf.* 4:27, 30; Luke 1:35; 1 John 2:20; Rev. 3:7. He is also referred to by the title ὁ ὅσιός i.e. the Pious One, but this title should be treated as a separate title and not used to interpret ὁ ἅγιος, pace Nineham, *Mark*, 79, and A.W.F. Blunt, *The Gospel According to St Mark* (Oxford: Clarendon Press, 1929), 148.

8   E. Schweizer, 'Er wird Nazoräer heissen (zu Mc 1:24; Mt 2:23)', in W. Eltester (ed.), *Judentum, Urchristentum, Kirche* (BZNW 26; FS J. Jeremias; Berlin: De Gruyter, 1960), 90-93; E. Schweizer, *Das Evangelium nach Markus* (Göttingen: Vandenhoeck & Ruprecht, 1967); F. Hahn, *Christologische Hoheitstitel: Ihre Geschichte im Frühen Christentum* (FRLANT 83; Göttingen: Vandenhoeck & Ruprecht, 1963, 1964), *The Titles of Jesus in Christology, Their History in Early Christianity* (H. Knight & G. Ogg, transls.; London: James Clarke & Co., 2002), 233. J.A. Bühner, *Der Gesandte und sein Weg im 4. Evangelium, Die kultur- und religionsgeschichtliche Grundlagen der johanneischen Sendungschristologie sowie ihre traditionsgeschchtliche Entwicklung* (WUNT 2,2; Tübingen, Mohr, 1977), 231.

9   W.R. Domeris, 'The Confession of Peter according to John 6:69', *Tyndale Bulletin* 44.1 (1993), 155-167; *Cf.* C.L. Blomberg, *The Historical Reliability of John's Gospel: Issues and Commentary* (Leicester, England: InterVarsity Press, 2001), 130; M. Mullins, *The Gospel of John: A Commentary* (Dublin, Ireland: Columba Press, 2003), 202, who quotes B. Witherington III, who in turn quotes Domeris; B. Witherington III, *John's Wisdom: A Commentary on the Fourth Gospel* (Cambridge, England: Lutterworth Press, 1995), 161.

10 R.H. Lightfoot, *St. John's Gospel: A Commentary* (C.F. Evans, ed.; Oxford: Clarendon, 1956), 170; A. von Schlatter, *Der Evangelist Johannes; wie er spricht, denkt und glaubt: Ein Kommentar zum vierten Evangelium* (Stuttgart: Calwer, 1960), *ad. loc*; B. Schwank, *Das Johannesevangelium* (Düsseldorf: Patmos-Verlag, 1966), 2.92; J. Gnilka, 'Die Erwartung des Messianischan Hohenpriesters in den Schriften von Qumran und im NT', *RevQ* 2 (1960), 423.

11 *Cf.* John 1:18*, 34, 49; 3:16, 18 (τὸ ὄνομα τοῦ μονογενοῦς υἱοῦ τοῦ θεοῦ); 5:25; 6:69*; 9:35*; 10:36; 11:4, 27; 19:7; 20:31 i.e. 13 times in all including variant readings (*).

12 *Cf.* John 1:51; 3:13, 14; 5:27; 6:27, 53, 62; 8:28; 9:35; 12:23, 34c, 34d; 13:31 i.e. 13 times in all.

13 *Cf.* John 1:18; 3:16, 17, 35, 36a, 36b; 5:19a, 19b, 20, 21, 22, 23a, 23b, 26; 6:40; 8:35, 36; 14:13; 17:1a, 1b i.e. 20 times in all.

14 Ps. 106:16.

it? And what of eschatological elements, if such are present? What are their roots? How do they influence the title of John 6:69? Add to this, the complexity of Johannine Christology and the question of its influence? And is there a soteriological presence in the title? From where and how are we to evaluate its development of this title in John?

2. The Johannine Use of Titles

The key titles[15] used by the fourth evangelist for Jesus in his Gospel are ὁ υἱὸς τοῦ θεοῦ, ὁ υἱὸς τοῦ ἀνθρώπου and Jesus' self-designation the absolute ὁ υἱός which occurs more frequently than any other title in the Gospel. It is not the task of this research to reiterate the scholarship pertaining to the titles ὁ υἱὸς τοῦ ἀνθρώπου and ὁ υἱὸς τοῦ θεοῦ, but only to make use of this scholarship as it relates directly to ὁ ἅγιος τοῦ θεοῦ.[16] R. Schnackenburg writes that Jesus' use of the absolute ὁ υἱός together with his use of 'Father' is the key to the understanding the evangelist's portrayal of Jesus, and of Jesus' words and actions as interpreted by him.[17] Schnackenburg goes on to distinguish the absolute use of ὁ υἱός from the title ὁ υἱὸς τοῦ θεοῦ.

> The Johannine Jesus does indeed speak of himself as the 'Son of God' (3:18; 5:25; 10:36; 11:4), and with the same meaning as when he says 'the Son', but it can be seen from the Gospel itself that the title 'Son of God' has a different root and a different *Sitz im Leben* (confessional formula: 1:34; 1:49; 11:27; 20:31) from the absolute use of 'the Son' which is reserved for Jesus alone.[18]

Schnackenburg mentions not only the Christian inheritance concerning the sending of Jesus, his knowledge of God (Matthew 11:27; Luke 10:22) and his use of 'Father' (Mark 14:36)[19] but contends that there are two other areas of influence that may have had a bearing on the fourth evangelist's 'Son-Christology'. Firstly, an influence from Judaism, and more specifically the Jewish doctrine of

---

15 For an exhaustive list of the titles for Jesus in the fourth Gospel see the appendices of the article by G. Van Belle, 'Christology and Soteriology in the Fourth Gospel', 435-462, especially 457ff.
16 For a brief overview of the recent scholarship on ὁ υἱὸς τοῦ θεοῦ, B.E. Daley, 'Christ and Christologies', S.A. Harvey & D.G. Hunter (eds.), *The Oxford Handbook of Early Christian Studies* (New York: Oxford University Press, 2008), 886-905; Extended works by D. Marmion and R. Van Nieuwenhove, *An Introduction to the Trinity* (Introductions to Religion; Cambridge: Cambridge University Press, 2010) and S. Davis, D. Kendall, & G.O'Collins (eds.), *The Incarnation: An Interdisciplinary Symposium on the Incarnation of the Son of God* (New York: Oxford University Press, 2002). For the recent scholarship of ὁ υἱὸς τοῦ ἀνθρώπου see R. Buth, 'A More Complete Semitic Background for bar-enasha "Son of Man"', C.A. Evans & J.A. Sanders (eds.), *The Function of Scripture in Early Jewish and Christian Tradition* (JSNT Suppl 154; Sheffield: Sheffield Academic Press, 1998), 176-189; G. O'Collins, Christology: *A Biblical, Historical, and Systematic Study of Jesus* (Oxford: Oxford University Press, 2009); B. Witherington, *The Jesus Quest: The Third Search for the Jew of Nazareth* (Downers Grove, N. J.: InterVarsity Press, 1995). See also M.M. Thompson, 'The Gospel of John', in J. Greene, S. McKnight & I.H. Marshall (eds.), *The Dictionary of Jesus and the Gospels* (Downers Grove, N.J.: InterVarsity Press, 1992), 368-383, esp. 376-379, for an introductory overview of the titles found in John.
17 Schnackenburg, *John*, 2.172. Cf. G. Wetter, *Der Sohn Gottes*, who suggests that it was not as Schnackenburg suggests, but rather the Hellenistic notion of Divine Man formed the key to the interpretation of Sonship in John; See also, Bauer, *Das Johannesevangelium*, p37f.; R. Bultmann, *Theology of the New Testament* (London: SCM Press, 1952), 1.130 –133; Hahn, *Titles*, 292-319. For views closer to Schnackenburg's, see O. Cullmamm, *Christology*, 270-305; E.M. Sidebottom, *The Christ of the Fourth Gospel*, 145-165; E. Haenchen, 'Der Vater, der mich gesandt hat', *NTS* 10 (1962/3), 208-216; J. Howton, 'The Son of God in the Fourth Gospel', *NTS* 11 (1963/4), 227-237. See further C. Mercer, 'Jesus the Apostle: "sending" and the Theology of John', *JETS* 35/4 (December 1992), 457-462, esp. 459, for the relationship with 'sending'.
18 Schnackenburg, *John*, 2.73
19 *Ibid.*, 177-180.

'the God-Messiah relationship as the Father-Son relationship'.[20] He asserts that the title ὁ υἱὸς τοῦ θεοῦ although originally messianic, was understood by the Gospel writer in a deeper sense as part of his 'Son-Christology'. Secondly, Schnackenburg contends that there is a Gnostic influence on John's presentation of the Father/ Son relationship, more particularly from the Odes of Solomon, the Gospel of Truth and the non-canonical Epistle of James.[21] Schnackenburg argues, with some conviction, for the continuity and disjuncture on the respective presentations of Father/ Son relationships in the Gnostic texts. However, we are aware that this view is outdated and there is evidence that the Gnostic texts to which he refers are influenced themselves by Christian thinking. However, that is not to say that it is not feasible that elements of the Gnostic myth related to Sonship may pre-date the Johannine presentation of Jesus in the fourth Gospel.

> The evangelist wished to give the Christian answer to the Gnostic question, and over against the mythical figure of the Gnostic redeemer to set the one true 'Son' who as man [sic] upon earth, truly reveals 'the Father' and leads the way to him.[22]

As the above quotation demonstrates there appears to be a mutual interaction of Sonship ideas. In his detailed study of the Odes of Solomon, J.H. Charlesworth appears to bear out the idea that there was a mutual influencing between the Johannine community during the writing of the Gospel and the Gnostic *milieu* of the time, thus supporting Schnackenburg's contention.[23] However, we will demonstrate that this view is not only outdated, but it lacks credibility.

More importantly, the fourth evangelist was concerned to combat certain 'false' teachings that Jesus was a Messiah [like David] as well as the notion that Jesus was perhaps the expected prophet-like-Moses.[24] In convincing fashion, M. de Jonge argues that although John acknowledges the belief that Jesus is both King and Prophet, both roles are re-interpreted and refined in terms of 'the unique relationship between Son and Father, as portrayed by the fourth Gospel'.[25] It is clear that John does not reject out of hand that Jesus is both Christ and Prophet, but that he points beyond the traditional understanding of these titles to the divine Sonship of Jesus—so Nathanael will see greater things[26] and the man born blind, knowing Jesus as both prophet and messiah, encounters him as the Son of Man.[27] According to de Jonge, the terms 'Christ' and 'Prophet' are not wrong but they are insufficient, 'they may be used in a wrong context and are, therefore, in need of further definition'.[28] The 'further definition' he speaks of is found in Jesus' teaching on the titles ὁ υἱός, ὁ υἱὸς τοῦ ἀνθρώπου and ὁ υἱὸς τοῦ θεοῦ;[29] when John uses both 'Christ' and ὁ υἱὸς τοῦ θεοῦ as a means for defining who Jesus is in 20:31 they stand together and a process of mutual

---

20 *Ibid.*, 180.
21 *Ibid.*, 181–184.
22 *Ibid.*, 184. We note too the important work of Colpe, 'New Testament and Gnostic Christology', 227-243.
23 J.H. Charlesworth, 'Qumran, John and the Odes of Solomon', in J.H. Charlesworth (ed.), *John and Qumran* (London: Chapman, 1972), 107-136, who opines that 'It is probable that the Odist systematically borrowed from John. The most probable solution at this stage in our research is that the author of John and the Odist shared not only the same milieu but perhaps also the same community' (p. 125).
24 Brown, *Community*, 43-45 and 171-182; Martyn, 'Glimpses', 163-166.
25 De Jonge, *Jesus*, 49-69, esp. 52.
26 John 1:50.
27 John 9:35, cf. 17:22. The reading υἱὸν τοῦ ἀνθρώπου seems preferable to the alternate υἱὸν τοῦ θεοῦ because it has better manuscript support.
28 De Jonge, *Jesus*, 83.
29 *Ibid.*, 69: 'Jesus is prophet and king because he is sent by the Father, and only as the Son sent by the Father'.

interpretation is to be understood, since neither alone can fully express Jesus' identity.[30]

The Gospel itself demonstrates that there are at least two pressures bearing down on the Johannine community. The first, and possibly the most obvious one, is the community's separation from the synagogue as a result of the decision to expel Jesus' followers.[31] The second arose within the community and most likely resulted from a division among community members who espoused variant Christological ideologies. Johannine Christology is developed not only in contrast with Jewish thinking, but also with other Christological views. The Johannine community does not only assert its identity by pondering over the true reason for its being separated from the synagogue, but by developing Christological motifs in explanation of that, it also tries to formulate its own standpoint, over against Christological discussions in the Church, particularly over against Christian arguments adduced in the debate between Christians and Jews.[32] J.L. Martyn's analysis of the historical development of the community is likewise cognisant of these very pressures and he locates them respectively to the middle and later period of the community's history.[33] Particular attention is given by de Jonge, to a group of so-called Christian-Jews who remained in the synagogue (8:31ff. and 12:42) and who are, as such, ἐν τῷ κόσμῳ.[34] The other group may have been those who were influenced by Gnostic thought and held a docetic view of Jesus.[35] In view of these pressures, the formulation of the community's Christology is vital within the historical development of the Gospel. Titles needed to be carefully chosen and placed within the complex Gospel formulation of Jesus, the incarnate Son of God.

> In the Johannine Christology, the most divergent impulses and aspects are merged into a consistent composition: along with the notion of the 'Son of Man' there is also that of the 'Son' who is sent by the Father and returns to him, and that of the Logos of the Wisdom type [...] The evangelist may and should be credited with the final amalgamation of the various elements.[36]

The amalgamation of the various elements is *the* most striking aspect of the Johannine use of titles. By drawing together diverse traditions from Christianity and Judaism and re-imaging them in light of his own Christological development, the writer of the fourth Gospel presents a single witness to God's divine Son. Probably the best example of this is how John presents the Son of Man. It seems to draw on the Synoptic tradition's understanding of the Son of Man and yet exhibits rather distinct traits. An example of this can be seen in the pairing of καταβαίνω and ἀναβαίνω, which has given rise to many theses over time, the most important of which is

---

30 De Jonge, *Jesus*, 52 writes, 'Titles like 'prophet', 'teacher sent by God', 'king', or even 'messiah' do not correspond completely with the real status and authority of Him to whom they point. The terms are not wrong but insufficient; they may be used in the wrong context and are therefore in need of further definition'. See also C.K. Barrett, *The Gospel According to St. John. An Introduction with commentary and notes on the Greek Text* (London: SPCK, 1978), 277. Painter, 'Farewell Discourses', 525-543.
31 Martyn, *History*, 47ff., and Brown, *Community*, p22, 40-43, noting that there are questions here that still await answers.
32 De Jonge, *Jesus*, 99.
33 Martyn, 'Glimpses', 160-175. See also Brown, *Community*, 23, who names the periods 'Phase 2' and 'Phase 3' respectively.
34 See de Jonge, *Jesus*, 29-47, esp. 31f.
35 Brown, *Community*, 111-116. E. Käsemann, *The Testament of Jesus*, 26, favours the fourth evangelist as in some ways a 'naïve docetist' himself. However, Brown's argument is favoured here.
36 Schnackenburg, *John*, 2.556.

Schnackenburg's contention for a connection with the Wisdom myth.³⁷

While the fourth evangelist's use of titles connects Jewish and Hellenistic thinking, neither offers an explication of his particular usage, and nor can Christian tradition supply all the answers. Therefore, it is imperative that our study takes account of the period of theological reflection that was brought to bear on all traditions that were to become part of the Johannine tradition. As such, we are aware of the need to be vigilant on two counts, firstly, how John used the Christological titles ὁ υἱός, ὁ υἱὸς τοῦ θεοῦ, and ὁ υἱὸς τοῦ ἀνθρώπου to interpret other Christian titles in the Gospel, cognisant of the importance of the Father-Son relationship. Secondly, the period of theological reflection that lies behind the Johannine use of titles prior to their incorporation into the complex theology of the final form of the Gospel. Such awareness will aid our study of John 6:69 and an appreciation of the theological and historical development of the title ὁ ἅγιος τοῦ θεοῦ.

But the titles in the fourth Gospel are not the only titles that may afford us some insight into the mindset of John. While ὁ ἅγιος τοῦ θεοῦ is unique to the sacred texts of early Christianity, other similar titles are to be found within the *corpus* of Jewish literature and in extra-canonical texts of Christianity. The exact title is not found in the period preceding the Gospels—as far as the evidence available at this time determines. Other, rather similar titles are in evidence, but the title *per se* is not found elsewhere. With only a few exceptions, the similar titles are to be found in three broad groupings of literature.

- The Jewish Scriptures with special attention to the Book of Sirach
- The Christian Scriptures
- The Documents of Nag Hammadi and Qumran

3. The Jewish Scriptures

In relation to our study of ὁ ἅγιος τοῦ θεοῦ the title most similar is to be found in the Psalms and is closely related to the priesthood. Psalm 106:16 reads καὶ παρώργισαν μωυσῆν ἐν τῇ παρεμβολῇ καὶ ααρων τὸν ἅγιον κυρίου. The Greek τὸν ἅγιον κυρίου translates the Hebrew קְדוֹשׁ יְהוָה. The reference for the text of Psalm 106:16 is to be found in Num. 16:7 where Aaron is called ὁ ἀνήρ ὃν ἂν ἐκλέξηται κύριος οὗτος ἅγιος a rendering of the Hebrew הָאִישׁ אֲשֶׁר־יִבְחַר יְהוָה הוּא הַקָּדוֹשׁ.³⁸ In Sir. 45:6 we read Ἀαρὼν ὕψωσεν ἅγιον ὅμοιον αὐτῷ ἀδελφὸν αὐτοῦ ἐκ φυλῆς Λευί· The reference to ἀδελφός refers back to Moses in 45:2 who was made like δόξῃ ἁγίων and also in 45:4 where Moses is sanctified by God and ἐξελέξατο αὐτὸν ἐκ πάσης σαρκός· the Greek verbs ἁγιάζω and ἐκλέγομαι are used respectively. We can infer from this that both Aaron and Moses are holy, though Aaron alone is called τὸν ἅγιον κυρίου. It would be wise at this juncture to leave the questions open as to whether one ought to differentiate between κυρίου and θεοῦ and, if so, how they ought to be distinguished one from another.

A second similar title is to be found in 2 Kings 4:9 and refers to the prophet Elisha. It reads

---

37 Schnackenburg, *Das Johannesevangelium*, 2.551-556; see also R.G. Hamerton-Kelly, *Pre-existence, Wisdom and the Son of Man, passim*; Talbert, 'The Descending-Ascending Redeemer', 441f.; for a contrary opinion, see M. Hengel, *The Son of God: the Origin of Christology and the History of Jewish-Hellenistic Religion* (London: SCM, 1976), 48-51.

38 Cf. the MT of Numbers 16:5 which reads

וּתְנוּ בָהֵן אֵשׁ וְשִׂימוּ עֲלֵיהֶן קְטֹרֶת לִפְנֵי יְהוָה מָחָר וְהָיָה הָאִישׁ אֲשֶׁר־יִבְחַר יְהוָה הוּא הַקָּדוֹשׁ רַב־לָכֶם בְּנֵי לֵוִי׃

Then he said to Korah and all his company, 'In the morning the Lord will make known who is his, and who is holy, and who will be allowed to approach him; the one whom he will choose he will allow to approach him', (NRSV translation).

in Greek ἄνθρωπος τοῦ Θεοῦ ἅγιος a rendering of the Hebrew אִישׁ אֱלֹהִים קָדוֹשׁ 'holy man of God'. Though somewhat removed from the title for Aaron, many scholars argue that it is logical to postulate a connection between Jesus as an exorcist and the prophetic tradition. Further, the words of the demoniac in Mark 1:24, par. Luke 4:34 are deemed reminiscent of 1 Kings 17:18 אִישׁ הָאֱלֹהִים [39] (addressed to Elisha) and the fuller text reads

וַתֹּאמֶר אֶל־אֵלִיָּהוּ מַה־לִּי וָלָךְ אִישׁ הָאֱלֹהִים בָּאתָ אֵלַי לְהַזְכִּיר אֶת־עֲוֹנִי וּלְהָמִית אֶת־בְּנִי׃

rendered in the Greek as καὶ εἶπεν πρὸς ηλιου τί ἐμοὶ καὶ σοί ἄνθρωπε τοῦ θεοῦ εἰσῆλθες πρός με τοῦ ἀναμνῆσαι τὰς ἀδικίας μου καὶ θανατῶσαι τὸν υἱόν μου. E. Schweizer suggests that in the Marcan text we have a synthesis of 2 Kings 4:9 with 1 Kings 17:18.[40] However, we argue that the connection between the Marcan text and the texts of 1 and 2 Kings is tenuous and that the most that can be said is that τί ἐμοὶ καὶ σοί, is a well-known form of challenge.[41] However, this does not mean that Jesus may have been seen as reviving the traditions of the prophets Elijah and Elisha,[42] such that 2 Kings 4:9 may be extremely important to the Synoptic perspective, but not so much for the Johannine.[43]

Finally, in certain of the Greek texts we see that the Nazirite, Samson, is called holy. For example, ναζὶρ Θεοῦ is replaced by ἅγιος θεοῦ, an indefinite form[44] but still close to ὁ ἅγιος τοῦ θεοῦ. So in Jdgs. 16:17 the text of the LXX Codex B reads ὅτι ἅγιος Θεοῦ ἐγώ εἰμι ἀπὸ κοιλίας μητρός μου· whereas the text of the LXX Codex A reads ὅτι ναζιραῖος θεοῦ ἐγώ εἰμι ἐκ κοιλίας μητρός μου. The Hebrew reads[45]

וַיַּגֶּד־לָהּ אֶת־כָּל־לִבּוֹ וַיֹּאמֶר לָהּ מוֹרָה לֹא־עָלָה עַל־רֹאשִׁי כִּי־נְזִיר אֱלֹהִים אֲנִי מִבֶּטֶן אִמִּי אִם־גֻּלַּחְתִּי וְסָר מִמֶּנִּי כֹחִי וְחָלִיתִי וְהָיִיתִי כְּכָל־הָאָדָם׃

In Jdgs. 13:7 we read, ὅτι Θεοῦ ἅγιον ἔσται τὸ παιδάριον ἀπὸ γαστρὸς ἕως ἡμέρας θανάτου αὐτοῦ, and Jdgs. 13:5 reads ὅτι ναζὶρ[46] Θεοῦ ἔσται τὸ παιδάριον ἀπὸ τῆς κοιλίας..., so it would appear that the translation raises the possibility for a known connection between the two titles. Schweizer made use of this possibility to suggest that the words of the demoniac in Mark 1:24 contained a play on the words 'Jesus of Nazareth' as equivalent to 'Jesus the Nazirite' basing this on the text

---

39 אִישׁ הָאֱלֹהִים can translate literally as 'man of the angels' or 'man of God'.
40 Schweizer, *Evangelium nach Markus*, 24.
41 Cf. Judges 11:12; 2 Samuel 16:10; 19:22 (MT 19:23); 1 Kings 17:18; 2 Kings 3:13; 2 Chronicles 35:21. See Bauernfeind, *Die Worte der Dämonen*, 3-10, 14-15, 28-31, and 68-69. See also the work of H. vander Loos, *The Miracles of Jesus* (Leiden: Brill, 1965), 380. Further see B. Chilton, D. Bock, D.M. Gurtner, J. Neusner, L.H. Schiffman, and D. Oden (eds.), *A Comparative Handbook to the Gospel of Mark: Comparisons with Pseudepigrapha, the Qumran Scrolls, and Rabbinic Literature* (The New Testament Gospels in the Judaic Contexts, 1; Leiden & Boston, MA: Brill, 2010), 83-84, which provides a list of the OT and extra-canonical texts that may have a bearing on the Marcan usage.
42 See G. Vermes, *Jesus the Jew*, 86-99, esp. 89. Also worth considering is the work of G.W. Buchanan, 'The Samaritan Origin of the Gospel of John', in J. Neusner (ed.), *Religions in Antiquity*, 166-170, wherein he gives a account of the list of parallels between the Johannine signs and the Elijah/Elisha epics.
43 This is explicated fully in chapter 2.2 of my dissertation.
44 A possibility allowed for by A.T. Robertson, *A Grammar of the Greek New Testament in Light of Historical Research* (London: Hodder & Stoughton, 1919), 796. We note that the verse is not mentioned in H. St. John Thackeray, *A Grammar for the Old Testament in Greek According to the Septuagint* (Cambridge: Cambridge University Press, 1909).
45 Which has been translated in various ways into English. A sample is provided below.
    - NIV = I have been a Nazirite set apart to God since birth
    - NASB and ESV = I have been a Nazirite to God from my mother's womb.
    - ASV and KJV = I *have been* a Nazirite unto God from my mother's womb:
    - YLT = for a Nazirite to God I am from the womb of my mother
46 So recorded on the LXX Codex B text while the LXX Codex A text reads the variant ναζειραῖον.

of Matt. 12:23.⁴⁷ This would mean then that the title, ὁ ἅγιος τοῦ θεοῦ, is then another affirmation of Jesus as Nazirite, ὁ ἅγιος as equivalent to ὁ ναζιραῖος. Schweizer also points out that in Jdgs. 13:5 (Codex A) and Matt. 2:23 the spelling of Nazirite is the same. His final conclusion suggests that it is the idea of 'consecration'⁴⁸ that is stressed by the play on words. We agree that the idea of consecration is important,⁴⁹ however, we note that the play on words is difficult to maintain as the text of Matt. 12:23 probably has been influenced by Isa. 11:1 and the messianic term חֹטֶר ⁵⁰ and not Jdgs. 13:5 (Codex A).⁵¹ Another title, 'the Holy One of Israel', does not merit our attention however.⁵² L. Morris remarks that 6:69 calls to mind the title 'the Holy One of Israel', which is used for יהוה, in the context of the covenant on a number of occasions.⁵³ We argue that the two titles, apart from sharing some words, have, in fact, little in common.⁵⁴ A more promising comparison would be the absolute 'the Holy One', which can be used interchangeably with 'the Holy One of Israel'. It is used frequently in later rabbinic works.⁵⁵ We note that in the Johannine literature outside of the Gospel, the absolute form ὁ ἅγιος is used with some indications that it pertains to Jesus' divine status. Therefore while we do not concur wholeheartedly with Morris' interpretation, we find some merit in his concluding that, 'It sets [Jesus] with God and not men'.⁵⁶

Finally, we consider the title found in Psalm 15(16),10b, which reads, οὐδὲ δώσεις τὸν ὅσιόν σου ἰδεῖν διαφθοράν. The expression τὸν ὅσιόν σου translates חֲסִידְךָ.⁵⁷ The Greek form of the title re-occurs in Acts 2:27 and 13:35, but refers directly to the Psalm and is applied to Jesus. Since the idea that Jesus is the messiah is evident in both texts from Acts, some have considered that the title is messianic and then apply this as evidence for a messianic interpretation for ὁ ἅγιος τοῦ θεοῦ in John 6:69.⁵⁸ This is misleading because although the RSV renders it 'Holy One' it is mistranslating the Greek ὁ ὅσιός that is itself a rendering of the Hebrew חֲסִידְךָ. Therefore, we

---

47   See the work of E. Schweizer, 'Er wird Nazoräer heissen', 90-39 on this. Matthew 12:23 reads καὶ ἐλθὼν κατῴκησεν εἰς πόλιν λεγομένην Ναζαρέτ· ὅπως πληρωθῇ τὸ ῥηθὲν διὰ τῶν προφητῶν ὅτι Ναζωραῖος κληθήσεται.
48   Schweizer, 'Er wird Nazoräer heissen', 92; Gnilka, *Markus*, 77; F. Mussner, 'Ein Wortspiel in Mk. 1:24', *BZ* 4 (1960), 285-286 makes a remarkably similar point; H.C. Kee. 'The Terminology of Mark's Exorcist Stories', *NTS* 14 (1967/8), 232.
49   Cf. Jeremiah 1:5
50   נצר n. meaning branch, sprout, shoot, used figuratively. *TWOT*, § 1408a. See also BDBG. 'Hebrew Lexicon entry for Netzer [sic]'. *The Old Testament Hebrew Lexicon.* http://www.studylight.org/lex/heb/view.cgi?number=5342 (Accessed on August 23, 2011).
51   R.E. Brown, *The Birth of the Messiah, A Commentary on the Infancy Narratives* (The Anchor Bible Reference Library; New York, N.Y.: Doubleday, 1977), 207. We note that in Modern Hebrew, Christians are called נוצרים. See also B.T. Sanh. 43a declares: 'He is to be stoned for sorcery and leading Israel astray'.
52   R.G. Kratz, 'Israel in the Book of Isaiah', *JSOT* 31 (2001), 103-127. Kratz demonstrates that the title the Holy One of God emerged in the development history of the book of Isaiah. Over the period of the transmission history of the book the names 'Israel' and 'Jacob' became interchangeable and the title 'the Holy One of Israel' emerged, usually as the portentate of doom. 'The construct expression applies the traditional attribute of God's holiness, as used in Isa. 6.3, explicitly to Israel and in this manner calls Israel as the people of God to account for their actions before God' (p.111).
53   We cite Isaiah 10:16; 40:25 and 45:18ff. as examples. See also, Procksch. 'ἅγιος κτλ.', 93f.
54   See Kratz, 'Israel', 127-128. Also see J.N. Oswalt, *Holy One of Israel: Studies in the Book of Isaiah* (Eugene, OR: Cascade Books, 2014) for a more complete study of the term.
55   See in Str-B 3, 762.
56   L. Morris, The *Gospel of John* (*NICNT*; Grand Rapids. MN: Eerdmans, 1971), 389f.
57   חסירך adj. meaning kind, faithful, pious/ godly, when used as a subst. faithful ones. See TWOT, § 698b.
58   Blunt, *Gospel According to St. Mark*, 148, wherein he says, 'The Holy One of God is a messianic title quoted as such in Acts 2:27 from Ps. 16:10'; K.H. Rengstorf, *Das Evangelium nach Lukas* (*NTD*; Göttingen: Vandenhoeck & Ruprecht, 1962, Ninth ed.), 70; F.C. Grant, *The Gospel According to Mark. Introduction and Exegesis, The Interpreter's Bible*, Volume 7 (New York, N. Y.: Abingdon-Cokesbury Press, 1951), 662, and also Nineham, *Mark*, 79, though to a lesser extent wherein he writes, 'Possibly a later Christian term (based on an association with Ps. 16:10 with the resurrection-See Acts 2:27)'. There does not appear to be any case where there is an obvious recognition that the title differs in Psalm 16:10/ Acts 2:27 and Mark 1:24 par. Luke 4:34 and John 6:69.

posit that a more correct translation for ὁ ὅσιός would be 'Pious One'. This is more apt as the LXX invariably translates חָסִיד as ὅσιός and never as ἅγιος or one of it cognates.[59] As such, the titles ὁ ὅσιός and ὁ ἅγιος have separate traditions.

4. The Christian Scriptures

The title ὁ ἅγιος τοῦ θεοῦ is found in Mark in the context of an exorcism (Mark 1:21ff.) and is repeated, with minor alterations, in Luke 4:31-37, but it is absent from Matthew. The Marcan version of the exorcism reads:

> They went to Capernaum; and when the Sabbath came, he entered the synagogue and taught. They were astounded at his teaching, for he taught them as one having authority (ἐξουσίαν ἔχων), and not as the scribes. Just then there was in their synagogue a man with an unclean spirit, and he cried out, 'What have you to do with us (τί ἡμῖν καὶ σοί) Jesus of Nazareth? Have you come to destroy us? I know who you are, the Holy One of God (ὁ ἅγιος τοῦ θεοῦ)'. But Jesus rebuked him, saying, 'Be silent (φιμώθητι), and come out of him!' And the unclean spirit, throwing him into convulsions and crying with a loud voice, came out of him. They were all amazed, and they kept on asking one another, 'What is this? A new teaching—with authority (ἐξουσίαν)! He commands even the unclean spirits, and they obey him'. At once his fame began to spread throughout the surrounding region of Galilee.

Two items come immediately to the fore.

i   *The mention of authority (ἐξουσία) in 1:22, 27.* Together with the pericopes preceding and following, i.e. the calling of the disciples (Mark 1:16-20) and Jesus' healing ministry—particularly of Peter's mother-in-law—(Mark 1:29-34), it presents something of the impact of Jesus' ministry on the region of Galilee. Such can also be said of the Lucan setting.

ii *The tension between the unclean spirit—πνεῦμα ἀκαθάρτον—and the Holy One of God*; between the demon and the agent of God, there is room only for enmity.

It is, therefore, apparent from the Markan (and Lukan) contexts that God's Holy One is he who carries authority over demons, an authority not brought about by incantation or spell of some sort, but by the authority of his word. The Holy One speaks and it becomes so.

Two other terms appear elsewhere in the Christian Scriptures, ὁ δίκαιος, and the authoritative ἐγώ εἰμι sayings. The title, ὁ δίκαιος, is found in 1 John 2:1; Acts 3:14, 7:52 and twice in the LXX in Isa. 53:11 (the righteous one, my servant) and Hab. 2:4.[60] There is also the concept of the righteous messiah in Psalms 17 and 37 and in the Qumran scroll, 4Q Patr. Bless Col. v.[61] which reads, 'until the Messiah of Righteousness (משיח הצדק) comes, the Branch of David'. An examination of the Jewish Scriptures' use of the term Messiah shows that the adjective 'righteous' is frequently

---

59 See entry for 'ὅσιός κτλ.', *TDNT* 5, 490-492.

60 Isaiah 53:11 reads, ἀπὸ τοῦ πόνου τῆς ψυχῆς αὐτοῦ δεῖξαι αὐτῷ φῶς καὶ πλάσαι τῇ συνέσει δικαιῶσαι δίκαιον εὖ δουλεύοντα πολλοῖς καὶ τὰς ἁμαρτίας αὐτῶν αὐτὸς ἀνοίσει and Hab 2:4 reads, ἐὰν ὑποστείληται οὐκ εὐδοκεῖ ἡ ψυχή μου ἐν αὐτῷ ὁ δὲ δίκαιος ἐκ πίστεώς μου ζήσεται.

61 Also known as 4Q252 is the Blessings of the Fathers. The context is the interpretation of Jacob's blessing on Judah (Genesis 49:10). See G. Brooke, *DJD XXII*, 185-207, pl. XII-XIII; PAM 43.253, 43.381; ROC 668, 670; J. M. Allegro, 'Further Messianic References in Qumran Literature', *JBL* 75 (1956), p174-176, pl. 1; J.T. Milik, 'Milkî-sedeq et Milkî-resaᶜ', 138; G. J. Brooke, 'The Thematic Content of 4Q252', *JQR* 85 (1994), 33-59; id., '4Q252 as Early Jewish commentary', *RevQ* 17/65-68 (1996), 385-401.

applied to Messiah and in particular to his role as bringing 'righteous judgment'. So it is not surprising that, in the Christian Scriptures the Greek equivalent ὁ δίκαιος is applied to Jesus. However, there is more to it than the direct application of a title from the Jewish Scriptures as applied to the Christian Messiah—the passages in Acts consistently emphasise Jesus' innocence and also place him is the long line of the prophets of old who were persecuted.

In Acts 3:14 we read ὑμεῖς δὲ τὸν ἅγιον καὶ δίκαιον ἠρνήσασθε καὶ ᾐτήσασθε ἄνδρα φονέα χαρισθῆναι ὑμῖν and further τίνα τῶν προφητῶν οὐκ ἐδίωξαν οἱ πατέρες ὑμῶν; καὶ ἀπέκτειναν τοὺς προκαταγγείλαντας περὶ τῆς ἐλεύσεως τοῦ δικαίου, οὗ νῦν ὑμεῖς προδόται καὶ φονεῖς ἐγένεσθε (Acts 7:52). We note here an ethical element is added in the usage of the title ὁ δίκαιος as it is applied to Jesus by the author of Acts. This is to say that Jesus as the Righteous One is the Messiah—the Jewish element is taken over—but further, he is the one crucified in spite of his innocence—the ethical element added by the author of Acts. This innocence is verified and proven by his being raised up by God (Acts 3:13) and given the task of turning people from their wickedness. There may be similarities with the Pauline concept of the second Adam (cf. Rom. 5:17 and 18) and to Isa. 53:11.[62] A connection to Isaiah is possible given that the presentation of Jesus in Acts 3:22-26 is that of a prophet-like-Moses particularly given the link with Acts 7:52.

In the first letter of John we read, Τεκνία μου, ταῦτα γράφω ὑμῖν ἵνα μὴ ἁμάρτητε. καὶ ἐάν τις ἁμάρτῃ παράκλητον ἔχομεν πρὸς τὸν πατέρα Ἰησοῦν Χριστὸν δίκαιον· καὶ αὐτὸς ἱλασμὸς ἐστιν περὶ τῶν ἁμαρτιῶν ἡμῶν, οὐ περὶ τῶν ἡμετέρων δὲ μόνον ἀλλὰ καὶ περὶ ὅλου τοῦ κόσμου (1 John 2:1-2) a theme that recurs in 1 John 2:29 ἐὰν εἰδῆτε ὅτι δίκαιος ἐστιν, γινώσκετε ὅτι πᾶς ὁ ποιῶν τὴν δικαιοσύνην ἐξ αὐτοῦ γεγέννηται. Both instances clearly demonstrate the ethical element in the use of the title, but with a slight change of emphasis. Here the effect is not so much to emphasise the innocence of Jesus, as to mark Jesus as belonging to the sphere of the Righteous— the sphere of God. As such, he becomes the advocate of all righteous believers who are in turn 'born of him' (1 John 2:29). Thus, it is in line with the dualism of the Gospel, which becomes more pronounced in this letter wherein humanity is divided into children of God[63] and children of the devil.[64] The marks of Jesus, the Righteous One, are also the marks of the believer's righteousness and anointing.

The second title of concern at this stage of our study is the use of the absolute ὁ ἅγιος, 'the Holy One', which is applied to Jesus, sometimes on its own as in 1 John 2:20 and sometimes with another title appended:

- ὁ ἅγιος καὶ δίκαιος 'the Holy and Righteous One' in Acts 3:14
- ὁ ἅγιος, ὁ ἀληθινός, 'the Holy One, the True One' in Rev. 3:7
- τέκνον... ἅγιον in the content of the annunciation narrative of Luke's Gospel: 'The angel said to her, "The Holy Spirit will come upon you, and the power of the Most High will overshadow you; therefore the child (τέκνον) to be born will be holy (ἅγιον); he will be called Son of God (ὁ υἱὸς τοῦ θεοῦ)"'.
- ἅγιος παῖς appears in Acts 4:27 and 30 a term that can be understood as either 'Holy Son' and so linking up with Luke 1:35 or as 'Holy Servant' establishing a possible link with the so-called Servant Songs of Trito-Isaiah.

We note that in the Acts there are references to the inclusion of a quotation from Ps. 2:1-2 where

---

62 R.H. Fuller establishes the link to Isaiah. See R.H. Fuller, *The Foundations of New Testament Christology* (Fontana Library of Theology and Philosophy; London: Collins, 1969), 47f.
63 1 John 1:12 and 3:1.
64 1 John 3:10 and John 8:44.

the term 'anointed' is used and this is applied to Jesus (Acts 4:27) as the one who works 'signs and wonders' (4:30). As such ἅγιος παῖς appears to have a thoroughly messianic framework of reference. Similar things can be said for the Lukan title τέκνον ἅγιον as the reference within the context to ὁ υἱὸς τοῦ θεοῦ successfully demonstrates (Luke 1:35). The Johannine references (1 John 2:20 and Rev. 3:7) show different connotations. Indeed the title used in Rev. 3:7 ὁ ἅγιος, ὁ ἀληθινός, 'the Holy One, the True One' is also used of God in 6:10, therefore it would be more accurate to call it a divine title.

5. The Documents of Qumran and Nag Hammadi

There is a well-attested understanding of holiness within the Qumran literature that includes the angels and the members of the community at Qumran. Terms to describe the angels include קודשים 'holy ones' are used frequently, which is similar to the usage found in the Jewish Scriptures as determining that these holy ones belong to God.[65] Further in CD-B 20:8 the expression קודשים עליון 'holy ones of the Most High' is found.

Although this has not been seen in relation to ὁ ἅγιος τοῦ θεοῦ before, perhaps because it was deemed inappropriate to consider it an angelic title, we note that in the Gospel of Thomas, Peter's confession reads 'You are like a righteous angel' (13:2).[66] The other title used of the angels is בני שמים 'sons of heaven' highlighting, perhaps, an orthodox sensitivity to avoiding the expression 'sons of God' in a manner analogous to the Matthean preference for 'kingdom of heaven' over against 'kingdom of God' which is used freely by Mark and Luke. Perhaps a similar sensitivity is evidenced in the frequency of the קדושיכה rather than the expression קדושים עליון, though we note that at least at 1QH 3:22[67] they appear as parallel, if not interchangeable, terms.

להתיצב כמעתד עם צבא קודשים ולבוא כיהד עם עדת בני שמים

Moreover, the parallel between קודשים 'holy ones' and בני שמים 'sons of heaven' opens possibilities for ὁ ἅγιος τοῦ θεοῦ and ὁ υἱὸς τοῦ θεοῦ in the Christian Scriptures. However, we must also be cognisant that in the Jewish and Christian Scriptures and other related texts קודשים and ἅγιος are applied with great frequency to members of a particular religious affiliation such as the members of the Qumran, Christians, the prophets of the Jewish literature as well as angels illustrates something of the problem in resolving its correlation for an interpretation for our text in John 6:69.

The last title we consider for now is found in the Melchizedek scroll of the Nag Hammadi writings,[68] wherein the priest is designated 'O Melchizedek, Holy One, High Priest, the Perfect

---

65 M.G. Abegg, Jr., with J. E. Bowley and E. M. Cook in consultation with E. Tov, *The Dead Sea Scrolls Concordance* (2 vols; Leiden: Brill, 2003) and K.G. Kuhn, *Konkordanz zu den Qumrantexten* (Göttingen: Vandenhoeck & Ruprecht, 1960), 189-191 for the list of the occurrences in the Qumran corpus.

66 Available at http://www.earlychristianwritings.com/thomas/gospelthomas13.html (Accessed on August 23, 2013). See also L.T. Stuckenbruck, *Angel Veneration and Christology. A Study in Early Judism and the Christology of the Apocalypse of John* (WUNT 70; Tübingen: Mohr, 1995).

67 See M. Mansoor (transl. & annot.), *The Thanksgiving Hymns*, in J. Van der Ploeg (ed.), *Studies on the Texts of the Desert of Judah*, Vol 3. (Grand Rapids, Michigan: Eerdmans, 1961), 116-121, esp. his translation of Psalm 6. Available online http://vinyl2.sentex.ca/~tcc/OP/Psalm6M.html (Accessed on August 23, 2011).

68 Not far from the village of Nag Hammadi in Upper Egypt, a group of farmers came across an entire collection of books written in Coptic, the language spoken by Egyptian Christians. This *corpus* of 1,200 pages is currently conserved at the Coptic Museum in Cairo. http://www.nag-hammadi.com/ (Accessed on July 23, 2010).

Hope and Gift of Life'.[69] However, the context does not enable a clarification as to why Melchizedek is so designated—whether it is on account of his priesthood or because of his divine qualities. There is simply not enough evidence on which to reach a firm conclusion.

6. Conclusion

By way of conclusion then, our study of titles in the New Testament has shown that there are none identical to that found in John 6:69 except for the Synoptic accounts of the demon possessed man in Mark 1:24, par. Luke 3:34. Therefore to gain some understanding of the title ὁ ἅγιος τοῦ θεοῦ in John 6:69 we reviewed the other titles used by John for, by or about Jesus namely, ὁ υἱὸς τοῦ θεοῦ, ὁ υἱὸς τοῦ ἀνθρώπου and the absolute ὁ υἱός. The most striking element of John's use of these titles is the the process of consolidation that he brings to them. The fourth evangelist presents a single witness to God's divine Son by drawing together diverse traditions from Christianity and Judaism and re-imaging them in light of his own Christological development. Of note is the pairing of καταβαίνω and ἀναβαίνω, which has given rise to the thesis that there is a Wisdom connection. Neither Jewish and Hellenistic thinking offers an explication of his particular usage, and nor can Christian tradition supply all the answers. Therefore the period of theological reflection that lies behind the Johannine use of titles prior to their incorporation into the complex theology of the final form of the Gospel needed to be examined.

Other titles worthy of further investigation include titles from the Jewish Corpus with priestly and prophetic elements. Of the three titles examined from the Jewish Scriptures for the priest Aaron (ὁ ἅγιος τοῦ θεοῦ: Ps. 106:16), the prophet Elisha (ἄνθρωπος τοῦ Θεοῦ ἅγιος: 2 Kings 4:9) and the Nazirite Samson (ναζὶρ Θεοῦ: Jdgs. 16:17), the Aaronite title of Ps. 106:16 would seem closest to ours and as such may hold some promise that Jesus may be cast in a priestly light. This is, of course, contingent that we take κύριου and τοῦ θεοῦ as being equivalent, the titles are very close, and the holiness of the priesthood is well-attested.[70] Of less significance is Jdgs. 16:17 (Codex B) and less again is 2 Kings 4:9, each being further removed from Mark. Similarly we find no merit in a comparison between ὁ ὅσιός and and ὁ ἅγιος as we have demonstrated that they have separate traditions.

From the Christian Scripture we have noted that the title ὁ ἅγιος τοῦ θεοῦ as used by Mark (par. Luke) shows that God's Holy One has authority over demons simply by the power of his word. Of course, the is only One who has power to begin things into being by his word and further, in New Testament cosmology the One with authority over demons is, of course, God! In Acts of the Apostles we noted that the title ὁ δίκαιος has taken over the Jewish concept that the Righteous One is the Messiah and has applied it to Jesus. However, we further noted that the author of Acts adds an ethical dimension—this Righteous Messiah died in spite of his innocence which is proven by his resurrection by God (Acts 3:13). This further supported by 1 John where Jesus belongs to the sphere of God so that all righteous believers are 'born of him' (1 John 2:29). So what we can say is that different writers of the Christian Scriptures used similar, yet distinct, titles and epithets to describe Jesus as holy and that they understand the aspect of holy in different ways—some as messianic, some as divine. Thus, while the concept of the holiness of Jesus appeared to have been well known to the writers of the Christian scriptures, it was clearly understood in a variety of ways.

---

69 See online at http://gnosis.org/naghamm/melchiz.html (Accessed on August 23, 2013).
70 Leviticus 21:6.

Further, we note the Christian references to the holiness of Jesus are worthy of further study. But we also note at this early stage that 'holy' as a descriptive may be attributed to an agent of God, divine, angelic, or human. Therefore, a fuller examination of possible links between ὁ ἅγιος τοῦ θεοῦ in John 6:69 and other references to the holiness of Jesus will form part any future study to determine if possible links to his messianic role or his divinity or both may be made.

Most promising is that possibility that John may have taken over the title ὁ ἅγιος τοῦ θεοῦ from Mark. But in evaluating the Johannine usage there are grounds for affirming a period of theological reflection upon the received tradition.[71] As a result, the Johannine use of ὁ ἅγιος τοῦ θεοῦ may have involved a process of re-interpretation and a reworking of the content such that it coalesces with the Christology and theology of the Gospel of John. There is something about this title that was too valuable for John not to include it in his Gospel. Yet, it is Peter who calls Jesus ὁ ἅγιος τοῦ θεοῦ and not the demoniac in the Capernaum synagogue. Why?

As we quest for the meaning of ὁ ἅγιος τοῦ θεοῦ in Jn 6:69 what we can say at this stage is that the traditions that the fourth evangelist has received have been molded to a Johannine end. The comparable titles have afforded us tantilising glimspes of possiblity, the priest par excellence of Psalm 106; the One with the authority to cast our demons as in Mark 1 (par. Luke 4); the righteous, innocent One of Acts 3; the One who is the the sphere of God in 1 John 2. Or does the foruth evangelist transcend that which he has received and fashion something new? One instincts would favour the latter, but that is subject matter for a book and not a brief article![72]

Debra Snoddy
Catholic Institute of Sydney

---

[71] J. Painter, 'Johannine Symbols: A Case Study in Epistemology', *JTSA* 27 (1979), 26-41 esp. 38.
[72] For a full exegesis of the study see my forthcoming volume on John 6:69, due to be published in 2018.

Thesis Summary:
The Kingship of Jesus in the Gospel of John[1]

SEHYUN KIM

This thesis, accepted by the University of Sheffield in 2010, studies kingship with reference to the Johannine Jesus: his identity and function. Post-colonialism, as a major methodology, leads to an avenue from which to read the Gospel of John in the more complex and wider context of the hybridized Jewish and Greco-Roman world in the first century C.E. This provides a new perspective on the kingship of the Johannine Jesus, whose kingly identity is characterized by hybridized Christological titles.

After an introductory chapter, opening up the question, the thesis falls into two parts of three chapters each, followed by a conclusion.

Chapter 2 discusses the textual features of the Gospel of John in relation to its purposes and its readership. Viewed as a postcolonial text the Fourth Gospel was written in a multi-cultural and hybridized society, and it is highly possible that this Gospel was composed with a variety of readers in mind, who were from multi-cultural environments. Through a survey of the two major backgrounds to the Gospel, both Jewish and Greco-Roman traditions, the thesis argues that the kingship of the Johannine Jesus is conveyed using various Christological terms. Although the meanings of these titles could be understood by readers from varied backgrounds, it is the combination of the two traditions that is important in order to understand the kingship of Jesus in this Gospel. In the mixture of meanings of the Christological titles from the two backgrounds, there is a commonality, centering on kingship. In particular, as a hybridized product (a post-colonial document) of this multi-cultural society, the Gospel accommodated various multi-cultural aspects. This Gospel was written for multi-cultural readers in order to present Jesus as king, to lead them to believe in him as the true king whom they would follow for eternity and to challenge them to live according to the ruling ideology of the Johannine new world. In this way, the Johannine Gospel encourages its readers, seeks to consolidate their faith in Jesus, and challenges them to live/ spread the Johannine ideology of the new world in/to the world.

Secondly, in discussing its chosen methodology, post-colonialism, the thesis notes that, because the Johannine world was under colonial power, the identity of the Johannine

> **This Gospel was written for multi-cultural readers in order to present Jesus as king.**

---

1 Sehyun Kim, "Kingship of Jesus in the Gospel of John" (unpublished Ph.D. thesis, the University of Sheffield, UK, 2010); supervisor: Professor Loveday Alexander. *This thesis will be published in 2018 by Pickwick Publications.

Jesus as de-colonizer could be recognized. Reading the Gospel as a postcolonial text shows the Johannine Jesus to be the solution to the conflicts among various groups. In order to attempt a postcolonial reading of the Gospel, particularly to clarify the kingship of the Johannine Jesus, the thesis surveys: 1) differences and similarities between the center and the margins (mimicry); 2) the subtle relationship between the center and the margins (ambivalence); and 3) hybridity and diaspora in post-colonialism, as major theoretical tools of post-colonialism. The relationship between the center and the margins in the Gospel is both complex and subtle, and the Gospel emerges as a discourse of resistance and emancipation.

> **The postcolonial hope is linked to the Johannine Utopia.**

Finally, this section argues that hybrid identity and diaspora are in a sense unavoidable in a colonial society, and it is necessary to admit that a postcolonial society is a hybridized and diasporic society. The postcolonial hope, therefore, is to make a new utopian society through mutual transactions between the center and the margin, thus overcoming institutionalized violence and suffering. The Johannine new world pursued in the Gospel is like this: entry into the new hybrid society, which overcomes institutionalized violence and suffering, means entering the new world of peace, forgiveness, service, freedom, and love. The postcolonial hope is linked to the Johannine Utopia, in which Jesus as the universal king reigns for all the people, regardless of whether their origins were at the center or the margin.

Chapter 3 investigates the Johannine Christological titles, which present the kingship of Jesus, for their distinctive usage. Important factors are identified for understanding the Johannine Christological titles as hybridized products of a hybridized society, and their distinctive usage in combination. The Johannine Christological titles are then discussed in terms of their implications for kingship (particularly, the Messiah, the Son of God, the Son of Man, the Prophet, the Savior of the World, and the Lord/ My Lord and My God).

The kingship of Jesus is a more prominent theme in the Gospel than is usually acknowledged, with John regularly emphasizing it. Of the many and various designations, portrayals, and titles, it is difficult to suggest one as the key term for Johannine Christology. However, the kingship of the Johannine Jesus qualifies as such a key. Although three Christological titles in the Fourth Gospel, 'Christ', 'Son of God', and 'Son of Man', are the major ones, they can be understood more fully in the light of other Christological titles used in the Gospel. So, how does this Gospel fully reveal the identity of Jesus? To answer this question, it is also important to keep in mind that the kingship motif permeates all these titles.

First, various titles used throughout the Gospel emphasize Jesus' identity and tasks as king. In this Gospel, the unique Johannine Jesus is created by an unparalleled literary use of the Christological titles, namely, by putting them in series, by synonymy, or by the employment of the various Christological titles in the same context. For example, John the Baptist refers to Jesus as *the Lamb of God*, and *the Son of God* (1:29, 34, 36), which point to Jesus as the Messiah in the following context. Then, Andrew confesses to Simon that he has found *the Messiah* (1:41; cf. 1:45). When Philip finds Nathanael, he says, 'we have found Him of whom Moses in the Law and *also* the Prophets wrote, Jesus of Nazareth, the son of Joseph', Nathanael doubts who Jesus is, saying, 'can *any good thing* come out of Nazareth?'. However, he later confesses directly to Jesus that he is *the Son of God and the King of Israel*, and Jesus does not rebuke him, or deny his identity (1:49ff).

Furthermore, Jesus admits himself to be *the Messiah* to the Samaritan woman (4:26) and she witnesses to his Messiahship to the Samaritans

(4:29). Consequently, the Samaritans confess that Jesus is *truly the Savior of the world* (4:42), a term which was used of the Roman emperors. In addition, after feeding five thousand men, the people confessed that Jesus is *truly the Prophet who is come into the world* (6:14). About this sign, the narrator comments that the crowd's intention is 'to come and make him *king* by force', even though Jesus rejects this understanding (6:15). In the dialogue between Jesus and his disciples, Simon Peter confesses directly to Jesus that he is *the Holy One of God* (6:69).

Moreover, during a controversy in the crowd, there is a question as to whether Jesus is *a good man* or a deceiver (7:12). In the following dispute, some confess that Jesus is *the Christ* or *the Prophet* (7:40-44), and, in relation to his origin, Jesus reveals that it was from above (7:28; 8:23; cf. 1:1ff). More strikingly, the man born blind confesses publicly that Jesus is a prophet (9:12), but when he meets Jesus after his excommunication (9:35) and Jesus reveals himself as *the Son of Man*, he worships Jesus (9:38) in a way that people might worship (bow down to) one who is God and King. Jesus' kingship is revealed more clearly as the narrative proceeds to its climax. When the Jews ask him to reveal plainly if he is indeed the Christ (10:24), Jesus reveals himself implicitly as *the Christ* who has power to control life and death and clearly reveals himself as *the Son of God* (10:36). Martha confesses directly to Jesus that he is *the Christ, the Son of God* (11:27) when she meets him before her brother's resuscitation. The multitudes welcome Jesus when he enters Jerusalem, confessing him to be *the King of Israel* (12:13). John is the only evangelist to include this detail. When the Roman soldiers come to arrest Jesus in the garden, they draw back and fall to the ground when Jesus identifies himself to them (18:6), reminiscent of the way in which people fell down before God, or before a king. At the trial by Pilate, the Jewish leaders accuse Jesus as an evildoer, and also for claiming to be *the Son of God* (18:30; 19:7). Furthermore, when Pilate asks him if he is the king of the Jews, Jesus identifies himself as a *king* (18:33, 36-37), although his kingdom is not of this world (18:36). Pilate refers to Jesus as *the King of the Jews* (18:39; 19:14-15). When he is crucified, the inscription written in Hebrew, Latin, and Greek, is put on the cross (19:16-22) to show ironically his universal kingship, since various titles employed to designate Roman emperors in inscriptions and papyri were also written in Greek or Latin. After death, he is buried in a new tomb in a garden (20:41-42) like the burial of Jewish kings (19:40-42). After Jesus' resurrection, Thomas makes the climactic confession to Jesus that he is '*My Lord and My God*' (20:28), a phrase applied to Roman emperors. Finally, the author reveals Jesus' identity as *the Christ and the Son of God* for which purpose this Gospel had been written (20:31).

Secondly, the Gospel of John contains Jesus' explicit avowals of his kingship (4:26; 10:24-25; 18:33-37). He is described as the king who wants to liberate the margins from the yoke of the Jewish religion as well as from the oppression of the Roman imperial power. He wants to lead them into the new world in which they can live together in harmony with less nationalism and without competition and struggles. It is necessary in connection with this viewpoint to say that there are a number of passages in which people convey their beliefs about Jesus in the Gospel. Furthermore, this shows that the various terms and motifs from the various backgrounds are used in this Gospel for the identification of Jesus. Therefore, some terms employed by the people to confess the identity of Jesus are related to Jewish expectations of the coming of the Messianic King, while other terms allude to royal titles in the Greco-Roman world. Various titles (the Son, the Son of God, the Son of Man,

> **Jesus reveals himself implicitly as the Christ who has power to control life and death.**

the Prophet, the teacher sent by God, king, or Messiah) could not correspond completely with the real status and authority of Jesus. Although not wrong, they are insufficient, and they require further definition to understand their full meanings in the contexts in which they are used. John presents all aspects of the identity of Jesus using various titles without negating any of them. The author also uses diverse Christological titles, weaving them together to express an overall view of the identity of Jesus.

It is important, then, that the titles employed to designate the identity of Jesus are able to reveal their fuller meaning when they are interpreted together in consideration with the meanings of other terms. Whether some terms were preferred by one group and others by another group, or whether the terms used imply conflict between the groups, the successive narrative locations of the titles in the Gospel, i.e. the Messiah/Christ and the Son of God, the Son of God and the King of Israel, etc. show that the author carefully put them together in order that the readers could come to know his identity without any misunderstanding caused by their different ethnic, cultural, or religious backgrounds.

Chapter 4 deals, in particular, with the title, 'the king of Israel/the Jews' which explicitly refers to Jesus as king. In fact, the Christological terms in John seem to be used to portray the Johannine Jesus as the universal king beyond the Jewish messiah and/or the Roman emperors. Particularly in the Passion Narrative, the term 'the king of the Jews' is used to show his universal kingship. The titles for Jesus are not always interpreted in the same way in different texts. Sometimes the Johannine titles are interpreted differently from the titles in the Synoptics. To explore this further, Greco-Roman and Jewish understandings of the office of 'king' were compared, before examining that title in the particular context of the Johannine Gospel. As the explicit vocabulary of king/kingdom, including 'the king of Israel'/ 'the king of the Jews' is used throughout the Gospel, but particularly in the Passion, demonstrate Jesus' kingship in terms of him being the king who represents the new Johannine world, namely, the kingdom of God. John challenges his readers to decide who they believe and follow: either the earthly king, Caesar, or King Jesus, who is presented as an alternative to Roman imperialism.

The second part of the thesis, investigates the function of the Johannine Jesus from a postcolonial perspective. Jesus is identified as king in the Gospel, which raises the question why the author described him as such. What prompted him to write his Gospel? Why did he characterize Jesus as king? In order to discover a possible answer, under the presupposition that the Johannine community of readers existed in a hybridized society and was in conflict with other groups at that time, the thesis proposed that the author needed to write the Gospel in order to consolidate them in their faith, to motivate them to evangelize the world, and to inspire them to seek as their goal the new world, where Jesus as their king reigns in love and freedom. To verify this, Chapter 5 attempts to identify and categorize the various groups in the Fourth Gospel, before Chapter 6 describes the message of the Gospel by considering the function and message of Jesus. The Johannine Jesus needed to be characterized as the king so that he would be seen as the one through whom a solution could be found to the conflicts faced by the readers. His kingship helps clarify their identity as followers of Jesus, and gives them a hope that will enable them to face persecution in the years to come. The unique message of Jesus in this Gospel promises to be the answer to each and every situation his followers might find themselves in.

Chapter 5 defines Rome as the colonizer, the center, which ruled over all the margins of the Empire, both at the time of Jesus and

> **The Johannine community of readers existed in a hybridized society.**

that of the Johannine community. From this perspective, 'the Jews'—and, in particular, the Jewish leaders—can be defined both as the colonized (the margins) under the Roman Empire, and as colonizers as well, for some were collaborators with the imperial power in the marginal society. The Gospel of John shows that there were those who had already admitted the imperial power of Rome to be the absolute power of domination. Their ambiguity and ambivalence towards Rome is well revealed in the Gospel. As the collaborators, the Jewish leaders eliminate Jesus in the same manner as their center, Rome, dealt with opposition. As the colonized, they kill Jesus so as not to be deprived of their position by the colonizer. Finally, evidence is assembled to show that the Johannine community, as the margin, experienced conflict with both the center and the collaborators. The Gospel as a postcolonial text challenges this marginal people to live in this colonized world with the principles of the Johannine new world: love, forgiveness, peace, service, and freedom.

Under these circumstances, the Johannine Jesus could be represented as the decolonizing king who has resisted the imperial power and the darkness, and who has liberated the margins from the suppression of the imperial power and the darkness. It is highly probable that a variety of special terms, which contained various different meanings before the era of early Christianity, were undergoing a change of meaning (hybridized meanings) in the multi-cultural environment of the Roman Empire. One of the reasons for this change would be related to 'asymmetrical conditions of power' at that time. The center having absolute power influenced the margins in every aspect of their society. The change of meaning(s) of specific terms through mutual transaction was not unknown, but mostly this came about through unequal exchange. It is the tendency of an imperial power as the dominant force at the center to force the change or modification of the meanings of terms (hybridity), and to choose as their dominant meaning that which corresponds with the logic of the center. Therefore, it is quite likely that the influence of the Imperial power can be detected in every aspect of society, including the combination of languages and the meanings of words. Greek was used as the dominant language, and its influence among other language speakers must have been formidable. It was impossible to reject the Imperial influence or not to be influenced by it. This tendency influenced the composition of the Gospel under Rome. Thus, it is probable that in these circumstances, the terms employed in the Gospel to indicate the identity of Jesus might undergo a similar process of meaning change, because the marginal societies, including the Johannine community, existed in the world under asymmetrical conditions of power. Accordingly, it is probable that John might have needed to adapt a variety of Christological titles, which were commonly permeated/linked with the kingship motif, in order to clarify the identity of Jesus in terms of kingship. Furthermore, he might have needed to arrange several of them in a particular passage, as mutual complements of one another in order to declare the identity of the Johannine Jesus as king, while avoiding being misunderstood by his readers.

> Jesus [...] the decolonizing king who has resisted the imperial power.

Thus, the Christological titles, which had also been changing in meaning, might be adapted in the Johannine narrative in order to create its own meaning in a unique way, which seemed to differ from those outside of Johannine Christianity. By employing Christological titles, which acquire new meanings in the Johannine text, the author might create and deliver a new identity for Jesus and deliver this understanding to the readers who were from a variety of backgrounds and were experiencing the mixture of meanings under the huge suppressing power of Empire. Under the circumstances, the change of terms might not only deliver new meanings to the readers inside Johannine Christianity, but it might also make the readers outside those circles better able to understand the meanings, because the terms were not totally changed. The Gospel proclaims a kind of postcolonial utopia, namely the kingdom of the Johannine Jesus, where Jesus as the universal king reigns. Moreover, it admits to and promotes the coexistence of various ethnicities and nations in the new world.

Chapter 6 defines the role of the Johannine Jesus, in terms of him being identified as a universal king, who functions as a de-colonizer, moving people towards his new world where they would live in harmony with love, service, peace, freedom, and forgiveness. This present world, from the time of the composition of the Gospel, is a world in which the margins were suffering from suppression, exploitation, and living in poverty. From ancient times, many empires have risen to power in order to establish their own ideologies but were later toppled by those who followed them. Many countries have claimed to stand for justice, freedom, peace, equality, wealth and happiness as their national foundations, but the accomplishment of their ideologies does not seem likely now, or in the future. Particularly, it seems to be more difficult to realize these ideologies in regions where religious, ethnic, and ideological conflict has been deeply rooted. So, is it possible to realize the new world in which the margins can still have hope, as they exist in this huge spiral of conflict and suffering?

the Gospel invites every reader into the new world, which transcends time and space.

The Gospel of John declares that this alternative world has been initiated in the coming of the king into the world (Prologue). Furthermore, this Gospel states that the expectation of the coming back of Jesus the king shows that the perfect place, the Johannine new world, will be given to all believers (14:2-3).

The Gospel presents a new way to overcome the present reality of this world, and a new ideological alternative to realize the better world, the new world. The appropriation of the Johannine new world and its realization in our future is an ongoing community effort. The time of the composition of the Gospel might have been a turbulent period. However, there have been similar situations throughout history. Although the specific situations faced by people at the time of the Gospel were different from those of other times, every era has had the margins and those who pursued utopia, in an attempt to present new alternatives to overcome their present limitations and problems. This Gospel represents one of these attempts in that it presents Jesus as an evident alternative in terms of pursuing utopia. It projects an alternative world of all-inclusive love and life. The Johannine Jesus has been given to the marginal people who have been caught up in oppression and conflict, violence and exploitation, persecution and death. He always comes as the liberator and gives them hope of the new world, in which he will reign as king. He opens the door to the new world to those still living in this world, and begins to reveal the ideologies of his rule. The Gospel delivers its message of the new world mainly through the kingship of Jesus, because in the Gospel he is described as the Lamb of God who takes away the sin of the world. In the Passion Narrative, he takes away the sin of the world on the cross, because he is the way to the Father. He went to the new world to prepare rooms for his followers and will return. He is the light to overcome the darkness of this world. Therefore, the Gospel invites every reader into the new world, which transcends time and space.

The Johannine Gospel leads the readers to see beyond this world/Rome by presenting Jesus as the universal king of the new world. In addition, this Gospel shows the ruling ideology of the new world through the teaching of the Johannine Jesus. This ideology (love, freedom, forgiveness, service, and peace) is different from that of the contemporary world of the Johannine community, the ideology of the darkness (suppression, exploitation, slavery, and so on). The Johannine Gospel also presents Jesus as the de-colonizer who comes to his own to liberate his people from darkness. Therefore, to know this Johannine Jesus, to believe in him, is the way of freedom. The only way of liberation from material suppression, tyranny and power, bondage of religions, and the limitation of a social position, is to believe in Jesus and to be his disciple. It is true that the conditions of the world in which the darkness reigned at the time of the Johannine Gospel is similar to that of today. To this world, the Johannine Gospel proclaims that the margins will be liberated from its reality, which is full of political, religious, and economic conflict.

Sehyun Kim
Korean School of Theology, Sydney College of Divinity

Book reviews

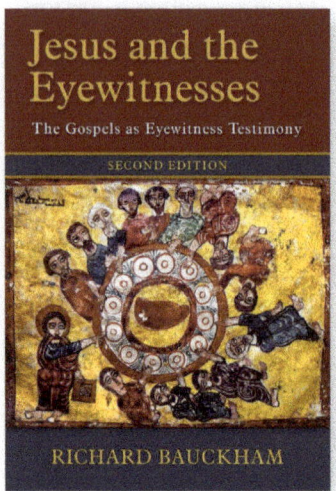

Richard Bauckham, *Jesus and the Eyewitnesses: The Gospels as Eyewitness Testimony* (Grand Rapids, MI: Eerdmans, 2017, 2nd edition). xiii + 704 pp. $50.00 USD. ISBN 0802874312.

After its release in 2006, the first edition of Richard Bauckham's *Jesus and the Eyewitnesses* made an impact in both academia and culture at large—winning the 2007 *Christianity Today* Book Award in Biblical Studies, and translated into five other languages. Released in April 2017, this second edition leaves the original eighteen chapters untouched and adds three new chapters.

The thesis of the first edition was that the 'Gospel traditions did not, for the most part, circulate anonymously but in the name of the eyewitnesses to whom they were due' (p. 8). Chapter 2 supports this thesis through Papias' testimony from the early second century. In chapter 3, Bauckham explores the many named and unnamed characters in the Gospels and suggests 'the possibility that many of these named characters were eyewitnesses who not only originated the traditions to which their names are attached but also continued to tell these stories as authoritative guarantors of their traditions' (p. 39). Chapter 4 utilizes Tal Ilan's *Lexicon of Jewish Names in Antiquity* (2002) to show that the relative frequency of the names in the Gospels corresponds to the relative frequency of Palestinian Jewish names from the same period. This statistically improbable feature is best explained by the fact that the Gospels get the relative name frequency correct because they are eyewitness testimony. Chapter 5 suggests that '[i]f any group in the earliest community was responsible for some kind of formulation and authorization of a body of Jesus traditions, the Twelve are much the most obviously likely to have been that group' (p. 96). Chapter 6 argues 'that three of the Gospels—those of Mark, Luke, and John—make use of the historiographic principle that the most authoritative eyewitness is one who was present at the events narrated from their beginning to their end and can therefore vouch for the overall shape of the story as well as for specific key events' (p. 146). Chapter 7 contains a nuanced argument that 'Mark's Gospel not only by its use of the *inclusio* of eyewitness testimony, claims Peter as its main eyewitness source; it also tells the story predominantly (though by no means exclusively) from Peter's perspective' (p. 179). Chapter 8 argues that some of the anonymous persons in Mark's passion narrative such as the woman who anointed Jesus (Mark 14:3-9), or the one who cut off the ear of the servant of the high priest with a sword (Mark 14:47), or the young man who fled naked (Mark 14:51-52), were kept anonymous because the 'need for 'protective anonymity' may have overridden the convention of naming the eyewitnesses' (p. 201). Chapter 9 critically examines what Papias probably meant by '[t]he Elder used to say:

Mark, in his capacity as Peter's interpreter [*hermēneutēs*], wrote down accurately as many things as he [Peter?] recalled from memory—though not in an ordered form' (p. 203; Eusebius, *Hist. Eccl.* 3.39.14); and Papias' comments on Matthew. Chapter 10 looks at three models of oral tradition: informal uncontrolled tradition (the form critical model), formal controlled tradition (Birger Gerhardsson, *Memory and Manuscript: Oral Transmission and Written Transmission in Rabbinic Judaism and Early Christianity* [Lund: Gleerup, 1961]), and informal controlled tradition (Kenneth E. Bailey, 'Informal Controlled Oral Tradition and the Synoptic Gospels,' *Asia Journal of Theology* 5 [1991] 34-51). In chapter 11, Bauckham looks at how the Jesus traditions were transmitted and chapter 12 furthers the case for eyewitness testimony over anonymous traditions. Chapter 13 examines the strengths and weakness of eyewitness memory. Chapter 14 argues that the Gospel of John is eyewitness testimony. Chapters 15 through to 17 contends that the witness of the beloved disciple is that of John the Elder – evidenced internally in the Gospel itself and how this fits externally with Papias, Polycrates and Irenaeus. Chapter 18, the last of the first edition, having argued that the Gospels are eyewitness testimony, argues that testimony 'is both the historically appropriate category for understanding what kind of history the Gospels are and the theologically appropriate category for understanding what kind of access Christian readers of the Gospels thereby have to Jesus and his history' (p. 473).

The second edition adds three new chapters, which respond to criticisms of the first edition and extend the argument. Chapter 19 revisits the eyewitnesses in Mark and responds to criticisms such as Jerome Murphy-O'Connor's *RB* 114 (2007), who thought Bauckham had not adequately shown the use of *inclusio* in relevant ancient literature. Bauckham now demonstrates this in the works of Polybius and Plutarch. Bauckham also presents evidence from Josephus's *Jewish War*, Plutarch's *Life of Pompey* and *Life of Antony*, and Corrnelius Nepos's *Life of Atticus*, that 'a literary device of "implicit eyewitnesses" that was employed by historians and biographers of the Greco-Roman world was a way of indicating the eyewitness sources of important events that the authors themselves could not claim to have witnessed, in a manner that did not disrupt the narrative flow of their stories' (p.534).

One telling admission by Bauckham is that he states: 'I know of no comprehensive study of the ways in which ancient historians indicated their eyewitness sources' (p.514). So, while the evidence he has presented is suggestive, a final verdict will await such a comprehensive study.

In an additional note Bauckham corrects some misunderstanding of his argument on onomastic analysis by Jens Schröter ('The Gospels as Eyewitness Testimony? A Critical Examination of Richard Bauckham's Jesus and the Eyewitnesses,' *JSNT* 31 [2008], 195-209) and Christopher M. Tuckett ('Review of Richard Bauckham, *Jesus and the Eyewitnesses*', in *RBL* [online at www.bookreviews.org/pdf/5650_6184.pdf]) stating that his argument was not based on the mere occurrence of common names but on their relative frequency. Consequently, the notion that 'the names were added in oral tradition, as the form critics tended to suppose' (p.544) is statistically unlikely.

Chapter 20 continues the discussion on who was the Beloved Disciple? Responding to Andreas Köstenberger (*Review of Jesus and the Eyewitnesses*, www.biblicalfoundations.org/jesus-and-the-eyewitnesses/) Bauckham argues that 'the internal evidence of the Gospel itself does not support the identification of the Beloved Disciple as John the son of Zebedee' (p.551). The internal evidence was something Bauckham felt was already sufficiently demonstrated by others and hence not detailed in the first edition. Bauckham's internal reasons for thinking why the Beloved Disciple is not John the Son of Zebedee are: (1) the focus on Jerusalem and Judea rather than

Galilee suggests '[t]hat the Beloved Disciple was a Jerusalem resident who did not usually travel with Jesus in Galilee' (p.563); (2) Different disciples are prominent suggesting a different 'circle in which the Beloved Disciple moved' (p.564); (3) The twelve are not prominent; (4) John's brother, James the son of Zebedee is only indirectly mentioned (John 21:2); (5) The Beloved Disciple is an eyewitness at the cross and '[w]hy should Mark resort to the women for testimony if one of the Twelve could have supplied it?' (p.570); (6) Jesus' preferential love for the Beloved Disciple 'despite the prominence of John the son of Zebedee in the Synoptics, there is no hint that he, unlike Peter or his brother James, was the disciple for whom Jesus had special affection. Yet precisely this is what characterizes the Beloved Disciple in the Fourth Gospel' (p.570-571); and (7) The distinctiveness of the Gospel of John is better explained 'if one of them is written from a perspective outside the circle of the Twelve' (p.571). Furthermore, Bauckham counters three alleged evidences for thinking the Beloved Disciple is John the son of Zebedee. Bauckham argues that the Gospel of John is still broadly of apostolic authority, and gives an interpretation of Polycrates that fits with his view. Finally, with respect to the death of John son of Zebedee Bauckham argues that 'it may be that in Papias and the martyrologies we have the surviving evidence that John the son of Zebedee suffered a violent death in Jerusalem long before his namesake wrote a Gospel' (p.589).

Chapter 21 confirms the end of form criticism. Responding to David Catchpole ('On Proving Too Much: Critical Hesitations about Richard Bauckham's Jesus and the Eyewitnesses,' *JSHJ* 6 (2008) 169-81) Bauckham states that one does not need form criticism to explain the differences between the Gospels.

While the second edition is a useful addition it is a little disappointing that one has to pay full price for only three additional chapters, especially when parts of those chapters have already appeared in some of Bauckham's published works since the first edition (such as: 'The Eyewitnesses in the Gospel of Mark,' *Svensk Exegetisk Årsbok* 74 [2009], 19-39; and 'The Gospel of Mark: Origins and Eyewitnesses,' in M.F. Bird & J. Maston (eds.) *Earliest Christian History: Essays from the Tyndale Fellowship in Honor of Martin Hengel* [Tübingen: Mohr Siebeck, 2012], 145-69). In addition, some of Bauckham's existing responses to his critics go into more detail than the new chapters, and as such one will still need to consult these (such as: 'In Response to My Respondents: Jesus and the Eyewitnesses in Review,' *JSHJ* 6 [2008], 225-253). In responding to the accusation that eyewitness memory is unreliable from Judith C. S. Redman ('How Accurate Are Eyewitnesses? Bauckham and the Eyewitnesses in the Light of Psychological Research,' *JBL* 129 [2010], 177-97); and Dale C. Allison (*Constructing Jesus: Memory, Imagination, and History* [London: SPCK, 2010], chapter 1), Bauckham defers to his article 'The General and the Particular in Memory: A Critique of Dale Allison's Approach to the Historical Jesus,' *JSHJ* 14 (2016), 28–51, and states more is forthcoming. Finally, in the preface to the second edition Bauckham states, 'I have not been able to put all my further thinking about the Gospels and the eyewitnesses into the additional chapters of this edition. Other work is in progress and will, I hope, be published in due course' (p.xix). So, while I am both glad for the new edition and that more work is coming, it isn't obvious why the three present chapters were published at this stage.

David Graieg
Sydney College of Divinity

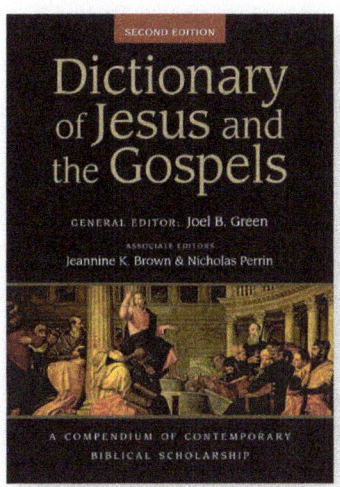

Joel B. Green, Jeannine K. Brown, Nicholas Perrin (eds.), *Dictionary of Jesus and the Gospels: A Compendium to Contemporary Biblical Scholarship* (Downers Grove: IVP Academic, Nottingham: IVP, 2013, 2nd ed.). Xxxi + 1088 pp., hardbound. ISBN 978-1-84474-876-1.

In the past three or four decades, research on Jesus and the Gospels has become an enormous and extremely diverse field regarding sources, methods, issues and applications. Full orientation of what is going on in international research is beyond most individuals. Scholars and students alike need reliable guidance as they approach the topic with whatever purpose. The first edition of the *Dictionary of Jesus and the Gospels*, edited by Joel B. Green, Scot McKnight and the late I. Howard Marshall (Downers Grove, Leicester: IVP, 1992), provided such guidance from a well-informed, balanced perspective informed by classical Christian faith.

The present second edition aims to fulfil the same purpose and stands in the same tradition. The editors describe the need for a second edition as follows:

> In recent decades some traditional viewpoints have been transformed, some overturned, others confirmed. New methodologies and approaches have been championed, some becoming commonplace. New studies have helped us to appreciate better the perspectives of the Gospel writers, and they have brought into sharper relief the challenge of Jesus' life and message. Those studies have also grown more numerous and, in many cases, more technical. (ix)

They emphasise the continuity with the first edition and describe the change in these terms:

> This revision of the *Dictionary* follows the same path, though now with new content and up-to-date bibliographies, as well as a host of new contributors. Some ninety percent of the original material has been replaced, with most previous entries assigned to a fresh list of scholars. A number of new articles have been introduced, and a handful of articles from the first edition have been updated in light of ongoing research. (ix)

The articles offer introductory discussions, comprehensive surveys and up-to-date bibliographies. They cover questions arising from the Gospels themselves, longstanding traditions and of interpretation of Jesus and the Gospels, fresh insights, various background issues, and the whole range of methodological approaches used in Gospels study.

Some 150 pages have been added in comparison with the first edition (933 pp.). Some articles of the first edition have been omitted altogether or the information was included elsewhere: 'Abiathar', 'Benefactor', 'Destruction of Jerusalem', 'Divine Man/ *Theios Aner*', 'Gospels, Historical Reliability', 'Judas Iscariot', '"L"-Tradition', 'Liberation Hermeneutics', 'Literary Criticism', 'Mary's song', '"M"-Tradition', 'Preaching from the Gospels', 'Ransom Saying', 'Rhetorical Criticism', 'Service', 'Simeon's Song', 'Taxes', 'Tradition Criticism', 'Truth', 'Zechariah's Song'. Some of these omissions are understandable, others, in view of the intended readership and provenience of the volume, perhaps surprising ('Gospels, Historical Reliability', 'Preaching from the Gospels', 'Ransom Saying', 'Truth').

The new articles in his second edition are: M.J. Smith, 'African-American Criticism' (6–10); J. Painter, 'Beloved Disciple' (69–72); R.W. Wall, 'Canonical Criticism' (106–109); R.J. Bauckham, 'Christology' (125–134); S.E. Porter, 'Criteria of Authenticity' (153–162); P.R. Eddy, 'Cynics and Cynicism' (162–165); D. Downs, 'Economics' (219–226); D.M. Peters, 'Essenes' (239–242); J.M. Scott, 'Exile and Restoration' (251–258); M.J. Smith, 'Feminist and Womanist Criticisms' (278–283); J.M. Scott, 'Gods, Greek and Roman' (228–335); S.F. Watson, 'Gospels, History of Interpretation' (352–359); J.B. Green, 'Historicisms and Historiography' (383–387); G.L. Parsenios, 'Incarnation' (399–403); S. Walton, 'Jerusalem' (408–414); A. González-Tejera, 'Latino/Latina Criticism' (501–505); V. Koperski, 'Mary, Mother of Jesus' (566–570); E.J. Schnabel, 'Mission' (604–610); J. Brown, 'Narrative Criticism' (619–624); P.R. Eddy, 'Orality and Oral Transmission' (641–650); E.B. Powery, 'Postcolonial Criticism' (680–684); C. Brown, 'Quest for the Historical Jesus' (718–756); M.L. Strauss, 'Sadducees' (823–825); A.D. Clarke, 'Slave, Servant' (869–874); R.B. Vinson, 'Songs and Hymns' (900–903); and A. Johnson, 'Theological Interpretation of the Gospels' (963–966).

The volume closes with a detailed Scripture index (1025–1070) and subject index (1071–1087). Future editions should contain articles on the portrayal of Jesus in the arts, literature and films, articles on the Jewish and Islamic study and reception of Jesus and articles on Jesus and the Gospels in the non-western and non-northern parts of the world (to follow e.g. the scope of the recent last volume of *The New Cambridge History of the Bible*, edited by John Riches, *The Bible from 1750 to the Present* [Cambridge: CUP, 2015]). Why is there an article on African *American* criticism, but not on African issues and contributions to the understanding of Jesus and the Gospels?

Like its predecessor, this is an excellent reference tool for scholars and students alike. The new edition with all the new material that is included is all the more welcome as other Bible dictionaries are either not as comprehensive or are also dated by now, such as the *Anchor Bible Dictionary*. The *Encyclopedia of the Bible and its Reception* (1, 2009ff) does not yet provide full coverage (Vol. 11, 2015 *Halah – Hizquni*) and is not as detailed on all the issues pertaining to Jesus and the Gospels. A good companion volume is Craig A. Evans's (ed.), *Encyclopedia of the Historical Jesus* (London, New York: Routledge, 2008).[1] The editors have the last word regarding their intention:

> When work began in the late 1980s on the first edition of the *Dictionary of Jesus and the Gospels*, New Testament scholarship informed by classical Christian faith was on the rise and had begun to make significant contributions to the discourse on Jesus and the Gospels. The landscape has changed since those days. In the intervening years, evangelical study spanning three generations of scholars has contributed to historical inquiry, to explorations of the particular contributions of each of the Gospel writers, and to reflection on the theological and ethical consequences of the fourfold Gospel. If interest in the historical Jesus in the popular media has waned somewhat since the 1990s, it remains no less crucial that critically responsible and theologically evangelical scholarship be placed in the hands of the larger church. In fact, to be evangelical and critical at the same time has been the object of the *Dictionary*. (x)

Christoph Stenschke
Biblisch-Theologischen Akademie, Forum Wiedenest, Bergneustadt, Germany/
Department of Ancient and Biblical Studies, University of South Africa (Pretoria)

---

[1] See my review in *RBL 05/2009*, www.bookreviews.org/BookDetail.asp?TitleId=7022.

BOOK REVIEWS

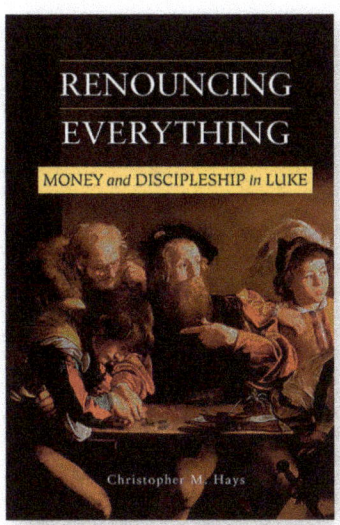

Christopher M. Hays, *Renouncing Everything: Money and Discipleship in Luke* (New York/Mahwah, NJ: Paulist Press, 2016). 118 pp. ISBN 978-0-8091-4991-9 (paperback), ISBN 978-1-58768-618-4 (e-book).

Christopher M. Hays is already well known to Lukan scholars because of his excellent monograph on Luke's ethical teaching regarding wealth, *Luke's Wealth Ethics: A Study in Their Coherence and Character* (WUNT II 275; Tübingen: Mohr Siebeck, 2010).[1] This is now popularised and summarized in *Renouncing Everything*, aimed at students and laypersons (p. xv).

Hays enters once again the well-traversed terrain of Luke's depiction of the 'wealthy' and 'poor' in Luke-Acts, the main scholarship of which is condensed by Hays for the general reader in a helpful bibliography (pp. 109-112). This brief and easy-to-read study of the wealth ethics of the Lukan Jesus and their impact upon the moral life of his 'Kingdom' community—including how it should inform the praxis of the church today in light of the Pentecost event—is a welcome addition to Lukan scholarship, not only for biblical scholars but now particularly for the general public.

At this juncture of Gospels research, Hays' focus upon wealth and the wealthy represents, to some degree, a welcome circuit breaker to New Testament scholarship on the ancient economy. In recent years scholarship on Poverty Studies in antiquity has been preoccupied with the question of precisely identifying the 'poor' and to what degree the constituency of the early house churches comprised the poor and destitute.[2] The problem is made more difficult by the absence of any full-scale monograph on poverty in the Graeco-Roman world covering the early imperial period,[3] although the (later) Jewish background

---

1 See also the important work of J. Marshall, *Jesus, Patrons, and Benefactors: Roman Palestine and the Gospel of Luke* (WUNT II 259; Tübingen: Mohr Siebeck, 2009). For a recent work on poverty and wealth in the New Testament era from a political perspective, see M.J. Sandford, *Poverty, Wealth, and Empire: Jesus and Postcolonial Criticism* (Sheffield: Sheffield Phoenix, 2014).

2 J. Meggitt, *Paul, Poverty and Survival* (Edinburgh: T&T Clark, 1998); S. Friesen, 'Poverty in Pauline Studies: Beyond the So-called New Consensus', *JSNT* 26 (2004), 323–61 (with responses by J.M.G. Barclay and P. Oakes in the same journal); idem, 'Prospects for a Demography of the Pauline Mission: Corinth among the Churches', in D. Schowalter and S. Friesen (eds.), *Urban Religion in Roman Corinth: Interdisciplinary Approaches* (Cambridge, MA: Harvard University Press, 2005), 351–70; W. Scheidel and S. Friesen, 'The Size of the Economy and the Distribution of Income in the Roman Empire', *JRS* 99 (2009), 61–91; B.W. Longenecker, *Paul, Poverty, and the Greco-Roman World* (Grand Rapids: Eerdmans, 2010). See the recent excellent coverage of the available first-century evidence for the urban poor by L.L. Welborn, 'The Polis and the Poor: Reconstructing Social Relations from Different Genres of Evidence', in J.R. Harrison and L.L. Welborn (eds.), *The First Urban Churches I: Methodological Foundations* (Atlanta: SBL, 2015), 189–243.

3 A.R. Hands, *Charities and Social Aid in Greece and Rome* (London: Thames and Hudson, 1968), 62–76; C.R. Whittaker, 'The Poor', in A. Giardina (ed.), *The Romans* (Chicago: University of Chicago Press, 1993), 279–99; V.J. Rosivach, 'Seneca on the Fear of Poverty in the *Epistulae Moralae*', *L'antiquité classique* 64.1 (1995), 91–98; R.P. Saller, 'Poverty, Honor, and Obligation in Imperial Rome', *Criterion* 37.2 (1998), 12–20; M. Atkins and R. Osborne (eds.), *Poverty in the Roman World* (Cambridge: Cambridge University Press, 2006). On poverty in later Roman antiquity, see P. Brown, *Poverty and Leadership in the Later Roman Empire* (Hanover: University Press of New England, 2002); idem, 'Remembering the Poor and the Aesthetic of Society', *The Journal of Interdisciplinary History* 35.3 (2005), 513–22.

is well serviced in this regard.[4] Furthermore, precisely because of the fragmentary state of the documentary and archaeological evidence, the 'poor' are difficult to identify and, worse, they routinely pass unnoticed in élite literary sources. Thus, Luke's graphic portrait of the extremities faced by the poor and, conversely, the indifference and exploitative attitudes displayed by the wealthy in his Gospel, provides invaluable first-century evidence regarding the unnoticed victims of the ancient economy, the voiceless underclass who are not normally heard in the Graeco-Roman documents and literature.

Hays' enlightening study of Luke's renunciation of, and demand for, the dispersal of wealth to the needy and, concomitantly, its radical implications for contemporary discipleship, underlines for modern believers that wealth ethics have to be thoughtfully and prayerfully considered before God. Hays argues (Chapter 7) that, for those in the acquisitive and consumptive West, a response characterised by genuine repentance and divine restoration ought to lead to a consideration of vocation and the experience of holistic sanctification (pp. 88-95). What, then, is Luke's unique contribution to the New Testament corpus in this regard, according to Hays?

Chapter 1 sets out the state of the scholarly debate about Lukan 'wealth ethics', that is, what Luke says, 'about morality and money, about how we should think of poverty, and what we should do with our possessions' (p. 2). Traditionally Luke's wealth ethics have been thought to pose an impractical choice between the divestiture of wealth and its necessary possession for beneficence. Luke's presentation is further criticised for being inconsistent with the wider evidence of his Gospel (pp. 2-6).

---

4   On charity in Second Temple Judaism, see H.H. Hamel, *Poverty and Charity in Roman Palestine, First Three Centuries CE* (Berkeley and Los Angeles: University of California Press, 1989); Y. Wilfand, *Poverty, Charity and the Image of the Poor in Rabbinic Texts from the Land of Israel* (Sheffield: Sheffield Phoenix, 2014); G. Gardner, *The Origins of Organized Charity in Rabbinic Judaism* (Cambridge: Cambridge University Press, 2015).

Scholars have proposed as solutions to this dilemma that Jesus is either (a) proposing an interim ethic confined to the disciples' journey to Jerusalem, (b) setting out the lifestyle required for the wandering charismatics of the 'Q community', (c) establishing the difference in wealth divestiture required for 'itinerant' disciples as opposed to 'non-itinerant' disciples, and (d) advocating divergent ethical choices for the individual to decide between (pp. 6-13). Either way, the 'intractable text' of Luke 14:33 (cf. 6:20), where Jesus categorically demands wealth divestiture on the part of *all* would-be disciples, remains a stumbling block for each interpretation (p. 12).

In Chapter 2 Hays argues readers to 'Let Luke be Luke' by respecting the genre of literature in which he sets out his wealth ethics: namely, ancient biography, with its strong focus on moral discourse, normative ethics, and exemplars. Referring to an important comment by the biographer Plutarch (*Mor.* 814a: p. 18), Hays notes that ancient biographers did not propose a slavish imitation of their subjects, unsuitable for the present times and conditions. Readers should, therefore, expect exactly the same strategy from Luke as a biographer. Exemplars, positive and negative, are set forth by Luke in a biographical narrative text, but in a context where 'the moral teaching of the text aims to generate contextually distinctive responses, rather than slavish copying' (p. 24). Hay's careful nuancing of Luke's intentions within the ancient genre of biography and, consequently, his elucidation of the type of moralistic expectations readers should have of the third evangelist, is a very important contribution to Lukan hermeneutics.

Having clarified genre considerations and expectations in their ancient context, Hays proceeds in Chapter 3 to propose that the centre of Luke's ethics is the double love commandment (Luke 10:27). Accordingly, an astutely conceived application of wealth ethics is 'part and parcel of the command to love one's neighbour' (p. 29). The radical renunciation of family and wealth envisaged by Jesus for his disciples (Luke 14:25-26, 33), including the *bête noir* text, Luke 14:33, is discussed. Hays argues persuasively that leaving 'all' is intended to be hyperbolic (pp. 31-34), with the word for renunciation, *apotassomai*, describing 'various forms of renunciation, temporary or permanent, internal or external' (p. 33). One wonders, however, whether Luke also includes in his wealth ethics the disciples' imitation of the mercy of God, especially given the sub-genre of Jewish/Christian biography with its focus upon *exempla*: 'Be merciful, just as your Father is merciful' (Luke 6:36). This is the rationale for loving, praying for, and being beneficent towards one's enemy and meeting their needs as required (Luke 6:35; cf. 6:31-31). At first blush, this would seem to be tangential as far as concern for the poor, but the strong hatred that a Pompeian graffito evinces towards the poor scuttles the idea that the poor were somehow excluded from the undefined category of 'enemy'. As the graffiti writer quips, 'I hate the poor' (*CIL* 4.9839b).

Hays addresses these issues more fully in Chapter 6, insightfully discussing the theology underlying Luke's social thought regarding wealth divestiture: namely, the mercy of God (pp. 68-69, including a discussion of Luke 6:36), Jesus' consistent combination in his teachings on wealth of the double Old Testament love commandments (Deut 6:15; Lev 19:18) (pp. 69-71), the dangers of wealth and God's provision for our needs (pp. 73-75), and, last, Jesus' teaching about the eschatological reversal awaiting the unrepentant rich and the elevation of pious poor (pp. 75-79). Jesus' teaching is set out clearly by Hays, with close attention to its Old Testament precedents (pp. 105-106), reminding readers of its 'powerful theo-logic [...] based on Luke's beliefs about God's character and operation in this world and the next' (pp. 79-80).

In Chapter 4 Hays addresses the distinction that modern scholars have made between 'itinerant' and 'non-itinerant' disciples. He shows that the divestiture of wealth applies to both groups, depending on personal factors unique to each group, and reflecting different expressions of total commitment to God. In sum, Hays concludes that Luke's divergent wealth ethics are not marked by contradiction but by harmony in pastoral praxis.

Chapter 5 summarises the outworking of this distinction in Acts by reference to the positive *exempla* (the Jerusalem community, Barnabas, Paul) and negative *exempla* (Annanias and Saphira). The following quotation effectively encapsulates Hays' conclusion about how the early church reconciled both types of disciples in a common gift-giving to the poor and needy (p. 65),

> Faithful disciples of Jesus follow Jesus' teachings on generosity and hospitality. Those who are non-itinerant work hard to care for the traveling itinerants and for the poor, whether in their own communities (Acts 20:34-35) or in other cities (11:27-30). Indeed, they even at times divest themselves of wealth in order to succour a needy brother or sister (4:33-37). Those figures whose wise behaviour rises to the level of being paradigmatic are the members of the Jerusalem community, who have all in common; Barnabas, who divests himself to care for the poor; and Paul, who works a job while preaching in order to have funds to provide for the needs of his travelling companions and the poor in his community.

This stylishly written, insightfully argued, and practically oriented book on Luke's wealth ethics demands two audiences. It is an invaluable introduction to a controversial area of Lukan social thought and theology for everyday readers, helping them to see how the contradictions and impracticalities of Luke's rendering of Jesus' teaching are in fact harmonised when one adopts a nuanced hermeneutic, which is one not of slavish imitation but rather one of differing contextual applications—as was expected by the ancient moralistic biographical genre in which Luke cast his narrative. But, equally, the book is a highly stimulating 'teaser' for New Testament scholars to read (and, indeed, to prescribe as part of their reading for courses on Lukan exegesis and theology). For those Lukan scholars who have not as yet read the original monograph upon which this book is based, they will inevitably be drawn by *Renouncing Everything* to investigate the full argumentation found in *Luke's Wealth Ethics*.

James R. Harrison
Sydney College of Divinity

BOOK REVIEWS

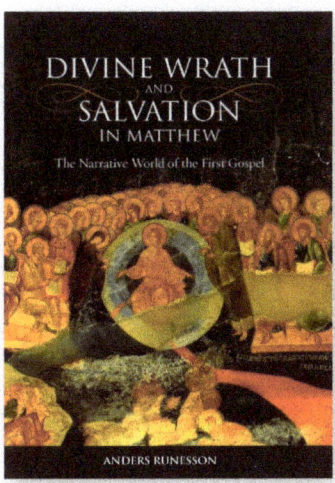

Anders Runesson. *Divine Wrath and Salvation in Matthew: The Narrative World of the First Gospel.* (Minneapolis: Fortress, 2016). xxxii+513 pp.
Print ISBN: 978-0-8006-9959-8
eBook ISBN: 978-1-4514-5225-9

As its title makes clear, this study focuses on divine judgement and salvation in Matthew. Runesson harshly criticizes the traditional Christian depiction of Israel as guilty (Matt. 27:25), condemned by God, and replaced by the church (p. 28) for being an anachronistic and antagonistic reading (pp. xviii-xix). Instead, he argues, reading Matthew in light of its theo-ritual[1] structure would help the reader realize that Jesus attacks only specific groups or individuals threatening them with divine judgement, while the crowds are exempted as victims of abuse (Matt. 9:36) (pp. 60, 339). Jesus proclaimed the eschatological kingdom and immense judgment on the religio-political authorities, who are accused of misleading the people (Matt. 15:14; 23:15-22) through their lax teaching of the law, and hence defiling the temple that became doomed to destruction as a result.

Jesus' death, contrary to common Christian theology, is not the cause of the destruction of the temple that has been already defiled (p. xxvi). Instead, it is the solution to such a theo-ritual dilemma, so that Jesus' ritualized death is the way of saving the Jewish people as a people (Matt. 1:21; 4:23; 10:6; 15:24) (pp. 58-61, 332). So, Jesus' atoning death makes possible the continuation of the Mosaic covenant after the fall of the temple (Matt. 26:26-29). The Mosaic covenant is thus not replaced, but continues based on Jesus' meticulous teaching of the law, which continues to have a valid salvific efficacy even after Jesus' resurrection (Matt. 5:17-20 and 28:18-20) (pp. 126-129). Hence, Matthew's Israel is still the centre of God's salvation into which non-Jews are to find refuge as the final judgement fast approaches (pp. xiii-xix). The non-Jews are the object of intense missionary activities and are envisioned as potential proselytes expected to adopt Jewish law—men should be circumcised to be considered true disciples (Matt. 28:18-20) (pp. 35-36, 431).

The genuine contribution of the book is its thorough engagement with a matrix of concepts that exhaust the different aspects and criteria of divine judgment, such as: sin and guilt, obedience and righteousness, repentance and forgiveness, faith and the person of Jesus, and covenant and grace (part I, chapter 2, pp. 53-205). Also, in chapter 3, Runesson goes on to apply the criteria of judgment on the different groups within the Jewish people (pp. 207- 325). He dynamically brings these concepts to the fore throughout the narrative world in Matthew (p. 19).

The main argument of the book is the centrality and continuing validity of the Mosaic law for how sin is defined, and for how salvation is realized and judgment is implemented. The criteria of judgement

---

1 By 'theo-ritual' structure, Runesson means a pattern in which theology and ritual cannot be understood separately. His frequent use of this term reflects his dissatisfaction with the academic tendency to systematize the religious thought of the ritually determined world view of Second-Temple Judaism (p. xv).

are concerned more with fulfilling Jesus' teaching of the law, not acknowledging his identity (p. 151). Jesus does not supersede the law, and loyalty to him means loyalty to his interpretation of the law. Agreeing with Fornberg, Runesson states that Jesus does not function as a judge, but rather as a lawyer / prosecutor at God's judgement, and he is certainly less important than the Spirit in this regard (Matt. 13:31-32) (pp. 155-157, 161, 333). The kingdom (and the law), not Jesus, is the primary message in Matthew, which becomes a universal reality when Jews and non-Jews follow God's law and thus accept the rule of the messiah (pp. 334; 433).

Runesson's thesis is not without problems. His main argument regarding the centrality of the law can be criticised. Jesus' fulfilling of the law and prophets until all is accomplished can be better understood, considering the consistent use of the fulfilment theme, mainly as an exclusive Christological claim (Matt. 1:22 till 26:54-56) that, in his life and ministry, Jesus is the one who brings about what the law and the prophets longed for (Matt. 11:13; 13:17).

What Jesus taught and did extends beyond mere interpretation of the law. Considering forgiveness, he is the one who has authority on earth to forgive sins (Matt. 9:1-8). Matthew is completely silent about Runesson's suggestion that the man's condition results from his wrongdoing to others and that Jesus overrides the role of the victim(s) to enable the man to bring sacrificial gifts to God in the temple. On purity, it is true that the point of controversy in Matt. 15:1-20 was the tradition of the elders, but what Jesus states twice (in v. 11 and 17) will inevitably challenge purity laws. For the Son of Man is lord of the Sabbath (Matt. 12:8).

Runesson's portrait of Jesus in relation to the law, which is so central for him, makes it difficult to understand why acknowledging Jesus as the Son to the Father is crucial to turning points in the narrative when teaching the law is not the crux. Such acknowledgement determines the person's status before the Father in heaven (Matt. 10:32-33; cf. 11:27). The church will be built upon it (Matt. 16:16-20). It eventually leads to his execution (Matt. 26:63-66).

Finally, contrary to Runesson's argument that the distinction between intentional and unintentional sins impacts the future of the Jewish crowds, who are exempted from any threatening divine judgment (p. 59-60), Jesus' speech to the crowds in parables, which he explains quoting Isaiah's prophecy, makes clear that they too come under divine judgment (Matt. 13:12-17).

Despite these criticisms, Runesson's book, in my view, will prove to be an essential text for Matthean students who are interested in the debate over the Jewishness of the Gospel.

George Bishai
Moore Theological College/
Alexandria School of Theology, Egypt

BOOK REVIEWS

Martin Spadaro, *Reading Matthew as the Climactic Fulfilment of the Hebrew Story*
(Eugene, Or.: Wipf & Stock, 2015). 316pp
ISBN: 13: 978-1-4982-0068-4
E ISBN: 13: 978-1-4982-0069-1

Reading Matthew as the Climactic Fulfilment of the Hebrew Story can be commended for three broad features.

First, the book pays careful attention to Matthew as a holistic narrative, drawing its thesis out of the rich narrative tapestry that is Matthew's Gospel. Although not often explicitly referring explicitly to the kind of narrative and reader-oriented devices Matthew uses to make an impact upon its readers, the book vigilantly reads each paragraph in the light of the whole Gospel and within the flow of Matthew's unfolding drama of Jesus.

So, for example, Matthew's 'parables discourse' in Matthew 13 is situated after the account of the mission of the Twelve in Chapter 10, and that of the rejection of Jesus' ministry in the Northern towns and villages, narrated in Chapters 11–12. The parables of Jesus are instruments to indict Israel for their sin, and after Jesus' mission is rejected in the North, Jesus' open proclamation of the kingdom is replaced by the enigmatic parables. By their rejection of Jesus' mission, the northerners have already shown themselves to be 'outsiders', and the parabolic teaching seals the deal, to allow 'the final and unavoidable wave of judgement' promised by Isaiah to fall on intransigent Israel.

Second, the book deals seriously with Matthew's historical focus on Jesus amongst first-century Israel. To put it somewhat simplistically, Christian Bible Reading habits have tended to favour what the text 'means for me now', over what the text meant about (and in) its original setting, and, despite claims to speak from historical concerns, Gospels scholarship has often not fared much better. Both readers and critics can be bedeviled with the moralistic assumption that the Gospels were written to change human behaviour, rather than to tell the news of Jesus' remarkable and dramatic presence amongst first-century Israel, with its implications for radically transforming subsequent human history.

Spadaro takes this obvious feature of Matthew's historical focus seriously. He combines what is said by the narrative in part and holistically with an appropriate historical imagination in order to listen for what Matthew says about Jesus in his first-century Israélite setting.

Thirdly, and perhaps most pertinently for Martin's major thesis, the book takes seriously Matthew's overt desire to explain the coming of Jesus Christ amongst first-century Israel as the climax and fulfillment of the Hebrew story, and of the Hebrew Scriptures. Perhaps it is here that Spadaro is at his best. Guiding the reader through Matthew's narrative about Jesus, he persuasively points out texts or patterns from the Hebrew Scriptures upon which Matthew potentially riffs.

As for the detailed argument, the book draws attention to the priestly nature of Jesus' Messianic identity, when set against the priestly element of Davidic Messianism. This helps to explain the clash between Jesus and the priestly classes of first-century Israel—which are, for Matthew, especially focused in the High Priest

Caiaphas himself. These religious and ruling classes occupied the place of the Christ, which they refused to lay aside when Jesus asserted his messianic claims. Whereas Jesus brought a message of judgement to recalcitrant and intransigent Israel, they refused it and rejected his Messianic claims. This clash between two priestly 'houses' led to Jesus' crucifixion, after which Matthew took up the task of placing Jesus' prophetic indictment of Israel down on public record, and demonstrating that it all happened according to the Scriptures. Caiaphas' house will not stand the test of time, but Jesus' house will remain forever. Jesus' story is the climactic fulfillment of the Hebrew story.

Peter G. Bolt
Sydney College of Divinity

BOOK REVIEWS

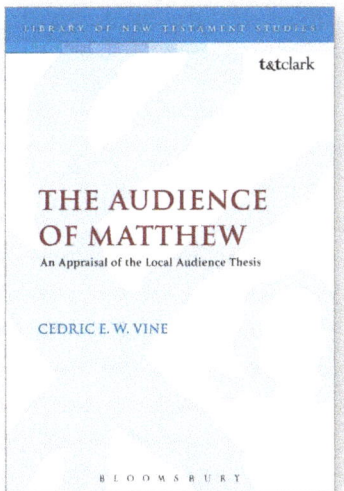

Cedric E.W. Vine. *The Audience of Matthew: An Appraisal of the Local Audience Thesis.* (LNTS 496; London: Bloomsbury T&T Clark, 2014). xiv+235 pp.
HB 978-0-56742-173-9
PB 978-0-5676-6448-8
ePDF 978-0-56761-320-2

The 'local audience thesis' is the claim that the original, intended or primary audiences for the Gospels were local communities, in limited geographical areas, and that the Gospels functioned as some sort of commentary or reflection on those communities, *for* those communities. This was a mainstay of twentieth century redaction criticism, with critics looking for possible editorial changes between the Gospels to make inferences about their historical setting. But it has also become a key feature of more recent claims that Matthew was writing for an audience/community that had not (yet) made a complete break with Judaism. Cederic Vine interacts with a number of these claims in this monograph, including those of Andrew Overman (who suggests a Jewish community in Palestine as the audience), Anthony Saldarini (a Christian-Jewish community in Syria) and David Sim (A Christian-Jewish 'law-observant' community in Antioch, in conflict with Pauline Gentile Christianity).

The local audience thesis was dealt something of a body blow in 1998 with a collection of papers edited by Richard Bauckham and published under the title *The Gospels for all Christians* (Edinburgh: T&T Clark), but it has proved remarkably slow to die, with a number of responses to Bauckham *et al* mounted its defence. Cedric Vine enters the fray against the local audience side (although he remains sceptical that one can infer anything definite concerning the identity of the Gospel audiences). The first argument is that local audience protagonists make a number of methodical errors in making inferences from the text (which may be true, but I did not feel was fully demonstrated). The second is that local audience protagonists ignore or down-play key features of the Gospel narratives such as plot development and characterisation (which is certainly true). And the third and fourth arguments have to do with orality—the likelihood that the Gospels were presented to an audience by performer/lector and received aurally. This is the most detailed part of the monograph, and useful in its own right quite apart from its (rather slight) contribution to its overall argument, orality being a neglected area of Matthean studies. Vine argues that listeners familiar with Mark would be extremely unlikely to be able to make the very fine inferences assumed by redaction critics and thereby engage with any supposed commentary on their own community experience. Indeed, an audience of such listeners would have been so diverse and heterogenous that it is a mistake to talk about 'their response' as a single entity.

Anyone looking for a comprehensive survey, analysis or critique of the local audience thesis in Matthean scholarship over the last hundred years or so is likely to be a little disappointed by this monograph. Of all the myriad ways one might conceive the audience(s) of the Gospels and their function and purpose, to suggest tightly defined local communities reading them as self-reflective narratives now seems among the least likely and most far-fetched of the options. There are thus many ways one might attack (or at least highly qualify) the local audience thesis, and it might be fair to say Cedric Vine chooses some of the less obvious routes. Still, they are interesting ones, and we can only hope they go at least some way to hastening the demise of an approach that has held back Matthean studies far too long.

Ben Cooper
Fulwood Bible Training, Sheffield, UK

www.ingramcontent.com/pod-product-compliance
Lightning Source LLC
Chambersburg PA
CBHW042038100526
44587CB00030B/4479